ALL I DID WAS ASK

ALL I DID WAS ASK

Conversations with Writers, Actors, Musicians, and Artists

TERRY GROSS

NEW YORK

Library of Congress Cataloging-in-Publication Data

Gross, Terry.
    All I did was ask : conversations with writers, actors, musicians, and artists / Terry Gross.—1st ed.
      p. cm.
    ISBN 1-4013-0010-3
    1. Fresh air (Radio program) 2. National Public Radio (U.S.) 3. Radio journalism—United States. I. Title

HE8697.95.U6G76 2004
791.44'72—dc22

2004042459

Hyperion books are available for special promotions and premiums. For details contact Michael Rentas, Assistant Director, Inventory Operations, Hyperion, 77 West 66th Street, 12th floor, New York, New York 10023, or call 212-456-0133.

Paperback ISBN: 0-7868-8820-2

FIRST TRADE PAPERBACK EDITION

10 9 8 7 6 5 4 3

For

Francis Davis

Anne Gross *(1918–2001) and* Irving Gross

Danny Miller

Although your name isn't on the cover,

this is your book, too.

CONTENTS

INTRODUCTION

I'm Terry Gross, and this is *Fresh Air* . . .

But this is a book, not a radio show. You may be wondering what the point is of reading interviews that were meant to be listened to. I've asked myself that. But in going through transcripts in preparation for this book, I was pleasantly surprised that so many of the interviews I remembered as having been good radio also made for enjoyable reading. In reading the ones gathered here—I probably shouldn't admit this—I've learned things from them that went right by me in the studio.

This book is different from the show in another way. It features only interviews with people in the arts. On our daily broadcasts, we try to offer meaningful discussion of the most pressing issues of the moment (too often of late, these have been issues relating to war and terrorism). Someone's new novel or movie or CD can seem trivial compared to the day's headlines. But whereas "timely" interviews can become dated very quickly, the pleasure we gain from the finest books and movies and music stays with us. So does our interest in the people who create them—which is why I'm hoping you'll enjoy reading this selection of interviews with writers, actors, directors, musicians, comics, and visual artists.

On the air, I make it a point to keep the focus on my guests. Here it seems fitting to share some of my thoughts about interviewing, and to give you an idea of what's involved in putting the show together. The interviews on *Fresh Air* sound conversational, or at least I hope they do. But they bear little resemblance to the conversations we have in daily life. Unlike an actual conversation, which requires only two people, a *Fresh Air* interview is a team effort. One of my producers finds and books the guest, a researcher locates the material I need to look at for background, an associate editor cuts the tape, and the executive producer decides on its final structure and length and whether it's worth putting on the air. The only people you're aware of when you listen to the interview, though, are me and my guest.

I violate many rules of polite conversation in my interviews, even when I'm making every effort to be respectful. You know what it's like when you're cornered by someone who can't stop talking? There's just no polite way of telling them to stop. If this were happening at a party, you could excuse yourself by pretending to spot someone else in the crowd you really needed to say hello to. Well, that kind of graceful getaway isn't an option for me in the studio—in addition to which, the problem isn't really that I'm bored, but that my listeners are going to be. Sometimes the guest is an expert on a given subject who's trying to provide more information than can be comfortably accommodated in a radio interview; he's so happy to be on public radio, where he doesn't have to answer in sound bites, that he can't stop himself from delivering a speech. But sometimes it's just a guest with what's facetiously called "the gift of gab," and there's no courteous way of telling him to cut to the chase. All I have with a guest is an hour tops, which means I have to make every minute count. So I do something I would never do off the air—I interrupt. I stop the interview to explain the peculiar demands of radio and suggest that shorter answers would be better. I risk momentarily embarrassing someone I regard highly enough to have on the show, because I trust that this little bit of advice will help him or her keep the attention of our listeners. Isn't that what we both want?

It doesn't always work. Sometimes a guest is just incapable of being concise, even though he knows better. A few years ago, for example, I taped an interview with Georgi Arbatov, once the Soviet Union's leading expert on the United States. His answers were so long that I found myself losing attention and felt confident our listeners would have the same problem. But he was impervious to my promptings for shorter answers. My final question to him was what advice he used to give Soviet leaders about making a good impression on American TV. "I've told Gorbachev more than once," he said emphatically and without missing a beat, "not to be so long-winded."

I also violate decorum by asking questions of my guests that you usually don't ask someone you've just met, for fear of seeming rude or intrusive. Within minutes of saying hello to a guest, I might inquire about his religious beliefs or sexual fantasies—but only if it's relevant to the subject he's come on the show to discuss. Or at some point during the interview, I might ask a question about a physical flaw of the sort that we gallantly pretend not to notice in everyday life. When I do this, my purpose isn't to embarrass my guest or to make him self-conscious. I'm trying to encourage introspection, hoping for a reply that might lead to a revelation about my guest's life that might lead, in turn, to a revelation about his art.

Sitting across the table from Chiwetel Ejiofor, the Nigerian-born star of Stephen Frears's *Dirty Pretty Things,* I couldn't help but notice that the scar on his forehead appeared larger than it had on-screen. I guess I was surprised to see it at all—I'd assumed it was the work of the film's makeup artists, a clue to the audience that Ejiofor's character was hiding a mysterious and dangerous past. I felt on safe ground asking Ejiofor about the scar only because an actor's face is part of his equipment and leading men are expected to be unblemished. He explained that the scar was from a car accident—the same one he'd talked about earlier, in which his father was killed. The incident, in which Ejiofor himself was badly injured, was so traumatic that he wasn't comfortable revealing more than that—which I found perfectly understandable. But he did say that he thought the accident had led him to become an actor. In his roles, he could express "frustrations, and sometimes angers, that are simply inappropriate in everyday life."

I also often ask my guests about what they consider to be their invisible weaknesses and shortcomings. I do this because these are the characteristics that define us no less than our strengths. What we feel sets us apart from other people is often the thing that shapes us as individuals. This may be especially true of writers and actors, many of whom first started to develop their observational skills as a result of being sidelined from typical childhood or adolescent activities because of an infirmity or a feeling of not fitting in. Or so I've come to believe from talking to so many writers and actors over the years.

EVERYTHING I'VE SAID SO FAR MIGHT lead you to think I believe that sitting in front of a microphone entitles me to ask practically anything. But I do respect my guests' privacy. I would never pressure anyone to reveal those thoughts and experiences he desires to keep private. The problem is you never know where someone is going to draw the line. A literary figure I interviewed a few years ago who was taken aback when I asked how his chronic illness affected his daily life was delighted by a question that gave him an opportunity to discuss how he developed his love of books by masturbating to pornographic ones as a child. I've learned the hard way not to make assumptions. That's why before beginning an interview, I tell the guest to let me know if I'm getting too personal, in which case we'll move on to something else (easy enough to do, because all *Fresh Air* interviews are prerecorded and edited).

Even this doesn't always prevent misunderstanding. "What is the use of this?" the actor Peter Boyle asked, moments before walking out in protest over my questions about his experiences as a member of the Christian Brothers monastic order before becoming an actor. "I made a movie, and you're asking me about all this stuff." Well, I had been hoping to find out if he ever drew on this experience for his roles. And I was fascinated by the paradox that this man who had once chosen the contemplative life wound up making his mark in the movies by playing a hard-hat killer in *Joe*. But you see the problem I sometimes face: A well-known actor or musician has been sent out on the road to promote his new movie or CD, and his idea of a good interview can be my idea of an infomercial.

Even so, I can understand Boyle's disinclination to talk to a perfect stranger (and to a national audience of strangers) about so meaningful a chapter in his life. "Being a celebrity can cause an accidental cheapening of the things one holds dear," Steve Martin once wrote in *The New York Times*. "A slip of the tongue in an interview and it's easy for me to feel I've sold out some private part of my life in exchange for publicity."

The other thing is that celebrities who believe interviewers are out to "get" them aren't just being paranoid. There is an entire industry devoted to digging up dirt on the private lives of celebrities, whether it's their drug habits or their sexual liaisons. Even at its most benign, celebrity journalism assumes that what appeals to us about our favorite performers is the power, wealth, and privilege they enjoy—not their work and the way it makes us feel that we have something in common with them.

All of which, I confess, sometimes leads me to question whether the autobiographical interview offers the potential for more than gossip or voyeurism. But only on my bad days. I try in my interviews to find the connections between my guests' lives and their work (the reason we care about them in the first place). I'd love to know how Chris Rock got to be so funny, how Dennis Hopper developed his screen presence, how John Updike became a great writer. Unfortunately, these kinds of questions are often unanswerable. Craft goes only so far in explaining how an artist uses his gift, and the gift itself is often inexplicable. Autobiography provides an alternate route—a seeming detour that may ultimately tell us something about an artist's sensibility and the experiences that shaped it. At the very least, the kind of interview I do offers me, and the show's listeners, an opportunity to learn more about someone whose work has moved and delighted us and perhaps, in some small way, altered our perceptions of ourselves and the world.

In his memoir *Self-Consciousness*, John Updike wrote that he was offering his as "a specimen life, representative in its odd uniqueness of all the oddly unique lives in this world." Ideally, this is something I would like all my guests to do. But I understand if they feel that starring in a new movie hardly requires them to reflect out loud on their inner lives.

I understand because this is something I myself have occasionally been reluctant to do when I'm the one being interviewed. Although I want to be as forthcoming as I ask my guests to be, I was brought up by parents who guarded their privacy and passed this instinct on to me. We lived in an apartment building where privacy was hard to come by, and this may have had something to do with it; you had to strain *not* to overhear the arguments of the families next door and those above and below us. Privacy, I think, was also a self-protective instinct for Jews of my parents' generation, who lived through the era of the Holocaust and the postwar witch hunts. Even though our neighborhood was about 99 percent Jewish—I grew up thinking the Catholic family across the street belonged to an embattled minority—the adults acted as if we dared not let the goyim know our business, because whatever disagreements we had among ourselves could be used against us. A few years ago, on one of my visits to Florida to see my parents, I showed them a copy of a magazine article that described me as totally unforthcoming and a mystery even to the people I work with. My mother's reaction on reading it: "You told them too much!"

The first few times I was interviewed, I was almost pathologically unforthcoming. Hoping to get me to talk about my childhood, one reporter asked me what I had wanted to be when I grew up. The answer was something not even many of my colleagues and closest friends know about me, so I was a little hesitant to come right out with it. But I figured that as an interviewer myself, I had a responsibility to answer truthfully. I told the reporter I had wanted to be a lyricist. "No, no," he said. "Tell me something interesting."

We might as well have ended the interview right there, because I was scared to trust him with anything personal after that. This experience and others like it have taught me that when an interviewee clams up, it's sometimes out of fear that the journalist he's speaking with won't fully comprehend what he's saying or simply won't care. This was an important lesson: It's one of the reasons I try to be well prepared for each interview, on the assumption that a guest is more likely to share his innermost thoughts with someone he senses has a good grasp of what he's all about.

In addition to allowing my guests to set the rules on what's private and therefore off-limits, I also encourage them to take advantage of the fact that the interview is being recorded and will be edited for broadcast. If someone is in the middle of an answer before he realizes what it was he wanted to say, he's welcome to go back and start again—we'll edit out the false start. I suspect that some of the journalists I look up to would take issue with me over this practice, but I'm doing radio—if an answer isn't clear, it's unusable. It's in everybody's best interest, including that of the show's listeners, if my guests are as clear, as concise, and as focused as possible.

When it comes to politicians and others in positions of authority, my rules are far less lenient. I don't elicit their help in drawing the line between public and private, nor do I allow them to start an answer over. Politicians are so skilled at manipulating the press—in staying on-message and evading any question that isn't to their liking—that it would be irresponsible on my part if I were to let them take back anything revealing that had just slipped out. The majority of my interviews are with people in entertainment and the arts, and with journalists and experts from every imaginable field we call on to analyze and explain important issues. It's my job to help these people, the experts as well as the artists, focus and present their thoughts. But this doesn't mean we shy away from controversy on *Fresh Air*. If we did, we would never have booked Bill O'Reilly.

We invited O'Reilly to be on the show because we wanted to be . . . well, fair and balanced. In September 2003, I had taped an interview with the liberal satirist Al Franken, who had devoted an entire chapter to O'Reilly in his best-selling book *Lies and the Lying Liars*

Who Tell Them. I had asked Franken a few questions pertaining to that chapter, and to a Fox News Channel lawsuit that accused Franken of violating its copyright with the book's subtitle "A Fair and Balanced Look at the Right." (A judge had ruled this claim "wholly without merit.") Before broadcasting the Franken interview, we wanted to be able to tell our listeners that O'Reilly would be on a future broadcast to present his point of view. So we scheduled an interview with him for early October, to coincide with the publication of his new book, *Who's Looking Out for You?*

One of the issues I wanted to pursue with O'Reilly was whether he uses his Fox News program to settle scores with anybody who takes issue with him. I read aloud from comments he had made on *The O'Reilly Factor* about Janet Maslin, a book critic for *The New York Times*, after she published a largely positive review of Franken's book in which she cited a couple of examples of how Franken "makes a bull's-eye of O'Reilly," including "[his] erroneous claim that he won a Peabody Award [which] evolved into even bigger fibs once it was challenged." Accusing Maslin of doing her paper's bidding, O'Reilly had responded by telling his viewers that her "gleeful libel demonstrates the viciousness that has enveloped the *Times*. I knew that once I took on *The New York Times*, the paper's character assassins would take dead aim on me." When I asked O'Reilly if he thought his accusations against Maslin and her editors might be a little disproportionate to what she'd actually written, he insisted that *"The New York Times* has accused me of everything you could think of because I criticize their secular editorial position, which bleeds over into the news pages."

Later on in the interview, still pursuing the theme of score settling, I brought up a review of *Who's Looking Out for You?* that had appeared in *People*. Kyle Smith, the reviewer, wrote that after he reviewed O'Reilly's previous book unfavorably, O'Reilly had denounced him as a "pinhead" and named the review "The Most Ridiculous Item of the Day" (*The O'Reilly Factor*'s regular closing feature). It was necessary for me to read from Smith's more recent review so that our listeners would know what we were talking about. But O'Reilly wouldn't let me finish reading the excerpt. Launching into a tirade, he accused me of throwing "every kind of defamation you can in my face," telling me I should be ashamed of myself for treating him differently than I had Franken and recommending that if this was my idea of journalism I should find another line of work. He then terminated the interview without having answered my question of whether he used his television show to get back at his critics. But that night, my interview with him was "The Most Ridiculous Item of the Day." He told his viewers that he'd "enjoyed telling that woman off" and continued to trash *Fresh Air* on several subsequent shows, repeatedly calling for an end to federal funding for public broadcasting. So maybe he answered the question after all.

Sometimes even what I figured would be a lighthearted conversation with someone from the world of show business can become confrontational. When I interviewed Gene Simmons, a cofounder of the comic-book-like heavy metal band Kiss, I expected we might share a laugh talking about what it was like for him to go on painting his face and strapping on a codpiece now that he was in his fifties. But neither of us wound up laughing, as you'll see when you read the interview. It's tough, not to say pointless, to pretend that you're conducting a typical interview when the guest says things like "if you want to welcome me with open arms I'm afraid you're also going to have to welcome me with open legs." I gave up trying. By the time the encounter was over, we sounded like two first-graders calling each other names, an indignity compounded by the fact that we're both middle-aged adults. Although the show's producers and I weren't even sure at first if the interview merited broadcasting, we eventually decided it made for gripping radio drama, even if it was unlikely to win any journalism awards. It ended up eliciting thousands of e-mails and drawing the attention of many newspapers and magazines. I guess this proves that controversy sells, and so does a good fight (or even a silly fight). But surely, some of this response was based on how totally out of character the whole thing was for National Public Radio. I suspect that if this had happened on commercial radio, the program director would have been in my office the next day encouraging me to fight with my guests all the time to boost our ratings. That's the sort of pressure that hosts on commercial radio and television come under. Thank goodness I'm not in that position.

I HAVEN'T YET MENTIONED THAT MOST of my guests are not in the studio with me. Bringing them to Philadelphia would be too expensive for us and too time-consuming for them. So instead we have them go to the studio of a public radio affiliate close to them and connect with me via satellite or digital lines. When I tell people this, they often assume that my lack of eye contact with guests makes interviewing them much more difficult than it would otherwise be. Truthfully, it often makes it easier. If you're a bit of a coward, as I am, it's easier to ask a challenging question when you're *not* looking someone in the eye—you can't be intimidated by a withering look. Paradoxically, geographical distance sometimes encourages a greater degree of intimacy, especially for someone who's inherently shy, like me. Neither I nor my guest has any reason to be self-conscious, as we might be if we were meeting face-to-face. We can go right to the heart of the matter. On the other hand, the long-distance interview might make it easier for a guest to behave obnoxiously or to storm out.

But I've already told you about Gene Simmons and Bill O'Reilly, haven't I? You're probably wondering when I'm going to stop stalling and tell you more about myself. "What does she look like?" I'm told that's the question most frequently asked about me. The book jacket ought to give you some idea, though it doesn't let you see how very, very short I am. I own a leather bomber jacket that I like to think makes me look reasonably hip. It's from Gap—Gap Kids, that is (the adult-size one was way too big for me). Inside, there's a label that reads: "This coat belongs to _____," in case some other kid has one just like it.

The second most frequently asked question about me is whether I'm straight or gay (this may be number one in San Francisco). Those people who swear I'm a lesbian offer two "clues." The first is my short haircut, which might be described as kind of cute or kind of butch. The second is that we've always featured a lot of openly gay guests on *Fresh Air*.

In fact, this used to get us into a lot of trouble with some of the stations that carried us—mostly in smaller cities where angry listeners complained that it was wrong to let gay people flaunt their sexual practices on the air, even though my interviews with them were about their lives and art, not the ins and outs of gay sex. This used to infuriate me. Program directors would never cater to listeners who objected that we had too many Jews or African Americans on the show, so why should they legitimize homophobia? One night on *The Simpsons,* a gay friend of Homer's broke the news to him that Tennessee Williams was gay. "How did he survive in the cutthroat world of theater?" Homer wondered. His friend explained that everyone who's ever written, acted in, or even seen a play is gay. A comic exaggeration, sure— but it would be ridiculous for a show that specializes in arts and culture to set a quota on gay guests.

Back to me. Because I don't preface my questions to gay guests by pointing out that I'm asking as a straight woman (it sounds like too much of a disclaimer), many listeners assume I must be gay. I'm flattered by the assumption, because it means my questions demonstrate some understanding of the subject at hand. I'm just as flattered when someone hears me talking to a novelist or musician and mistakenly assumes that I write or play an instrument. The confusion about my sexual orientation has led to some pretty amusing scenarios. About ten years ago, when my husband, the writer Francis Davis, won an arts fellowship, I went with him to a reception honoring him and the other recipients. My mother-in-law came with us, and at one point I saw her laughing at something the wife of one of the other fellows had just said to her. She later explained that the woman had pointed at me and whispered, "Terry Gross is here. Did you know she's a lesbian?"

That's one of the reasons I love working on radio: You might be a public figure but you're essentially just a voice, and this lets each person who listens form whatever image of you he or she wants—tall or short, fat or thin, sex bomb or schoolmarm, straight or gay. The invisibility of radio was something I took comfort in early in my career, when I felt so physically unassuming that I might as well have been invisible, and when I actually was—it felt right. All you are on radio is a mind and a disembodied voice, and for someone as physically self-conscious as I am, this can been liberating.

OF COURSE MY LISTENERS ARE INVISIBLE, too—at least to me. I'm always amazed by the diversity of the show's listeners and the settings they listen in. One of my favorite fan letters was from a prison inmate who wrote to tell us he was grateful that his local station carried *Fresh Air* at 4:00 P.M.—"a convenient and quiet hour, because prisoners have to be counted at 4:30." You never know how the program fits into someone's day.

I've been hosting *Fresh Air* almost my entire adult life. In 1975, when I was twenty-four, I was hired by David Karpoff, the program director of WHYY-FM in Philadelphia (then called WUHY-FM) and the creator of *Fresh Air,* to replace Judy Blank, who was leaving her position as the program's host and producer. The program I inherited was a local show, broadcast from 2:00 P.M. to 5:00 P.M. each weekday—the same time slot as *This Is Radio,* the program I had been co-hosting at WBFO-FM in Buffalo, on the university campus. But not only did I have no cohost on *Fresh Air,* I had no staff. I was on my own until January 1978, when a student from Temple University showed up at the station and asked if he could work as an unpaid intern on *Fresh Air.* After bumming a cigarette, he told me that he was studying film at Temple; that he played piano in a salsa band and taught music therapy at a senior citizens center; that his record collection included albums by Charlie Parker, Charles Mingus, and Lenny Bruce; and that he was a big fan of the movie *Taxi Driver*—an ideal résumé, as far as I was concerned.

Danny Miller is still with *Fresh Air* twenty-five years later and counting, only now he's our executive producer and it's impossible for any of us to imagine what the show would be like without him—or if there would even still be a show. Danny approves every piece of tape that goes on the air, determines its final length, and evaluates whether we're presenting an issue fairly. He also rules on which words are unacceptable for broadcast and need to be bleeped or edited out of interviews, readings, lyrics, and film clips. When he decides no bleep is necessary, he has the peculiar task of writing Sensitive Language Advisories to program directors, explaining why our broadcast is going to include such words or phrases as "wanker," "jerking off," "big dick," "floppy penis," "sanctimonious prick," "happy twitching in his shorts," "cunnilingus," "big jugs," "wipes his ass," "red-hot poker up his ass," or "for me to poop on." I often find these advisories quite entertaining, though I doubt program directors find them amusing.

But Danny's contributions to the show and to keeping our workday harmonious hardly end there. He oversees everything, and his office is the place to go when you have a problem—a dilemma with an interview, a budget question, or something personal. He always has a solution.

Let me give you some idea of how the show is put together. We have three interview producers. Amy Salit handles the book interviews, Naomi Person deals with film and TV, Monique Nazareth focuses on issues in the news—but they all produce interviews related to issues that interest them, and all of them are free to set up music interviews. Phyllis Myers produces the reviewers and commentators who help to keep us and our listeners up-to-date on the latest books, movies, CDs, and TV shows.

The one indispensable element to a good interview is a good guest, and this is something our producers take care of beautifully. Once a guest is booked, Jessica Chiu, our researcher, finds me the material I need to prepare. After an interview is recorded, one of our associate producers—either Jessica, Patty Leswing, or Ian Chillag—edits the tape in collaboration with the interview producer, rearranging the order of the questions, if necessary, but also taking out the bluster, the dead ends, the redundancies, and the "like"s, the "you know"s, and the "um"s that would drive even our most devoted listeners crazy if they ever heard them. It doesn't end there: The tape is passed back and forth among the interview producer, the associate producer, and our executive producer, and re-edited until everyone is satisfied—or until the show is ready to begin and we run out of time.

The edited interviews and the music CDs are rolled in during the broadcast, around my live introductions and announcements. There's a hell of a lot going on, in other words, and all of it is smoothly coordinated by our director, Roberta Shorrock. Our engineer, usually Julian Herzfeld or Audrey Bentham, handles the technological end. Ann Marie Baldonado takes the most entertaining interviews and reviews of the week and re-edits them into our weekend edition, *Fresh Air Weekend*. When it's all over and listeners call to say they loved or hated what they just heard, the person they're likely to speak with is Dorothy Ferebee, our station services coordinator.

I'm lucky to work with people who are not just talented but fun to spend the day with—which is probably more than they can say about me, since I tend to be edgy and preoccupied when facing a deadline, which I am most all the time, even when I go home. The problem is that those of us who are lucky enough to do work that we love are sometimes cursed with too damn much of it. Each weeknight, I work straight through the evening preparing for the next day's interviews. If a friend happens to call, I reluctantly have to cut the conversation short and get back to work. My efforts to be a well-prepared and sensitive interviewer sometimes make me an insensitive friend. I often ask my guests about the paradoxes in their lives. I guess that's one of mine.

THOUGH THE INTERVIEWS COLLECTED HERE WERE edited before their original broadcasts, editing them specifically for the page required a few additional steps. Of necessity, we've had to leave out authors' readings and music and film excerpts that you might remember hearing when these interviews were broadcast on *Fresh Air*. It became necessary to rewrite some of my questions to close some of the gaps we were left with as a result. With the exception of the occasional John Updike, no one speaks readable, perfectly grammatical sentences. So we've edited the answers my questions elicited for clarity and concision, while sticking as closely as possible to each interviewee's actual speaking style. As for my questions, I've frequently taken advantage of the opportunity to clarify my wording, though I've resisted the temptation to make myself sound smarter or more clever.

A note about the arrangement of the interviews: Rather than group together writers in one section, musicians in another, and so on, Margaret Pick (my collaborator on this book) and I have mixed them up to provide for variety and contrast, in keeping with the spirit of *Fresh Air*. But we have attempted to take advantage of certain "affinities" between interviewees. For example, it seemed logical to have Paul Schrader, Jodie Foster, and Albert Brooks follow one another here because they all worked together on *Taxi Driver,* and because each had something to say about that movie. In many cases, the "affinity" isn't so obvious; some of the sequencing is purely intuitive. The original broadcast date is given at the end of each interview.

With one exception, all of these interviews were recorded after *Fresh Air* became a daily national program in 1987: The interview with James Baldwin was recorded in 1986. Regular listeners of *Fresh Air* are likely to be surprised by the absence of certain of the show's most frequent guests. Frankly, so am I. It's just that in putting this book together, I found that several of what I'd always thought of as my favorite interviews sounded much better than they read. Richard Price and Scott Spencer aren't included here, even though these are two of my favorite novelists. This is my fault, not theirs: I've interviewed Price many times, always keeping the focus on his latest book or screenplay, which means that each of the interviews I did with him now sounds a little bit dated. Sadly, the same is true of my many interviews with Spencer.

The best part of producing a daily show is knowing that many listeners come to consider you a regular companion. The worst part is hardly having a minute between one deadline and the next and doing everything in a hurry. I almost always wish I had more time to prepare for interviews, and more time to spend with each guest. The interviews presented here were conducted on the run and are by no means "definitive." But I hope you'll accept them in the spirit in which they're offered, as entertaining and thought-provoking conversations with people I believe are worthy of your time.

One last thing: Although this book represents the work of many people, I take full blame for all the questions you think I should have asked but didn't.

PHILADELPHIA
January 2004

ALL I DID WAS ASK

Don't Do It

Nicolas Cage

*He's still very sensitive about the perception that he's wacky,
because his performance isn't that. It's all hard work. Nothing
in it is arbitrary.*

Mike Figgis, director of *Leaving Las Vegas*, to Steve Daly, *Entertainment
Weekly*, March 15, 1996

Nicolas Cage might be as famous for his obsessive preparation as
he is for the riveting performances he gives as a result of it. Cage
has starred in both lighthearted comedies and weighty dramas, brood-
ing independent films and big-budget action blockbusters. His best-
known movies include *Leaving Las Vegas* (for which he won an
Oscar), *The Cotton Club, Rumble Fish,* and *Peggy Sue Got Married*
(all directed by his uncle Francis Ford Coppola), *Birdy, Moonstruck,
Raising Arizona, It Could Happen to You, Red Rock West, The Rock,*
and *Con Air*. But everyone has his or her own favorites among Cage's
movies—even if no one else's would, my list would have to include
Vampire's Kiss and *Amos & Andrew.*

What appears below combines questions and answers from
each of Cage's two visits to *Fresh Air*. Our first conversation was in

1990, when Cage was promoting David Lynch's *Wild at Heart*. We spoke again in 2002, when Cage starred in *Windtalkers,* a film about World War II directed by John Woo, who had also directed him in *Face/Off* five years earlier.

TERRY GROSS: You've watched yourself die time and time again in movies. Does it put you in touch with the inevitability of your own death? Do you take it personally when you see yourself die in a movie?

NICOLAS CAGE: Well, I see it very much as a performance. My own feelings about death are almost Japanese in thinking. There is a samurai philosophy that you have to earn your right to die. Death has always been sort of a friend to me, because I've never ignored the fact that it's going to happen, I'm very accepting of it. It's always been something that I wear on my shoulder that says, "Get to work, because you only have so much time."

TG: Is that an attitude you've worked on or one that just came naturally to you?

CAGE: It started when I was about fifteen. I remember that I didn't really believe in heaven or hell at that time. But I did believe in death. So I made a vow to myself that if I could achieve certain goals in my life that I would be okay with my death. I've since changed my views somewhat, but I don't see death as a horrible thing.

You know, there's a 50 percent chance it could be really amazing, because no one really knows what it is. I had to go through my will the other day with my attorney, and questions came up like, "What is it that you want if, God forbid, you're in a car accident? Do you want to be in a coma or do you want them to pull the plug?" And I'm, like, "God, I've got to think about this." But I said, "Well, you know, I hear coma's not a bad place, so maybe not, but what I do know is that I don't want to be bombed out of my skull on some massive dose of morphine. If I go into the next life, I want to go in aware. If there is a next life, I'd like to be aware." So I had them write that down.

TG: Don't you think, though, you might want the pain dulled if—

CAGE: Yeah. I mean, that's the tricky part. Remember those Buddhists that set themselves on fire during the Vietnam War? How do they get to that point to be so in control of their state to not even flinch when they're burning to death? I think it's a life's work to actually prepare yourself for the moment of death.

TG: Are your ideas about death in any way connected to your approach to acting? Do you see acting as an altered state, or an act of willed consciousness?

CAGE: It's strange. I do see it as an altered state. I think that's a good way of putting it. As crazy as it sounds, I almost see it like channeling spirits.

TG: You've been in a couple of films directed by John Woo. You've said about Woo's films that even though there is "a lot of death in them, there's also the notion of being closer to God." Do you ever wish that you could have that kind of faith, too? Maybe you have it. Maybe I am making an assumption.

CAGE: No, I do have faith. I believe in God, and I am a Christian.

TG: I know that you've gone to extremes to develop that altered state of consciousness to get into a role.

CAGE: Well, yeah, I had to learn publicly through trial and error. Sometimes I fell on my face. Sometimes it worked. I started when I was seventeen, and I really didn't have that much training. So I did all the things that I'd heard the other great actors had done, like staying up all night to do a scene the next day to look tired. In *Cotton Club* I was playing a crazy gangster who was very feared in Harlem. I would walk down the street in New York and really believe I was this psychotic killer. I brought all that stuff to the scene. And it worked. But needless to say, I wasn't liked very much. I mean, I do have a life. I don't really want to live the part anymore. So I stopped doing that. I realized I could get there without all that intense "living the role" kind of a thing.

TG: What did you do when you were taking the "living the role" thing to extremes?

CAGE: Well, once I went down to Christopher Street, and there was a guy selling remote-control cars for fifty bucks, and I said, "Let me see that." I put it in the middle of the street, and I jumped on it and smashed it. All the pieces were flying around. All the people just scattered, saying, "Oh, you're crazy." I did give the guy fifty bucks for his car, but it helped me believe that I could create fear in people—which is what that character did in the movie.

TG: Before that, you had no confidence that you were capable of generating fear in people?

CAGE: Well, I'm not a violent guy. I'm not a fighter. When I was playing that role, I was young. I was experimenting with trying to evoke fear, so that I could believe it in myself for the character. But I've learned that it's not necessary. It's a lot more creative and thoughtful to just act the role.

TG: Let's talk a little bit about *Vampire's Kiss*. This is the movie where you ate the cockroach. It's a wonderful film. You play a character who's a very obnoxious literary agent. After he's bitten by a woman he sleeps with, he starts to believe that she is a vampire and that he is turning into one. He shrinks at the sign of the cross and asks people to put a stake through his heart to take him out of his misery. It's an incredibly original performance. You must have watched all the new and old horror films to get the classic vampire gestures for the movie.

CAGE: Well, I was exposed to the movie *Nosferatu* at a very early age because my father was teaching film. The original *Nosferatu*, starring Max Schreck, the black-and-white, silent vampire movie, gave me nightmares for years. Those images, especially his body language, his gestures and movements, stayed with me. I always thought it would be great to be able to incorporate that kind of silent film acting into modern film. They used their bodies more because they had to compensate for the lack of sound.

With *Vampire's Kiss,* I saw an opportunity to explore that German Expressionist style of acting, like in *The Cabinet of Dr. Caligari.* I figured the only way I could pull it off was if the character was insane, because you can't really act like that in modern film in a normal format. People just wouldn't get it. But if the character is insane, and especially if he thinks he's turning into a vampire, there's a wonderful landscape of things you can do. So I brought those old-style gestures to the character.

TG: Let's get to the cockroach-eating sequence. There's a scene where you are in your kitchen, after you've concluded you're turning into a vampire. There's a cockroach crawling across the burner of the stove. You scoop it up in your hand and eat it. We don't see you swallow it in the movie. But we do see you chewing on it. There's no edit, so it's definitely the real thing that's gone into your mouth.

CAGE: Yeah, definitely the real thing. Originally, they wanted me to eat raw eggs, and that didn't do anything for me.

TG: Sylvester Stallone had already done that.

CAGE: Yeah, exactly. And I wanted to tie in the Renfield thing—Renfield from the *Dracula* novel where he was eating the bugs and stuff.

TG: Renfield is Dracula's assistant. He's in an insane asylum and he eats insects.

CAGE: Right. And it was a slow progression for my character, Peter Loew. First he's eating pistachios, then he's eating a cockroach, then he finally eats the dove. Ultimately he bites a girl's neck, kills her, and drinks her blood. So it was this progressive building from pistachio to girl. The cockroach was one of the steps in the disintegration of Peter Loew.

So I said, "I want to try eating a cockroach." Everybody was like, "You've got to be crazy!" And I said, "Yeah, I—I know what you mean. I really don't like cockroaches myself." They wrangled up three New York cockroaches out of somebody's basement, and the day arrived where I had to do it. I saw the bug when I walked on the set. The legs were kicking. The antennas were going. It looked huge. I almost said, "Guys, I can't do it." I figured that it would be a cop-out, because I'd set it up and made them wrangle for cockroaches for weeks.

I put the cockroach close to me. Every muscle in my body was saying, "Don't do it." The wings were going. And then I—I did it. And—I couldn't sleep for about three days. I couldn't eat. But well, I did it. And there it is.

TG: **Did you call a doctor first and ask if chewing a cockroach could kill you?**

CAGE: Yeah. They said it would be okay. What I did was I rinsed my mouth out with hundred-proof vodka and sterilized my mouth before I did it. And then when I spit the cockroach out, I sterilized my mouth again.

TG: **What did it taste like?**

CAGE: Oh, you know, I couldn't remember. All I know is it was soft. It was not crunchy. It was soft. And it was—it was just a nightmare.

TG: **Did it ever come back and haunt you?**

CAGE: When I talk about it like this and I start thinking about it, I get goose bumps. I'm starting to get the willies again.

TG: **There are at least two different threads to your career: one, the more action-oriented roles, and the other, the more introspective roles like *Leaving Las Vegas* or *Red Rock West*. Did you ever expect to become an action hero when you started acting? Were you ever physical in that kind of way, or athletic, when you were young?**

CAGE: I always liked action films as a boy, but I was probably the last person on the list for starring in an action movie, even though I wanted to. I had heroes like Clint Eastwood and Sean Connery, who I was lucky to work with in *The Rock*.

I always saw it as escapist entertainment, which to me is just as valuable as the thought-provoking and introspective work that actors do in art films or indie films, because, to be honest with you, there are times when I don't want to think. I just want to get my mind off my problems, and have my popcorn and escape.

To answer your question, I was not someone who was perceived as action material, and then Jerry Bruckheimer cast me in *The Rock*. But even so, I was playing a nerd who becomes an action hero. I was trying to build my foreign market up, and I thought more people would see the work, and I thought, "Well, why not try to do something with action movies? Just because it's a genre picture doesn't mean you can't create a character."

What I found was that I have to be very quick on my feet and very succinct about what it is I want to say, because it is a formula. They want to get to the car chase or to the explosion, so whatever acting you do, you've got to do it fast, which is frustrating, but it's also good training. It does distill your acting down to the precise essence of the character.

TG: **Since becoming an action hero, you've had to change your body, pump up a lot. Has it also changed your sense of self?**

CAGE: Well, no. Actually, the truth of the matter is that I've always been physical. I started working out when I was twelve years old.

TG: **What motivated you to do that when you were so young?**

CAGE: I wanted to look better and feel stronger. Then I got addicted to it. It became a place where I could put my anger. As a young boy growing up, I had a lot of anger that needed to be directed or focused, and working out helped me with that. To this day, I've used exercise as a place to sort of clear my head and relax, although I do prefer to look trim.

TG: **The movie you received an Academy Award for, *Leaving Las Vegas*, was based on a story by a writer who was so depressed that he killed himself before the movie was made. Could you comprehend that level of depression?**

CAGE: Well, I made a choice early on in the rehearsal process that I wasn't going to play him depressed, because I always felt that there's nothing sadder than a person who's in a sad situation and doesn't know it. Consequently, I thought that Ben Sanderson—even though the truth is that he is so depressed that he's going to drink himself to death—on the surface, had freed himself. And he'd be smiling and laughing a lot. I thought that would make it even more sad.

I saw Ben as somebody who had let go and was not afraid to die, and therefore, he could do anything. He was going to have four weeks to do it, and he was going to have one big party; and he was responsible about it. He cashed out. He cleared his debts, and he wasn't going to be a burden to anybody anymore. He wasn't going to be a burden to his boss. In fact, he feels bad that he upset his boss.

TG: **I read that your mother suffered from depression. My guess is that she wasn't the kind of wisecracking depressive that your character is in *Leaving Las Vegas*. Did your experience of her depression inform your performance?**

CAGE: Oh, yeah. I mean, I'm sure it did. I think there are moments in the movie where I watch and I go, "Well, that's Mom." But these are things that happen almost by accident. I don't think about it.

TG: **Your character is drunk during a lot of *Leaving Las Vegas*. Did you drink while preparing for the role in order to get a sense of what goes on mechanically when you've had a lot to drink?**

CAGE: I did, in fact, drink on a couple scenes in that movie because I wanted it to be extremely real. I would drink on my own and then videotape myself getting drunk so that I could see what I was like. Then I destroyed the videotape, but I would use that experience as a way to get into the character. There is one scene in the casino where I freak out, and I smash the table and break a glass and start shouting, where I am completely inebriated for real. So much so that I had to crawl to my room after I had done the scene. I don't think I ever made it into my hotel room. I actually fell asleep outside the door and woke up in the morning in the hallway.

I don't recommend it for actors, I mean, I don't know how healthy it is. But I was experimenting with the idea of being out of control in art. Being in control while being out of control is the goal.

So I said, "Well, this scene—I don't have a lot of dialogue, and I'm going to go out of control here. I want to create that kind of connection with the audience where they feel as if there's danger in the room, and I want them to freak out with me." That's why I did it.

TG: Was the director, Mike Figgis, disturbed when he saw how drunk you were? Did he know what you were up to?

CAGE: He was a part of the process the whole time. He knew that I was going to go there, and he concurred.

TG: The movie *Face/Off*, which you starred in with John Travolta, is a great action film that's also very funny. It was directed by John Woo, who also directed you in *Windtalkers*. You play a sadistic criminal, and John Travolta is an FBI agent on your trail. For reasons too complicated to explain here, you surgically trade faces and then have to impersonate each other. It must have been fun to copy each other's mannerisms within the performance. What did Travolta pick up on about you?

CAGE: Well, he picked up the way I tend to elongate my words when I talk, sort of like, "There's a glass aahbject that I'm really interested in baahying, Jaahn."

TG: Did it make you self-conscious to hear him doing a takeoff on you?

CAGE: Well, I didn't know that I had that manner of speaking, but now I do, so now when I hear myself, I'm thinking, "My God, am I becoming a caricature of myself?"

TG: Is that self-consciousness potentially dangerous?

CAGE: I don't know that it's dangerous. When I first started acting, I felt that my voice was not interesting at all. It occurred to me that all the great actors I loved were stars like Bogart, or Cagney, or Brando, or Eastwood, who have voices you can imitate; and it's fun to be able to imitate them. I worked very hard to understand what was distinctive about my voice and tried to accentuate it. But at first, I was doing everything I could *not* to use my voice. Even in *Peggy Sue Got Married,* I used the voice of—I think it was Pokey—from *The Gumby Show,* which was really a stretch.

TG: **Your voice is very colloquial-sounding, yet you have this impeccable pronunciation.**

CAGE: My father is a literature professor, and I remember, he always spoke with this distinction in his voice, and I guess that was a choice for him. He told me that because he's a literature professor, he wanted to speak with distinction and to speak accurately with proper English. I'm an amalgamation of my father and also this kid who grew up in Long Beach, California, surrounded by people who did not speak with distinction.

TG: **How did you know, as a child, that you wanted to act?**

CAGE: I was six years old, sitting on the living room carpet, watching our old, oval-shaped Zenith TV, and I remember, I wanted to be inside that TV so bad. That's my first cognizant recollection of wanting to act. I couldn't understand how people got inside the television set, and I wanted to go there.

TG: **Several of your early films were directed by your uncle Francis Ford Coppola: *Rumble Fish, Peggy Sue Got Married,* and *Cotton Club.* You're a Coppola, why did you change your name to Cage?**

CAGE: I went in to read for *Rumble Fish.* And to my surprise they said, "Well, we'd like you to be in the movie." I was still Nicholas Coppola, and I felt a lot of pressure from the other actors, thinking I didn't have the goods because it was a case of nepotism. It made me a little stiff. So I changed my name.

TG: **Why did you choose Cage as your last name?**

CAGE: I used to read a lot of comic books. There was a [Marvel] superhero, and his name was Luke Cage, Powerman. I thought it was a cool-sounding name. Then I was listening to John Cage's music, which I found very stimulating. And I decided to use it. It sounded right to me. Simple and to the point.

TG: I've read that you have a tattoo of a lizard on your back. When you see your back in a mirror, doesn't it give you the creeps?

CAGE: No. That's part of the reason why I put it on my back. I really don't see it that often.

TG: Why did you get the tattoo?

CAGE: Well, it was Halloween 1984, and I had broken up with my girlfriend, and I felt like I had to do something radical. I guess I was getting ready to become a man. It was my way of saying, "I'm my own person—I'm breaking free of the family." I was the first one in the family to get a tattoo. In retrospect it was kind of a walkabout, if you will, or a bar mitzvah.

TG: How did you show it to your family?

CAGE: I said, "Dad, I got a tattoo." I lifted up my shirt. He saw it, and his face went white. He had himself a martini. And that was that.

July 27, 1990, and June 13, 2002

LIKE A SKINNY BOXER

Chris Rock

At the time Chris was coming up, the Def Comedy Jam *style became the dominant African-American style of comedy. The shock was in the language. But Chris was going with the shock of ideas.*

Lorne Michaels, to Christopher John Farley, *Time*, July 20, 1998

We're very big on popular culture at *Fresh Air*. Along with a bust of George Foster Peabody that fell off the Peabody Award we received in 1994, among the items you'll find on the desk of Danny Miller, the show's executive producer, are a plastic figure of Lisa Simpson, *Scarface* refrigerator magnets, and a John Holmes ("Johnny Wad") Big Boy Ruler, which Danny might prefer I didn't mention. Oh, and one more thing—a Nat X action figure replete with Afro, dashiki, and a button you can push to see him give the black-power salute.

Nat X was one of Chris Rock's regular characters on *Saturday Night Live*—a black-militant TV host whose show was only fifteen minutes long because "the man" was afraid to give him a half hour. (Remember the "whitey-cam"? It let us see what Nat X would look like behind bars, which was where "whitey" thought he belonged.)

Rock was an *SNL* cast member for three years, beginning in 1993. In his HBO comedy specials, he takes on racial and political issues that many comics would consider to be too controversial or in bad taste. But some of his funniest television appearances have been as the host of the MTV Video Music Awards, a capacity in which he has taken wicked delight in mocking fellow celebrities. I spoke with him in 1997, just before the premiere of his HBO series *The Chris Rock Show*.

TERRY GROSS: **Probably the most controversial part of your stand-up act, in the early days of your career, was talking about what you describe as "the civil war between black people." You ask, "Who's more racist, black people or white people?" The punch line is "Black people." When you wrote this, were you thinking about experiences you had, or people you know?**

CHRIS ROCK: Well, I'm just interpreting. Everything I said in that routine, my mother said. My father said. I heard it in barbershops. It's not like I invented anything. You know, these views have been out there forever. Just nobody said it.

TG: **If a white comic said exactly the same thing, would it have a completely different meaning?**

ROCK: Yes, it would. Why would a white comic want to say what I said, though? In what context would that ever be necessary?

TG: **Well, what is the difference between you saying it and a white comic saying it?**

ROCK: I can say it. What's the difference between someone calling your kid an idiot and you calling your kid an idiot? It's a big difference. It's a huge difference. Your kid knows what you mean when you say it. Your kid knows you just mean he's messing up. But when somebody else says it, boy, that's mean.

TG: **Did you go through a radical black-consciousness period when you were in your teens?**

ROCK: No, you know, when I was in my teens—that's like the eighties—

it wasn't exactly the most conscious decade. I was bused to school as a kid.

TG: **From where to where?**

ROCK: From Bed-Stuy to Gerritsen Beach, and to Bensonhurst. I was getting called "nigger" since I was in the second grade. I was always in tune with my blackness, from the time I was in the second grade.

TG: **Were there a lot of other people from your neighborhood who got bused to Bensonhurst?**

ROCK: There was about five of us.

TG: **Five? That's all?**

ROCK: Yeah, you know, when I say "the neighborhood," I'm just talking about, like, a two-block radius. When you grow up in a bad neighborhood, there's not a lot of venturing out. So my neighborhood was like two blocks to me. Then the rest of the neighborhood—I didn't go anywhere 'cause anything could happen. My mother wasn't having it.

TG: **How many African American students would you say there were in the schools that you got bused to?**

ROCK: I was the only black kid in my grade a couple of times. I was the only black boy, and then there were two black girls, for most of my grade school. The girls had each other. I was by myself. It's weird. Even though I would get beat up, of course, my best friend would end up being white. Then he'd get beat up for being my friend. It's a weird circle of events.

TG: **Do you think that being so alienated as a kid contributed to your being a comedian?**

ROCK: Yes, I was alienated. I had nothing else to do. You know, I always loved comedy. I had nothing to fall back on. I have no real skills. If I picked up a paper right now and went through the want ads, there's nothing I could get that would pay me more than the minimum wage. So I loved comedy, got into it, was a little twisted. My schooling had twisted me somewhat. It really helped me out.

TG: I have a question about your voice. Onstage, when you're doing comedy, your voice is much deeper, louder, and rougher than your voice in conversation, which is higher and lighter—almost sweeter, if I could use that word.

ROCK: Well, thanks.

TG: I wonder why you are not comfortable with that voice onstage? Do you feel you need a harder-edged voice to do your comedy?

ROCK: Well, you know, the money's on the line. People are paying twenty-five dollars. They want a performance. They don't want me, they want me to be better than me. I gotta look better than me. I gotta be taller, louder, funnier. When you're onstage, it's kind of like being a woman. It's put on the makeup; do the hair. You know, nobody wants *me*. They want *Chris Rock*! I'm just Chris. By the same token, I couldn't walk through life acting the way I act onstage.

TG: Well, right, without getting hit a lot.

ROCK: Right. Exactly.

TG: Did being skinny affect how people thought of you or how you see yourself as a comic? Were you kind of scrawny as a kid?

ROCK: I'm scrawny now as a man. Totally. Being skinny has affected every aspect of my life—every decision I make; everything I put on. Put it this way: Look at my stand-up. I always say stand-up comedy and boxing are pretty much the same. You know, boxing is to sports what stand-up is to entertainment, 'cause there's just a guy out there by himself. I perform like a skinny boxer. My size has me so insecure; I'm always working twice as hard. I don't have the ability to knock you out. So you take my hour special and anybody else's hour special—I probably have twice as many jokes packed into it. Being skinny has totally affected me, and totally, totally, totally weirded me out.

TG: Speaking of boxing, when you were young, did people try to pick fights with you and take advantage of your size?

ROCK: Totally, totally. The only reason they don't do it now is 'cause, you know, I'm "me."

TG: **Right. You're famous.**

ROCK: That's the only reason.

TG: **Did you learn to fight?**

ROCK: When you're as small as I am, it doesn't really matter.

TG: **Did you try martial arts or anything?**

ROCK: You know, what's the point? Some big guy will just grab you and throw you down.

TG: **Well, did you try to cripple your opponent with comedy?**

ROCK: Wow, I just stayed out of situations where fights might occur. I don't drink because I can't fight. Wherever alcohol's served, there's a bouncer 'cause people get out of hand. I'm too little to be around guys that get out of hand. So I can't drink. Woe is me.

February 6, 1997

BEING SQUARE

John Updike

*The ideal novel, Stendhal once observed, is like "a mirror that
strolls along a highway. Now it reflects the blue of the skies,
now the mud puddles underfoot." It's a definition happily and
abundantly fulfilled by John Updike's four Rabbit novels:*
Rabbit, Run, Rabbit Redux, Rabbit Is Rich *and now* Rabbit
at Rest.

> *Taken together, this quartet of novels has given its
readers a wonderfully vivid portrait of one Harry (Rabbit)
Angstrom, a small-town Pennsylvania basketball star turned
car salesman, and in chronicling the passing parade of Harry's
life, the books have also created a Kodachrome-sharp picture
of American life—the psychic ups and downs; enthusiasms
and reversals experienced by this nation as it moved from the
somnolent '50s through the upheavals of the '60s and '70s
into the uncertainties of the '80s.*

Michiko Kakutani, *The New York Times*, September 25, 1990

One of my favorite literary memoirs is John Updike's *Self-
Consciousness,* in which Updike unflinchingly reveals the psori-
asis, the stuttering, and the other physical and emotional problems at
the root of his insecurities. Another of my favorites is Nicholson
Baker's *U and I,* a creepy, laugh-out-loud-funny examination of why

Updike's literary abundance leaves Baker feeling inadequate. At one point in *U and I,* Baker measures his own stumbling performance in a radio interview (one on *Fresh Air,* he later told me) against Updike's stellar performance on a 1983 public-television documentary. "[I]n one scene," Baker writes, "as the camera follows his climb up a ladder at his mother's house to put up or take down some storm windows . . . he tosses down to us some startlingly lucid little felicity, something about, 'These small yearly duties which blah blah blah,' and I was stunned to recognize that in Updike we were dealing with a man so naturally verbal that he could write his fucking memoirs *on a ladder!*"

Unlike Baker, I don't have to compete with Updike—his "startling lucidity" makes an interviewer look good. That's one reason he's been a frequent guest on *Fresh Air;* the other is my deep admiration for his writing. This interview is different from the others I've done with him, and different from the others collected in this book. It was recorded in front of an audience in 1997 at the Free Library of Philadelphia as part of its author lecture series. Although I generally prefer the intimacy of talking with a guest in a studio, I am willing to admit that the performance aspect of facing an enthusiastic audience like the one we had at the Free Library can keep both the interviewer and the interviewee on their toes.

TERRY GROSS: **Has aging been an interesting process for you because it offers new territory to write about?**

JOHN UPDIKE: It's true. Every day, you are older than you've ever been before. In a sense, you are blazing a trail, and sending back news to the younger of what it's like. The older I get, the more I think of my parents. My father lived to be seventy-two, and my mother to quite a good age, eighty-five, although that was not as old as her father became. He lived to be ninety. So yes, I am aware of aging, but I do it in a hopeful spirit because, with any kind of luck, I have fairly long-lived genes and see this as a territory with some advantages. It's certainly more peaceful than your middle years, and certainly your sense of yourself is more solid than it was when you were an adolescent. Many of the questions you ask of life have been answered.

TG: **Are there things that you feel haven't been said about aging that you are trying to explore in your writing now?**

UPDIKE: One's witness is individual. I don't know as I have any special news about aging. Getting old is more and more the usual thing. An old person used to be a survivor and was kind of heroic for having survived. In Africa and China, they would look to their old people for wisdom because to have lived a long time was a great accomplishment. It's not so great for a twentieth-century American. Instead of playing less, you tend to play more. I know that my contemporaries, as they retire, have ever more time to play. I am invited to join in this kind of return of childhood, but I'm still trying to work. When you're a self-employed writer, there's nobody to tell you to retire. So you go on until you drop. What else can I say about aging? I say that the sex instinct does not die, that it remains, inconvenient as it sometimes is.

TG: **Speaking of your life in New England, you said, "My impersonation of a normal person in Ipswich became as good as I could make it." If you were impersonating a normal person, who was the real you?**

UPDIKE: I never felt quite normal. It always seemed to me that other people knew more than I did and were possibly having more fun. I was an only child, so I was denied the companionship and the life lessons that siblings give one. I lived with four older people: my mother's parents and my own parents. I had several afflictions, which, while not fatal, served to intensify my sense of being a boy apart. I stammered a certain amount, not so much that I didn't keep trying to get the word out, but enough to annoy me and probably annoy those around me. I had a skin condition; although nonfatal and nonpainful, it was humiliating.

Then, added to this, this wish to be a writer was unusual in small-town Pennsylvania. Being a writer was a very odd idea that wouldn't have occurred to me, but it *had* occurred to my mother. She was really the person in the family called to write. She was the one I watched tap away at her typewriter. She was the one who kept at it and implanted in me something of an ambition.

TG: While you were writing about the middle class, the middle class went crazy. People were doing drugs and drinking a lot. Marriages were breaking up, and new relationships were forming; there were affairs on the side. Was this an interesting time to be writing about the middle class?

UPDIKE: It turned out to be. I didn't plan these events. I was, like many in the fifties, married young. The most feasible way of getting a woman to go to bed with you was to marry her. The intention was to create little nuclear households of happy children, and humming appliances, and a collie dog in a station wagon. And I acquired all of that, not the collie, but a golden retriever, which seemed close enough.

And then, in the revolution of the sixties, that world really came apart. In 1963, when John Kennedy was shot, somehow, that let loose a lot of demons; the discontent that the fifties conformity had imperfectly masked really let loose. We were a little old for the revolution. By this time, we were parents of small children, four, in my case. I suppose there was a general wish to join in the fun. So we had our own little sexual revolution, suburban sexual revolution, which took the unhappy form of divorce, often. Very few of those fifties marriages survived, locally.

But, yes, I wrote about couples. Trying to describe this generation, for which the various faiths, patriotic and religious, had faded and for whom, unlike today, their professions offered no deep diversion. The men had jobs, but they only worked nine to five. Jobs were, by no means, as consuming; you did them on the side. But your real life was the social life, the parties where you would take your wife and look at the other wives. It was a world in which people tried, in the absence of another compelling religion, to make a religion of each other, a kind of cult intermingling. It was the heyday of the Julia Child dinner party. It was the heyday of the Sunday afternoon volleyball game. It was a lot of "rubbing elbows," my father used to call it.

TG: The first *Rabbit* novel was published in 1960, about three years after Jack Kerouac's *On the Road*. In the beginning of the novel, Rabbit leaves his wife. He is restless, unhappy, frustrated. And he takes off in his car and drives south. He has no idea where he is going, he can't tell if he has gotten there yet because he has no destination, and he ends up just turning around and going back home. It's an interesting counterpoint to *On the Road*, which is about the fun and the adventure and the excitement of being on the road.

Did you ever feel that you were missing out on the adventure that other writers of your generation were having—the sense that the road is filled with mystical adventures, lots of sex and drugs and freedom, and exciting things to write about? You were creating beautifully crafted, intricate prose, a direct counterpoint to the jazz improvisational style of the Beat writers of your generation.

UPDIKE: They didn't feel like my generation. They felt like a slightly older generation. I *was* sort of jealous of Kerouac. I *did* think he was having more fun than I was, and I resented that so much that I didn't read *On the Road* for years after it came out. My Pennsylvania small-town farm boy mentality argued against this vision of being on the road; it seemed to me we couldn't all be on the road, all the time. Nothing would get done. And the reality surely is that we are all a party to a social contract. And when one unit in the social web takes off, there are tugs and breaks he leaves behind him. So that *Rabbit, Run* was, in some sense, a kind of an anti–*On the Road*. Yes, he breaks away, and there is that within us which cries out for freedom, which rebels against the constraints. Rabbit is faced with an alcoholic and pregnant wife and a dead-end job of no great charm, a glorious past as a high school athletic hero, and a general sense of being caught. He is a rabbit in a trap. So he breaks out. But then I thought it was more realistic that such a person would get lost on the road after one glorious burst of freedom, and return to where he came from. That was my take on *On the Road* and its philosophy.

TG: Did you worry that hipsters were going to think you were square?

UPDIKE: I *am* square. I suppose being square didn't frighten me too much. To me, the act of creating poems and stories that got into print was so otherworldly that I thought I was cool. It was cool to try to perceive a pattern, to make tales out of this grayish, middle-class, amorphous life around one. I was a happy man.

TG: You write in your memoir, "My success was based, I felt, on a certain calculated modesty, on my cultivated fondness for exploring corners—the space beneath the Shillington dining table, where the nap of the rug was still thick; the back stairs, where the vacuum cleaner and rubber galoshes lived . . . I had left the heavily trafficked literary turfs to others and stayed in my corner of New England to give its domestic news."

"Domestic news" has traditionally been the territory of women writers, whereas men traditionally wrote about adventure, war, and the big issues of the day. Do you feel that you brought a male point of view to a territory that had, for the most part, been women's territory in fiction?

UPDIKE: That hadn't occurred to me. My concrete objective was to get enough stories in *The New Yorker* that I could support my own domestic scene, which rapidly included four children. And *The New Yorker* ran, almost entirely, stories about domestic situations. Shawn, who was then editor, had a personal aversion toward violence. You never saw what would pass for an adventure story in *The New Yorker*. So I was really one of the crowd. And in some way, the American home was where it was at in those years. I didn't feel I was cultivating a backwater. I thought that this was standard for everybody, more or less, except Jack Kerouac. He, funnily enough, kept coming back to his mother. Neal Cassady and Ginsberg were fine for a while, but he'd come back to Momma Kerouac and eat her home cooking for months at a time. So, so much for you, Jack Kerouac.

TG: In writing about domestic life, you, of course, also wrote about sex. I have a quote on that subject from Nicholson Baker's *U and I*—the "U" being Updike, and the "I" being Baker. It's a memoir about Baker's obsessive relationship, as a reader and a writer, with you and your work. He writes, "Updike was the first to take the penile sensorium under the wing of elaborate metaphorical prose." He goes on, "Updike brought a serious morally sensitive National Book Award–winning prose style to bear on the micromechanics of physical lovemaking." What do you think of that?

UPDIKE: "Micromechanics." They don't feel micro when you are doing them.

TG: How about this idea of the "National Book Award–winning prose style" applied to lovemaking?

UPDIKE: It's a very jaunty piece of criticism and not untrue. It seemed to me important in writing about people to be able to describe the sexual transactions between them. For many people, it's the height of what they know. All their poetry is in their sexual encounters. Anyway, it clearly seemed a writer should be free to describe it.

One didn't entirely lack models for sexual realism, even in the late fifties and early sixties. There was James Joyce's Molly Bloom soliloquy, in which the sex, quite explicitly, is rolled into the general continuum of her awareness. It's really a beautiful example of lots of sex but probably not more sex than there really is. In Molly Bloom, you get a feeling of the sexual basis of our existence. D. H. Lawrence's *Lady Chatterley's Lover* was around, first as a rumor and then as an actual book that we could read. Certain eighteenth-century fiction writers described things more or less as they were, like *Moll Flanders*. So it wasn't entirely new. What may have been new, and what Baker highlights, is that my prose style was heavily influenced by Proust, who I read in my early twenties; I *did* try to bring to certain couplings a Proustian eloquence, just as I would bring that same eloquence to anything I was describing.

TG: You've described yourself as shy and priggish as a young man. Was it hard, being shy, to write sexually explicit material?

UPDIKE: No. It's just what a shy and priggish person would do. Writing is an act of aggression. A person who is not aggressive in his normal, may I say, intercourse with humanity, might well be an aggressive writer. I had the courage of my convictions, and the conviction was that this was worth doing, and that after Freud no one needed to argue the importance of sex in our lives.

TG: **Have some people misinterpreted the sexual aspects of your writing?**

UPDIKE: No. Some have complained about it. But I don't think anybody misread it, or maybe they did. I don't know. You can't keep track of the misreadings. It was said early and late that there was too much of it. But it didn't seem to be too much to me. *Rabbit, Run* was so alarming to the readers at the publishing house in 1959 that Alfred Knopf, who was then very much in charge of the house, liked the book, but had lawyers read it. The lawyers said, "This won't do. You'll be put in jail by southern sheriffs." How southern sheriffs could have gotten to Alfred Knopf, I don't know. I was then twenty-six, and this was my second novel. I was pleased he liked it, and displeased that there was a shadow over it.

Apparently, once you have asked for legal advice, if you don't take it, you are in worse shape than if you hadn't asked at all. So by having asked and received an answer, he had, in a sense, committed himself either to refuse the book or have some trimming done. I liked Alfred, and I liked the house. I liked the way the books looked and didn't think I'd get a better deal anywhere else. So I did consent to do a little legal trimming, done very tastefully, I thought, and delicately. A young lawyer and I sat elbow to elbow in this sunny room taking out certain words. He didn't want contact. He didn't mind the words so much. He just didn't want to see the people rubbing against each other. And so the text, somewhat modified, came out. The English publisher, Victor Gollancz, would not publish it even though it had been modified.

And, of course, it was on the eve of the revolution. You had *Lolita* coming out. And you had the *Tropics* books in pipeline, *Lady Chatterley*. In the end, it was nothing, and no southern sheriff even threatened to put either of us in jail. So, in a way, it was all a wasted effort.

But to make a long story short, those passages where Rabbit and Ruth explore each other, discovered each other, were very crucial, I thought, to a book about a man's quest. Certainly here was the peak of a certain kind of quest, and as far as ecstasy and purity and light, he wasn't going to find it anywhere else. So I thought it was very worth trying to describe.

TG: You were fourteen when you wrote your first short story, which is reprinted in a book called *First Words: Earliest Writing from Favorite Contemporary Authors*. Would you read the first couple of sentences from this story?

UPDIKE: This begins, "My employer, Manuel Cetaro, pushed the letter across the desk at me. It was written in a large masculine hand with no curlicues and a firm downstroke."

TG: On first reading that, I was so impressed with the line about the "firm downstroke" and the penmanship. This is fantastic detail for a fourteen-year-old. I know that your mother was an amateur graphologist. I think there is a lesson in this: The more you know, the more interesting detail you can put in fiction.

UPDIKE: Fiction is very greedy. It will take all you know and then some. The first novel I tried to write, I was struck by this—the appetite of the blank page for ever more information, ever more data. An empty book is a greedy thing. You are right: You wind up using everything you know, and often more than once.

October 14, 1997

A MAN'S VOICE

Johnny Cash

*Johnny Cash became an overnight sensation in 1956, when
he recorded "I Walk the Line" for Sun Records. But it was his
many years of singing as if he knew from personal experience
all of humankind's strengths and failings—as if he had both
committed murder and been accepted into God's light—that
made him a favorite of liberals and conservatives, MTV and
the Grand Ole Opry, Gary Gilmore and Billy Graham.*
Francis Davis, *The Atlantic Monthly,* March 2004

In the 1990s, a generation of listeners too young to remember
Johnny Cash from "Folsom Prison Blues," "I Walk the Line," "Ring
of Fire," or his other country hits of the 1950s and 1960s discovered
him through the CDs he made for Rick Rubin, a producer more identified with rap and heavy metal than with Cash's mature, plainspoken
country music. On his recordings for Rubin, Cash sang a mix of traditional ballads, his own new songs, and moody cover versions of
songs by artists ranging from Leonard Cohen and Loudon Wainwright III to Beck and Nine Inch Nails.

When I spoke with Cash in 1997, following the publication of
his autobiography, *Cash,* he apologized for sounding a little under the
weather. Canceling the remaining stops on his book tour a few days
later, he revealed that he had been diagnosed as suffering from a rare

illness with symptoms similar to those of Parkinson's disease. This was a misdiagnosis: The real culprit was autonomic neuropathy, a degenerative complication of diabetes that attacks the nerves and muscles that control the body's involuntary movements, including the respiratory and digestive systems.

As time goes by, more and more of the people in *Fresh Air*'s archives pass on, and although this saddens everyone who works on the show, we gain some consolation from being able to let our listeners hear from them again on tape. We rebroadcast this interview with Cash as our memorial to him following his death in 2003, at the age of seventy-one.

TERRY GROSS: **You grew up during the Depression. What are some of the things your father did to make a living while you were a boy?**

JOHNNY CASH: My father was a cotton farmer first. But he didn't have any land, or what land he had, he lost it in the Depression. So he worked as a woodsman and cut pulp wood for the paper mills. He rode the rails in boxcars, going from one harvest to another to make a little money picking fruit or vegetables. He did every kind of work imaginable, from painting to shoveling to herding cattle. All the things he did inspired me so—from being a soldier in World War I to being an old man on his patio, sitting on the porch watching the dogs.

TG: **It's interesting that you say your father inspired you so much. I'm sure you wouldn't have wanted to lead his life, picking cotton.**

CASH: I did. Until I was eighteen years old, that is. Then I picked the guitar, and I've been picking it since.

TG: **Did you have a strong motivation to get out of the town where you were brought up, and get out of picking cotton?**

CASH: Yeah. I knew that when I left at the age of eighteen, I wouldn't be back. It was common knowledge among all the people there that when you graduated from high school, you'd go get a job, you'd do it on your own. First, I hitchhiked to Pontiac, Michigan, and got a job working in the Fisher Body plant, making those 1951 Pontiacs. I worked there three weeks, got really sick of it, went back home, and joined the air force.

TG: **You have such a wonderful, deep voice. Did you start singing before your voice changed?**

CASH: When I was young, I had a high tenor voice. I used to sing Bill Monroe songs. And I'd sing Dennis Day songs that he'd sing on *The Jack Benny Show*.

TG: **Oh, no.**

CASH: Yeah. Every week he'd sing an old Irish folk song. Next day, in the fields, I'd be singing that song. I loved those songs and, with my high tenor, I thought I was pretty good. Almost as good as Dennis Day.

When I was seventeen, my father and I cut wood all day long. I was swinging that crosscut saw and hauling wood. I walked in the back door late that afternoon, singing "Ev'rybody's gonna have religion in glory, ev'rybody's gonna be singin' a story." I'd sing those old gospel songs for my mother, and she said, "Is that you?" I said, "Yes, ma'am." She came over and put her arms around me and said, "God's got his hands on you." I still think of that, you know.

TG: **She realized you had a gift.**

CASH: That's what she said. Yes. She called it "the gift."

TG: **How did you feel about your voice changing? It must have stunned you, if you were singing like Dennis Day and then suddenly you were singing like Johnny Cash.**

CASH: Well, I don't know. I felt like my voice was becoming a man's voice.

TG: **As your voice got deeper, did you start singing different songs?**

CASH: Mmm-hmm. "Lucky Old Sun." "Memories Are Made of This." "Sixteen Tons." I developed a pretty unusual style, I think. If I'm anything, I'm not a singer, I'm a song stylist.

TG: **What's the difference?**

CASH: Well, a song stylist takes an old folk song like "Delia's Gone" and does a modern, white man's version of it. I would take songs that I'd loved as a child and redo them in my mind for the new low voice I had.

TG: **You say in your book that you briefly took singing lessons and your singing teacher told you, "Don't let anybody change your voice." How did you end up taking lessons in the first place?**

CASH: My mother did that. She was determined that I was going to leave the farm and do well in life. She thought, with the gift, I might be able to do that. She got a washing machine in 1942, as soon as they got electricity, and took in washing. She sent me for singing lessons, for three dollars per lesson.

TG: **You were living in Memphis when you got your first break in the music business. How did you wind up there?**

CASH: Well, I got married and moved to Memphis after I finished the air force in 1954. I got an apartment and started trying to sell appliances at a place called Home Equipment Company. But I couldn't sell anything and didn't really want to. All I wanted was the music.

TG: **By the time you got to Memphis, Elvis Presley had already recorded "That's All Right Mama" for Sam Phillips on his label, Sun Records. You called Phillips and asked for an audition. Did it take a lot of nerve to make that phone call?**

CASH: No. It just took the right time. I was fully confident that I was going to see Sam Phillips and record for him. So I called him and he turned me down flat. Then two weeks later, I called. Turned down, turned down again. He told me over the phone that he couldn't sell gospel music. So I didn't press that issue. But one day I just decided that I'm ready to go. I went down with my guitar and sat on the front steps of his recording studio and met him when he came in. I said, "I'm John Cash. I'm the one that's been calling. And if you'd listen to me, I believe you'll be glad you did." He said, "Come on in." That was a good lesson for me to believe in myself.

TG: **What was the audition like?**

CASH: It was about three hours of singing with just my guitar.

TG: **Of all the songs that you played for him, what did Phillips respond to the most?**

CASH: A song of mine called "Hey, Porter," which was on the first record. But he asked me to go write a love song, or maybe a bitter weeper. So I wrote a song called "Cry, Cry, Cry" and recorded that for the other side of the record.

TG: **This record launched your recording career. What was it like when you started touring and you were recognized as you traveled around the country?**

CASH: Well, I started playing concerts from Memphis to Arkansas to Louisiana and Tennessee. Played the little towns there. I would go out myself in my car and set up the show in those theaters. Along about three months later, Elvis Presley asked me to sing with him at the Overton Park Shell in Memphis. I sang "Cry, Cry, Cry" and "Hey, Porter." From that time on, I was on my way. I knew it. I felt it. Elvis asked me to go on tour with him and I did. I worked with Elvis on four or five tours in the next year or so. I was always intrigued by his charisma. You couldn't be in the building with Elvis without looking at him. He inspired me so, with his fire and energy, and that helped me.

TG: **It's funny, I think of your charisma and his charisma as being very different. He would move around so much onstage. I think of your charisma as being very still.**

CASH: Mmm-hmm. Mmm-hmm. Well, I'm an old man next to him. I'm four years older than he was. I was twenty-three when I started recording and Elvis was nineteen. I was married. He wasn't. We didn't have a lot in common, but we liked each other and appreciated each other.

TG: Did you want the kind of adulation he was getting from girls who came to see him perform?

CASH: I don't remember if I wanted it, but I loved it. Yeah, I did.

TG: What were the temptations for a young married man, like yourself, on the road, slowly becoming a star?

CASH: Fame was pretty hard to handle, actually. The country boy in me tried to break loose and take me back to the country, but the music was stronger. The urge to go out and do the gift was a lot stronger. The temptations were women, and then amphetamines. Running all night, in our cars on tour, the doctors got us these nice pills that gave us energy and kept us awake. I started taking those, and I liked them so much, I got addicted to them. Then I started taking downers, or sleeping pills, to rest after two or three days. I was taking the pills for a while, and then the pills started taking me.

TG: It was in the late 1950s that you started doing prison concerts, which you eventually became very famous for. What got you started performing in prison?

CASH: Well, I had a song called "Folsom Prison Blues" that was a hit just before "I Walk the Line." People at the state prison in Texas heard about it and got to writing me letters asking me to come down there. So we went down. There's a rodeo at all these shows that the prisoners have there. In between the rodeo things, they asked me to do two or three songs. I did "Folsom Prison Blues," which they thought was their song, you know, and "I Walk the Line," "Hey, Porter," "Cry, Cry, Cry." Then the word got around, and the requests started coming in from prisoners all over the United States.

I always wanted to record a show in prison, because of the reaction I got. It was far and above anything I ever had in my life—the complete explosion of noise and reaction that they gave me with every song. I kept talking to my producers at Columbia about recording one of those shows. "It's so exciting," I said, "that the people out there ought to share that and feel that excitement, too." So a preacher friend of mine set it up for us, along with Lou Robin and a lot of people at Folsom Prison. We went into Folsom on February 11, 1968, and recorded a show live.

TG: You've almost always worn black during your career. And I was interested in reading that your mother hated it.

CASH: Yes, she did.

TG: So we have something in common. Mothers who don't like black.

CASH: Mmm-hmm, yeah. But I love it.

TG: Me, too. But you gave in for a while, didn't you, when she started making you bright, flashy outfits. Even a nice white suit. What did it feel like to be onstage in bright colors? Or all in white?

CASH: Well, it was okay. I would wear anything my mother made me. But I decided to stick with black because it felt good to me onstage. That figure there in black and everything coming out his face. That's the way I wanted to do it.

TG: You married June Carter, now June Carter Cash, in 1968. In many ways, the Carter Family is the "first family" of country music. How did you meet?

CASH: I met June backstage at the Grand Ole Opry when I did my first appearance as a guest artist. We started touring together in Des Moines in January 1962. We've been together ever since. I met her family on our second tour together because I'd asked them to all come and be a part of the show. I got into those people and became one of their family. It felt good to go out with them.

TG: What was it like, traveling with a family instead of being on your own?

CASH: I really don't like to do an appearance without June Carter. What would it be like, being alone? It would be awfully lonely to me.

I'm very comfortable with how we do it, with my wife and my son on the show, and a daughter or two. It feels so good. I would hate to think that I had to do it all alone.

TG: **Did it change your life to have a family that really understood the performing life because it was their life, too?**

CASH: Very much so. Yeah. Right.

TG: **What was the difference? I mean, why was that so important?**

CASH: Well, there's something about families singing together that is just better than any other groups you can pick up or make. If it's family, if it's blood-on-blood, then it's gonna be better. The voices, singing their parts, are going to be tighter, and they're going to be more on pitch. Because it's bloodline-on-bloodline.

November 4, 1997

LIFT EVERYTHING UP

Charlie Haden

No other instrument in jazz is more essential than the bass,
both backbone and heartbeat, and Haden is its master.
Francis Davis, *The Atlantic Monthly,* August 2000

Charlie Haden first gained widespread notice in 1959 as a member of the Ornette Coleman Quartet, a group that toppled many
of the conventions of modern jazz, including the role of the bass. I've
interviewed Haden several times over the years, but we didn't discuss
his work with Coleman in either of the two conversations I've ex-
cerpted here (from 1996 and 1999), which focus more on Haden's
childhood and his life now.

 Charlie is one of my favorite musicians. One of the things I like
about him is that he respects songs as *songs,* not just as vehicles for
improvisation. He's recorded a number of my favorites from the
1930s, 1940s, and early 1950s—and introduced me to a few wonderful ones I didn't know. The interview I recorded with him in 1996, following the release of his CD *Now Is the Hour,* is one that I'm

especially proud of—not on account of the questions I asked, but because it played a part in encouraging him to sing again.

TERRY GROSS: **You're the most melodic bass player I know. In your role as a composer and bandleader, how do you hear the bass fitting in to the ensemble?**

CHARLIE HADEN: The role of a bass player is to lift everything up and make it deeper and more full-sounding. When I was a kid listening to classical music on the radio, or even country music, when the bass player stopped playing, the depth left the music for me. That's why I always wanted to play bass. It's important for bass players to enhance everything *behind* the solos in order to inspire the other musicians to play better than they've ever played before. That's what I try to do.

TG: **When you're improvising, there's a sense of melodic sweep to the lines that you play that I don't usually hear in bass playing. Most bass players think harmonically, and think about rhythm, but not so much about melody.**

HADEN: Well, I was brought up with melodies all my life—even before I was two years old when I started singing on my parents' radio show every day. My mom told me once, "You know, when you were a baby I used to rock you to sleep, and hum all these old songs like 'Barbara Allen,' 'Mansion on the Hill,' 'Silver Threads Among the Gold,' and 'Wildwood Flower.'" While she'd be humming in the rocking chair, my brothers and sisters would be walking through the living room, and they'd start humming the harmony with her. They all knew how to do that by ear because everybody sang all the harmony parts on our radio show. Then my mom would sometimes switch to the harmony, and they would switch to the melody.

One day she was humming to me and I started humming the harmony along with her. She said, "Well, I guess that's a signal it's time for you to join us on the show." So I started singing on the radio show when I was twenty-two months old.

I tell my students at Cal Arts that they should be able to harmonize every melody they know by ear, every harmony part. It's so important. I was really lucky to be brought up around melodies of the

Carter Family and the Delmore Brothers and Hank Williams, and all those people that my parents knew. It was a strong musical training, and I acquired a melodic sense very early on.

TG: **When you were a boy and your family had that country music radio show, what part did you sing?**

HADEN: I sang all the harmony parts. I loved it. Every day my parents would choose the songs that we were going to play out of their vast library of songs from the Carter Family and the Delmore Brothers and all the hymns that we had. We would go over them. Then we would go on the air. Sometimes we had radio studios in our homes wherever it was we were living. We moved around a lot. But mostly we would go to the studio at the radio station and do our show every day. I loved going to the studio. I liked the air-conditioning and the acoustical tile and the big windows that had triple, quadruple glass. This was back in 1945 through '49. It was a great experience.

TG: **I can't believe you had radio studios in your home. Would you do remote broadcasts from your own home?**

HADEN: Yeah. Where I was born in Shenandoah, Iowa, we were on a radio station called KMA. It's still there. Then my dad moved our family to Springfield, Missouri, in the Ozark Mountains. My father's mother and father had a farm outside Springfield, and my dad always wanted to farm, so he got this farm down the gravel road from them. I went to a one-room schoolhouse there. My dad had the radio station come out and hook up a remote in our farmhouse—a thing that rings when you turn the crank. Well, he used to turn this crank, and the ring would go into the studio in Springfield. That was the signal for us to go on the air, and we'd start the theme song. We did our show from our farmhouse for several years before we moved into the city and went over to the station every day.

TG: **Did you play in churches and at revival meetings in addition to singing on the radio?**

HADEN: We played in churches and personal appearances all over. My parents were on the Grand Ole Opry quite a few times.

TG: **Did singing in churches and other religious events give you a sense that music has a spiritual dimension to it?**

HADEN: Well, the hymns especially. And then, I don't know why, but when I was around nine years old, I was the only child out of six kids she would take to the African American church in Springfield. We would quietly go in the entrance, and we would sit in the back row, and we would just listen to the choir. It was one of the most beautiful things that I've ever experienced in my life, to hear the spirituals and the gospel music. I'll never forget that. Yes, I had a feeling right away that there was spirituality in music. When you talk about jazz, I believe 85 to 90 percent of improvisation in jazz is spiritual. You can go to school and learn the academics of music, and the fundamentals of scales and chords and composition, but when you start to play, you tell a story to people and take them on a journey. It's all about spirituality.

TG: **You had polio as a child and stopped singing.**

HADEN: Yeah. I had bulbar polio. There was an epidemic going on in '52. We were in Omaha, Nebraska; we had a television show there. This was right before my dad retired from music. And I got this virus. I was really lucky, actually, because most of the hospitals were filled with polio patients with paralyzed lung function and legs. Mine hit my vocal cords—the left side of my throat and my face. Eventually I got over it, but the range in my voice left me. I couldn't sing. I loved singing, but I wasn't able to sing anymore.

TG: **Once you discovered you couldn't sing, did you turn to the bass?**

HADEN: I was playing my brother's bass before I had polio. He wouldn't *let* me play his bass, but every time I could, I'd sneak around and play it. I loved playing the bass with records that we had. I was fourteen and in the ninth grade in Omaha, and they had an orchestra in my school, North High. The director wanted me to play bass.

When he found out that I played bass, he said, "We need another bass in the bass section of the orchestra." And I said, "I can't read music." And he said, "Well, I can teach you." So he took me down to the band room. His name was Sam Thomas. I'll never forget it, man. He showed me the first page of the Simandl book, the bass method book. All the open strings were there. And he said, "Now I want you to practice playing these with the bow. This is a G. This is a D. This is an A and an E. Practice this while I'm gone. Then we'll start on the half position, and we'll go to the first position to where you press down the strings." And he said, "You're playing this anyway by ear with the little band you have here at school. But now you're going to know how to read it." And I said, "Great."

He left the room, and I started getting real nervous. I mean, I got this anxiety attack. I said to myself, "Oh my . . . !" I looked at these notes, and I was bowing. All of a sudden I thought I was having a heart attack. Can you imagine having a heart attack at fourteen? So, man, I grabbed my chest. I put the bass down. I ran out in the hall to the water fountain and started drinking all this water. A couple of students came up to me—my friends—and said, "What in the world's wrong?" I said, "I think I'm having a heart attack." They said, "Charlie, you're out of your mind. You're not having a heart attack." I said, "I think I am." And Sam Thomas came back and he was cracking up, man. He said, "You're not having a heart attack, Charlie. You're just learning how to read music."

TG: I would like to ask you about a problem you have now with ringing in your ears. I imagine it must affect your music in some way. I know a lot of musicians develop this problem from being either too close to loud amplifiers or too close to drums. How bad is it for you? Does it drown out the music? How does it affect what you hear?

HADEN: I also have a condition called hyperacusis, which is extreme sensitivity to loud sounds. While I'm here talking to you, I've got the volume on these headphones almost off. If someone were to drop a fork on the floor, or any sudden loud sound, it's like hitting me in the head. It really hurts me. The doctors tell me that there's a membrane in the middle ear that protects the ear from loud sounds. It's not working in my case. So it's like the volume is turned up in my head.

Everything is three times louder for me than normal hearing. Whenever I take a hearing test, I hear so well I go over the limit.

Most people with tinnitus lose their hearing. But in my case, my hearing's just becoming more and more acute. I hear this ringing in my head that is so loud that if most people heard what I hear, they would run down the street screaming. But I've adjusted to it over the years. I just made it a part of my life, and I put up with it. But if I stop and think about it, I get real depressed. So let's change the—no, I'm just kidding.

TG: **Well, does it drown out the music that you play?**

HADEN: Oh, no. No, it doesn't. I wear earplugs when I play.

TG: **So that the other musicians' sounds aren't too severe for you?**

HADEN: Yes. So it will soften the decibels. Right.

May 29, 1996

At the end of this interview, Haden explained that the title song from his CD Now Is the Hour *was a Maori folk song. I asked if he would sing it—and he did, reluctantly, in a soft, sweet voice whose honesty I found wonderfully affecting. Afterward, I told him how much I liked his singing and urged him to try doing it on record. Much to my delight, three years later, he did. The Art of the Song* concludes with him singing the traditional ballad "Wayfaring Stranger."

TG: **This is the first vocal performance you've recorded since you used to sing with your family when you were a child. What made you decide to sing on this CD?**

HADEN: After polio paralyzed my vocal cords, I stopped singing. Eventually, I got my vocal cords back, but I lost the range in my voice.

After that, I focused all my musical melody-energy on my playing. I never thought about singing again after that. I didn't even sing in the shower. It wasn't that I was afraid to, it was just over for me. Recently, some people have been saying, "You used to sing, how come you don't sing anymore?" Ruth, my wife, who's a singer, has said, "Why don't you sing?"

Then I was on your show a while ago, and we were talking about "Now Is the Hour," and you asked me to sing it. I was very reluctant, and I couldn't believe that you asked me. I finally gave in and sang, and you called back later and said that you thought it was great and that I should sing sometime on one of my records. And I said, "Well, thanks for the compliment, Terry, but—"

It was kind of humorous to me. I never took it seriously, until we started planning this record. I was going through music, and I ran across some from our family's radio show back in the forties. I saw this song called "Wayfaring Stranger" that my mom used to sing on our show. I remembered how beautiful it was.

I thought, "This isn't a song for Shirley Horn or Bill Henderson [the album's featured vocalists] to sing, but it should really be sung, because the words are so beautiful." I said, "Well, the only way it could be sung is if I sing it." And I thought, "Oh my goodness, that's not going to work."

I called Jean-Philippe Allard, our executive producer, in Paris, and I said, "You know, I might sing on this record." There was a big silence. And he said, "Pardon?" I said, "I might sing." Another long silence. "Pardon?"

Anyway, I told Alan Broadbent, the pianist and arranger on this CD, "Write the arrangement as if somebody's going to sing it, and if I don't make it, I'll play it on the bass."

I didn't want to get my mind set, like, "Oh, I'm a singer, and I've got to sing this like a singer, and it's got to be perfect." I really love singers who sing the way they speak. When they stop speaking and start to sing, they don't change their voice or the way they say their words in any way. It's just natural and honest. A lot of singers, as soon as they begin to sing, everything changes. All of a sudden they're somebody else. So I'm not doing it as a singer; I'm doing it to tell a story of where I come from.

TG: I really love this performance, and I'm so glad that you decided to sing on "Wayfaring Stranger." The lyrics are filled with metaphors about death, like—

I'm going home to see my father
I'm going there no more to roam.
I'm only going over Jordan
I'm only going over home.

What did the words mean to you as a child when you heard your mother sing it? Was it a frightening song to you? Did it make you think of death?

HADEN: No, actually it was a very soothing song. It's just the opposite. It's a song about life. I remember a very funny thing that my mom told me. Once when I was four years old—we were living on the farm outside Springfield, Missouri—she was working around the house, and all of a sudden she heard me screaming in the living room. She thought something horrible had happened to me. She ran in the living room; she said, "Charlie, what's wrong?" And I looked up at her, and I said, "I don't want to die!"

And she said, "Jesus, Charlie. What in the world are you talking about?" She was cracking up. I always had this deep need for the beauty of life and a sense of how precious every moment is. This song evokes that for me.

TG: **What happened to you that day? What were you thinking about that made you think, "I'm going to die"?**

HADEN: I think somebody close to us had just died, and they had a funeral. And I was thinking, "Oh God, someday that's going to happen to me," you know, and here I am four years old, and I start screaming.

TG: **Are you shy about singing now, in a way that you're not about playing bass?**

HADEN: Probably. That's the first time I've sung in about forty-five years, so I'm very shy about it. I always want to do everything the best I possibly can. I play bass every day, but I don't sing every day.

TG: **Well, I do hope you sing more.**

October 7, 1999

EROTIC CHEESE AND CRACKERS

Mary Karr

The Liars' Club is a classic of American literature. . . . Mary Karr conjures the simmering heat and bottled rage of life in a small Texas oil town with an intensity that gains power from the fact that it's fact.
James Atlas, *The New York Times Magazine*, May 12, 1996

After reading a few good ones in the late 1980s and early '90s, I believed that the memoir was becoming the most provocative form of contemporary literature. Then everybody started getting into the act. Soon I was taking home memoir after memoir by authors with few profound experiences and nothing resembling an inner life. Some of them didn't even write especially well. My motto has become a line spoken by Dennis Hopper in the movie *Search and Destroy:* "Just because it happened to you doesn't make it interesting."

Happily, there are still exceptions. In her first book, *The Liars' Club,* published in 1995, Mary Karr wrote compellingly of having twice been sexually abused as a child in Texas. *The Liars' Club* was critically acclaimed and became a national best seller. *Cherry,* her second memoir, dealt with ordinary teenage experiences—conflicts with parents and teachers, crushes on boys, the difficulty Karr had in figuring out who she really was and what she wanted to do with her life. There was certainly nothing ordinary about the way that Karr described the self-consciousness and insecurities surrounding early sexuality from the vantage point of a teenage girl but with the mature insights of a writer confident of her own voice.

TERRY GROSS: **You write that in the town where you grew up, the community was more tolerant of physical affliction than social handicaps. Were you or your family considered socially handicapped?**

MARY KARR: That's an understatement for what my family was considered. I mean, I've often said a dysfunctional family is a family with more than one person in it. My mother was married seven times, and this was the anesthetized fifties. I grew up in a working-class, swampy backwater in east Texas. My mother had been to art school, had married seven times, twice to my father, and guzzled a lot of vodka. My father was a pretty hard hitter. So, yeah—I mean, I think my family stood out.

TG: **But some of your mother's eccentricities probably had a positive influence on your life. She was a painter. She liked art. She liked to read.**

KARR: My mother was one of those women who had a big tower of books by her bed. And this was in a town that didn't have a bookstore. The only bookstore in my town sold those little Day-Glo icons that you set on your dashboard. In fact, I don't remember if they even sold books, although it was called a bookstore. Reading saved my life. Poetry saved my life. My mother believed in the life of the mind. She would drive us to see opera or to see a play, if we could afford it, and if we all could get loose from our various obligations. She was tolerant of change, and a lot of moms aren't tolerant of the changes I went through at this age.

TG: **You say that poetry is one of the things that saved your life growing up. What was the poetry you particularly loved?**

KARR: I could do Shakespeare. You could whap me upside the head, and it would come out. "Of comfort no man speak. Let's talk of graves, of worms and epitaphs. Make dust our paper, and with rainy eyes write sorrow on the bosom of the earth." I mean, it doesn't get any better than that.

TG: As the title of your memoir *Cherry* implies, the book is about teenage sexuality and those early sexual awakenings, which you write about so eloquently. Your mother was a teacher and had seen a lot of pregnant teenagers, so she put you on the pill at age fifteen—just in case. Did that encourage you to be sexually active earlier than you might otherwise have been?

KARR: Absolutely. I think she was trying to be progressive and certainly trying to prevent my getting knocked up, which was a common occurrence in the town I grew up in. I had friends who were pregnant and married at fourteen. But at the time, I wasn't even dating. I was this skinny, borderline tomboy—a recovering tomboy. What's amazing to me about this book is that everybody thinks the title, *Cherry,* is ironic. Despite my mother's sexual openness, which nudged me to be sexual long before I was prepared for it, it's a book about discovering an innocence that I didn't believe I had. It's in no way ironic.

TG: You write that people talked about being deflowered as if "something you owned was stolen, something of worth ruined." You had been raped at the age of seven. Did that experience make you feel that some part of you was already ruined?

KARR: Exactly. When I first started writing the book, I was thinking of it as a book about the loss of innocence. It became for me a rediscovery of an innocence I didn't know I had, and an innocence, given my reckless behavior, I probably didn't deserve. After I began to write the book, I threw away about five hundred pages because they were all about this steamy sexuality. I was superimposing the libidinal feelings of a forty-year-old woman onto myself at twelve. I kept throwing them out because the pages seemed so perverted, and they were perverted. They also happened not to be true. At a certain point, I clicked that,

"Oh, I remember. I wanted this guy to skate over to me with a long-stemmed red rose." All my fantasies that I found so thrilling at that time were very courtly. The scenes that I've been told are very racy are entirely chaste.

TG: **In retrospect, what was different about the way you experienced your early sexuality versus the way boys you knew experienced their sexuality?**

KARR: Well, the culture doesn't have a language for girls being sexual at this age. There's no word comparable to "chubby" for a girl to describe arousal that's so childlike and innocent and silly. I think of my son teasing his friends, "Boy, I bet you take really long showers." Or my nephew came to visit me once when he was about fourteen and we were flying up from Texas. He had a locked briefcase with him. And I said, "So what's in there, your *Playboys*?" He turned to me very sharply and said, "You looked." I can't think of anything comparable for girls. That's partly because the way we feel doesn't ding the cultural bell as erotic. I wasn't hardwired to get the deed done, in the way a seventeen-year-old boy might have been.

TG: **You write about how, after smooching with a boy, the next morning you'd look in the mirror and say to yourself, "What was I thinking?" Looking in the mirror, you'd think, "I'm not the person I thought I was."**

KARR: Yeah, I used the phrase that there was some schism between that wild luxury of kisses and this scabby-looking girl who still looks partly like a child. Yeah, I went on a date with a kind of regular fella, you know, nice. I had no particular passion for him and wound up kissing him. The feelings were so out of line with my relationship with this guy. I avoided this boy like the plague because I was so embarrassed by having made out with him at the drive-in.

TG: **Oh, and I liked this, too. Once, before being with a boy, you said you wanted to take a shower and brush your teeth, but you thought that being concerned with hygiene at such a time would** sound so uncool. You also aren't sure that cleaning up would help. You say, "It's the whole blunt corporeal exchange that's eating away at you."

KARR: This particular boy, who was my first lover, was really a very sweet boy and smart and kind, but as soon as we'd slept together, I had that sense of "Oh my God." Everything we'd been doing before was what *I* liked. Kissing and staring into each other's eyes for hours on end. I could see that for him it had all been erotic cheese and crackers that was sort of beside the point. Once you crossed over that line, his experience was very different than mine. And yet I had envisioned him as my soul mate, this boy who understood everything about me, and we were so similar and it was so great that we'd found each other so young because we were going to have this fabulous life together. I was fifteen years old. Yeah. And to suddenly see in this guy's face that, in fact, he's hardwired to get the deed done. Our experiences were so different.

TG: In your early teens, what were the books and movies, or the TV shows and music, that formed your romantic fantasies?

KARR: Oh, it's funny. I think of that Nick Hornby novel *High Fidelity*, about how you're shaped by pop music in this awful way. Books—oh, gosh. *Anna Karenina* was my favorite novel. It's still one of my favorite novels, this romantic tragedy in which a woman betrays her husband. Then, because of the nature of the betrayal, she winds up a suicide. That couldn't be more operatic, or unfortunate, in terms of where a woman's libido is going to lead her. I listened to a lot of blues. I grew up not far from where Janis Joplin was born. The idea that you were going to suffer at the hands of some man was built into the deal.

TG: You mentioned *Anna Karenina* and suicide. You tried suicide when you were in your teens. You swallowed a whole bunch of Anacins. What provoked that?

KARR: In retrospect, I don't think of it as "trying suicide" so much as a gesture. It didn't feel quite as dramatic as I meant it to be. I intended the scene in the book to be comical, because I put on my black dress and lay down and crossed my hands over my chest. My neighbors were yelling at each other outside the window, and I thought, "You know, Socrates didn't have to deal with this." My attempt with a handful of Anacin lacked that drama. My home was unstable and I was depressed. Whether that suicide attempt was hormonally prompted or endemic to my nature, certainly it's a result of having a very chaotic household.

TG: **When you realized that your suicide wasn't going to have the gravity of Socrates', did it ruin the romance of suicide and make it not worth messing around with again?**

KARR: After that, I never turned a hand to myself. Now when I'm upset, I sometimes consider homicide. But it stopped seeming like a solution. Certainly, there's a lot of great art that surrounds that kind of despair. I just wrote an introduction to *The Waste Land* for the Modern Library. That's a classic example of someone creating a psychic landscape where suicide might, indeed, be a logical extension. But it seems to me now very cowardly. My mother had threatened suicide. She never did anything about it, but I think when she was overwhelmed, that frequently was her solution. I don't get that kind of black depression these days, but my head will start prattling at me. Now I'm better at turning the volume down on it.

TG: **How do you do that?**

KARR: Physical exercise, which generates endorphins. If I'm feeling bad, I talk to people. I have a number of friends. And I'm not above going to see a mental health professional. I'm happy to get professional help, if it'll shut my head up. But you know, it's the way all of us heal ourselves. You find people to love you, people who will buy your act. To have someone sitting across from you with a caring expression when you're talking about your pain is comforting. I also go to church. I converted to Catholicism. So I pray.

TG: **When did you convert?**

KARR: '97.

TG: **How come?**

KARR: My son came into my room one Sunday morning when he was about five years old and said, "I want to go to church." I wanted to read *The New York Times,* so I said, "Why?" And he said, "I want to see if God's there." I thought, "Oh. I didn't like soccer either, but I went and stood out on the frozen field and watched him run up and down." So we did this thing we called God-O-Rama, where anybody we knew who had a spiritual practice of any kind, we went with them. So we went to a number of Jewish temples, including conservative temples and small, private groups. We went to Baptist churches, Episcopal, Unitarian. We even did a Buddhist zendo. We never made it to a mosque, but I found myself in a Catholic church that a friend of mine, Tobias Wolff, invited me to. I was very moved. If you had told me I would join the Catholic Church, I would have laughed myself sick. And I'm sure I'm not the pope's favorite Catholic. But I go to church every Sunday, and I pray every day. It puts me in perspective. It puts my difficulties in their right size.

TG: **Your first memoir, *The Liars' Club,* was a best seller and it was also important in popularizing the memoir. Do you keep a journal now?**

KARR: Oh, goodness, no. I don't have time. And I lead a pretty banal life. In many ways I'm a soccer mom. I teach at Syracuse University. I'm a single mom, although my ex-husband is great and we co-parent really well, and he's very involved in raising our son. I live in Syracuse in this Country Time lemonade–commercial sort of life; that's the way it looks. All the things that everybody in the fifties tried to escape, I'm trying to re-create. Literally, I have a picket fence. I stand out on the soccer field and watch kids run up and down, and shoot hoops in my driveway when my son comes home from school.

TG: **What about memory, though? Your two books of prose have been memoirs. Writing them required remembering. Sometimes memories start to disappear, you're able to remember less, and you begin to distrust the things you are able to remember. Isn't** there the temptation to keep a journal just to preserve what you've experienced?

KARR: If I were going to do that, I'd strap a video camera to my head. For me, memoir is an act of memory and not an act of history. It's remembered experience; it's not lived experience. There are all kinds of theories about ways we remember, and I have no doubt that I do have a better long-term memory than most people. I wrote this book and gave it to all my friends. No one said, "That didn't happen," or "That didn't happen that way." People told me things I didn't remember, or they augmented events, or told me how they felt, in ways that I had no way of knowing. But memoir is a corrupt form. Memory informs imagination, and imagination informs memory. So when people ask me how I remember all this stuff, I always say, "Well, obviously, I don't; I just think I do," which I think is true.

October 2, 2000

A New Gift

Andre Dubus

*His is an unapologetically sacramental vision of life in which
ordinary things participate in the miraculous, the miraculous
in ordinary things. He believes in God, and talks to Him and
doesn't mince words. . . . He is open to mystery and of all
mysteries the one that interests him most is the human
potential for transcendence.*

Tobias Wolff, introduction to *Broken Vessels*

One summer night in 1986, the writer Andre Dubus was driving
on a Massachusetts highway when he saw a man and woman
standing by their car in another lane. After pulling over to lend assistance, he was hit by an oncoming car that also struck and killed the
young man whose car had broken down. As a result of the injuries he
suffered, Dubus never walked again; he fell into a depression so deep
that he feared he might never write again. But he gradually sum-
moned the will to produce three more books of short stories and essays. He was awarded a MacArthur Fellowship, and a book of his
short stories, *Dancing After Hours,* was a finalist for a National Book
Critics Circle Award. "Dubus has made of his wheelchair a place to
see the world more clearly than ever," Tobias Wolff wrote in an introduction to *Broken Vessels,* a collection of autobiographical essays that
Dubus published in 1991.

I interviewed Dubus in 1991, five years after his Good Samaritanism almost cost him his life—and eight years before the surprise heart attack that killed him at the age of sixty-two. (After his death, his short story "Killings" was adapted into the movie *In the Bedroom*.) I began the interview by asking Dubus to read from "Light of the Long Night," an essay from *Broken Vessels*, in which he described the night of the accident.

> *I remember the headlights, but I do not remember the car hitting Luis Santiago and me, and I do not remember the sounds our bodies made. Luis died, either in the ambulance, or later that night in the hospital. He was twenty-three years old. I do not remember leaving the ground my two legs stood on for the last instant in my life, then moving through the air, over the car's hood and windshield and roof, and falling on its trunk. I remember lying on my back on that trunk and asking someone: What happened?*
>
> *I did not lose consciousness. The car did not injure my head or my neck or my spine. It broke my right hand and scraped both arms near my wrists, so my wife believes I covered my face with my arms as I fell. I lay for a while on the trunk, talking to a young man, then to a woman who is a state trooper, then I was in an ambulance, stopped on the highway, talking to a state trooper, a man, while he cut my trousers and my right western boot. That morning my wife saw the left boot on the side of the highway, while she was driving home from the hospital in Boston. The car had knocked it off my foot. The state troopers got the boot for my wife, but I did not leave the hospital with a left foot or, below the middle of my knee, a left leg.*

TERRY GROSS: **You know, one of the reasons I asked you to read this story, instead of asking you to tell it, is that I thought you might be tired of telling it.**

ANDRE DUBUS: I am. You know, five years I've been telling the story. Actually, the first few years it used to scare me, and I'd have to take a Xanax to tell it.

TG: Have you told it enough so that it's just a story now?

DUBUS: Actually, I told it to some teenage girls I was teaching only last fall. I had a new girl that night. She asked what happened, and another girl started telling her because I didn't want to. She wasn't telling it right, so I told it. When they left, I started paying bills, and I got very anxious. I wondered, "What's wrong?" Then I thought, "Well, you just told a story about almost getting killed, and you told it at night," which I usually try to avoid doing. "It's messed you up."

TG: Why is it harder to tell it at night?

DUBUS: Oh, I think it has to do with darkness and death. When I got home from the hospital in September '86, I got frightened every day at sunset. I'd take a Xanax when the sun went down. To this day, I sleep with my bedroom door open, and all the shades up, because being closed in reminds me of the hospital. There were windows, but they looked down over an alley. There was not much light.

TG: This is the story that's most changed your life, and it's probably the story you've told the most over the years. How has the telling of the story changed over time?

DUBUS: It hasn't changed much. Since writing it out, I've come to terms with the lives of the other people involved. In other words, I've done some forgiving, which was necessary. Especially of the driver who ran over us. Of course, she should be forgiven. It was only an accident. But I took it personally for about eight or nine months. Nearly five years away from it, I'm even more deeply grateful and awed that I was struck by a fast-moving vehicle on the highway and emerged as healthy as I did. I could be dead.

TG: You met the driver?

DUBUS: No, I never met her. As a little boy brought up in a Catholic school, I learned to pray for people you don't like. I started praying for her, using her name, because I really felt hatred. I knew the only way to get rid of it was prayer.

Finally, after a few months, with help from somebody who was praying with me, I saw it from the woman's point of view.

TG: **Have you been able to find a way of telling this story so that what people feel isn't pity, but a larger sense of the fragility of life?**

DUBUS: Every time I tell it, it's always with awe and gratitude. Since my injury, because of the mutual help that we go for, I've met a lot of injured people. Everyone I know who's crippled has used the words *gratitude* and *grateful*.

That's always the way I remember it. Well, I remember it with fear, too. A nurse told me no one ever remembers the point of impact. But I know two people who do, and I'm hoping that I never remember that.

TG: **Do you think it's a blessing that you don't remember?**

DUBUS: It's a great blessing. I remember the headlights. Then I remember being on her trunk. Then learning that I never lost consciousness. My eyes must have seen that grill and the hood and windshield coming. I'm very glad that I don't remember it.

TG: **You're a very literary man. You read a lot. You write a lot. Do you feel that what you learned from literature, from the greatest writing that you read, helped you in any way?**

DUBUS: Oh, yes, I do. If I had been younger, or even older, and had a different background, I may have had a worse response. Growing up with the passion of Christ as your example of "This is how things are going to be" gives you the expectation of suffering. I started reading serious literature when I was about eighteen. Most literature is about what? People who love each other, people who hurt each other, people who lose. You could say I've been spending most of my spiritual and mental life dealing with the suffering of others—from Christ to Natasha in *War and Peace*.

TG: **Has your reading changed in recent years?**

DUBUS: Yeah, I tend to read more of the New Testament and less of anything else. The first year of my injury I didn't notice it until someone said to me, "What are you reading?" I said, "I'm only reading the New Testament and histories of marines." The guy said, "Well, that makes sense." Then I realized I was doing both for my spirit. Trying to get courage, endurance, grace, wisdom.

TG: What did the marines give you?

DUBUS: Vivid examples of people suffering and enduring and having true grit and resilience. I was in the marines, so I need that spirit. It became very important to me after I got run over.

TG: You've talked about forgiveness and the New Testament. How long did it take you to forgive the person who ran you down?

DUBUS: About from July until the following May.

TG: You're laughing, but you know that's not a very long time at all.

DUBUS: That was pretty long. I am also laughing because my anger really wasn't rooted in anything reasonable. I thought she should have sent me flowers and a card in the hospital. But I'm sure her attorney said, "Don't even lick a postage stamp with his name in your mind, or you'll get messed up."

I'd mention her name every morning, and I prayed for her because I knew that I couldn't go around hating somebody. It just destroys you. You can't carry that around in your heart. Finally, the grace came to me—to be in the car, as she would have been, on that night—driving. I realized she didn't do anything wrong. She just had a bad night. She wasn't drinking. She wasn't on drugs. She just didn't see us. You know, she didn't break any laws.

TG: How long did it take you to start writing again after the accident?

DUBUS: I'm still working on that. I'm still writing. I wrote ten essays, and I've written four stories. I got hit in July. I wrote a very short story in January. I was trying to write in the hospital. I've always been writing since the accident.

But it's been very difficult to create something whole. I'm starting to understand now in my fifth year. The healing is long. People have told me this all along. The body, the spirit, the mind—they're all damaged. Everything is going to come back slowly. I'm starting to believe it now.

TG: So is it mostly physical distress that's held you back from writing more?

DUBUS: I don't really know. Only in the past few weeks, I've begun to feel energy and peace that I have not felt since being hurt in '86. I've begun to feel almost as well as I remember I used to feel.

On Thanksgiving of '86, I was still in a cast. I was home. I was hurting. Tobias Wolff, who's a wonderful writer and friend, called. As soon as he said, "This is Toby," I started crying. I said, "Toby, I cannot write, why can't I write?" This was three or four months after I got run over. He said, "Because your body's broken, and your body and spirit are one, and they are both mending."

I still have aches and pains and fatigue every day, but I think a new gift is coming. I really do. I think writing is going to become more like what it was before I got run over than what it's been since I got run over, which has been like chasing a piece of paper blowing on a windy playground.

TG: In one of the new pieces in your new collection, you say that the best person for a crippled man to cry with is a good physical therapist. Do you have a sense of what's best left to a professional as opposed to someone you're intimate with, someone in your family?

DUBUS: I went to a professional psychologist in 1989, nearly three years after the accident, because I woke up every morning crying. One morning I couldn't stop. What the professional did in one hour was to get me to contact two other crippled friends. One came over two days later and taught me to drive a car. I saw the professional therapist for about six or eight weeks. He was very good. He said,

"You're not depressed, you're sad because you lost your legs. You'll always be sad, and you'll never replace them." Which is exactly what all the friends I called said. "You'll always wake up missing your legs and you'll never get over that."

I had made the mistake of expecting to wake up one day as you do from the flu, and say, "Wow, that was tough. Now I feel great, I'm myself again." I lay there crying for a few days. I would call myself a bad cripple. I was angry at myself for not being a cheerful cripple. Then I found out from the other guys who are more experienced cripples than I that they weren't cheerful either. They had just learned to expect to wake up feeling this and to expect to go through this each day and night. It's nice to have that brother- and sisterhood.

TG: **You use the word *cripple* to describe your condition?**

DUBUS: I do, but I think that's because I'm a writer. I've never liked euphemisms. I don't say "passed away." I say "dead." One of my older children came to me in the hospital and said, "You're not disabled, you're physically challenged." I said, "No, you're physically challenged. You're breathing hard from climbing the stairs. I'm disabled." My friends who are active disabled people like to be called "disabled." But *cripple* is a good old-fashioned word for me. That's what I would have written even before the accident if I had written this story about somebody else who was crippled.

June 25, 1991

Andre Dubus III

Not long after Andre Dubus's death in 1999, I spoke with his son Andre Dubus III, who had just published his second novel, *House of Sand and Fog*. (The book spent several months on the paperback best-seller list the following year, after Oprah Winfrey selected it for her book club. It was adapted into a movie in 2003.) This is the part of my conversation with him in which we spoke about his late father.

TERRY GROSS: **I was very sorry to hear about the death of your father. Had he been sick?**

ANDRE DUBUS III: No. No, it was one of those terrible sudden deaths. As you know, because you've interviewed him over the years, he was in a wheelchair the last twelve and a half years of his life, and that's not easy on anybody. But that notwithstanding, he was in pretty good physical shape.

Just in the last few months, my brother and his partner built a really long, straight ramp out from my father's house, and he did sprints on it in his wheelchair. In the summer, he swam laps in his pool. He shadowboxed and lifted weights. He took good care of himself. So, you know, he was sixty-two and we didn't—no, it was a shock. He got in the shower and had a heart attack and died.

TG: **One of the many things you do is carpentry, and I understand that in his papers your father asked that you build his coffin. What was your reaction when you found that out?**

DUBUS: Well, it was not in his will at all. It actually came up this way: My brother and I were busting his chops over the last story he'd written, called "Sisters." It's a Western, and the hero builds a coffin for a man and digs the grave and does it all in about three and a half hours.

My father was a master writer, but he never worked with his hands, and my brother and I have always done this kind of work. Boy, we really gave him grief for that, because there ain't no way you can build a box that can hold a 200-pound man in three hours, let alone with hand tools. And then dig a hole around trees with roots.

We gave him a lot of heat for that and were having fun doing it, out on his deck this past summer. He said, "Well, when you build my coffin you can take all the time you want. I want it to be straight pine. I want to be buried on my land."

That was this past summer. I was on this book tour in San Francisco when I heard, and all I wanted to do was get back and hug my children, and then go find my brother and build the coffin. And we did.

We gathered at the lumber store, my brother, Jeb, and me, and we designed it through tears. It was such a stark experience. Then we bought the wood; we spent about an hour picking it out in the lumberyard where we'd been for years on jobs. We went to a shop, and from about five at night until nine in the morning we built my dad's coffin out of pine. It was a beautiful night. There'd be this masculine sparring, and then we'd be hugging each other and crying, and then we'd be ripping a piece of wood on a table saw, and laughing and crying. There'd be long moments of stillness and quiet. Over the course of the night, his friends would come by. One of my father's priests stayed until three in the morning and helped us sand. Friends came at dawn with beer and sandwiches. We took a break. When it was finally done, I lay in the coffin and had them shut it so I could feel what it was like. I was also testing to see if the lid was the right height and there was enough curve to it.

Then we dug the grave. We ended up buying a plot of land a half mile from my dad's house. The farmer who we bought it from said that she'd have her hired hands dig it by shovel. She didn't have a backhoe. When we heard that we said, "Well, no, we'll be happy to dig it. If anybody's going to be digging this grave by hand it will be his sons."

My brother, Jeb, and I and our good friend Bill, who's like a third son to my father, dug the grave. The funny thing is it took eight hours. Building the coffin with power tools took two men about twelve hours and digging the grave with three men took eight hours. The veracity of that detail was off in that story my father wrote.

TG: **So you were right to criticize your father.**

DUBUS: Yeah. He needed to redo that one.

TG: **Did he, by the way, redo it?**

DUBUS: No, he didn't. He said, "No, there was sand near those roots and he happened to have the tools."

May 4, 1999

THE CRAFT ITSELF

Uta Hagen

In this world of crassness and commercialism, Ms. Hagen,
like Puccini's Tosca, lives for Art.
David Hyde Pierce

David Hyde Pierce paid this high tribute to Uta Hagen after playing opposite her in a Los Angeles production of *Six Dance Lessons in Six Weeks,* in 2001. Hagen made her Broadway debut in 1938, playing Nina in Alfred Lunt's production of Chekhov's *The Seagull.* In 1943, she starred opposite Paul Robeson in a production of *Othello* that has since entered the realm of legend. She originated the role of Martha in Edward Albee's *Who's Afraid of Virginia Woolf?* in 1962, and she has also appeared in several movies and television dramas. But Hagen was a revered acting teacher as well as one of this country's most celebrated stage actresses. Jack Lemmon, Jason Robards, Geraldine Page, Matthew Broderick, and Lily Tomlin are a few of the well-known actors who studied at the HB Studio, which Hagen established in the mid-1940s with her late husband, Herbert Berghof. And with her books *Respect for Acting* and *A Challenge for the Actor,* she's influenced an untold number of actors who never set foot in her studio.

Hagen died in 2004 at the age of eighty-four. I spoke with her six years earlier, when she was starring in the off-Broadway production of Donald Margulies's *Collected Stories.* You never know what someone is going to be reluctant to talk about. Who could have guessed that Uta Hagen, an actress famous for imparting wisdom to others in her profession, would be unwilling to discuss her craft? Instead of backing off, as I usually make it a point to do when a guest indicates that I'm trespassing, this time I persisted. In the generally quiet and cordial atmosphere of *Fresh Air,* this civilized disagreement created quite a stir. Listeners loved it. Here's an excerpt.

TERRY GROSS: You once said that at your age of seventy-nine, it's hard to find roles that aren't about Alzheimer's disease.

UTA HAGEN: Isn't that the truth? Work that has to do with intelligent people and functioning people is very difficult. It's a wonderful world.

TG: Let me ask you a question that I hope you don't misinterpret, but I think most people find that once they're in their thirties their memory isn't as good as it was. Everyone I know seems to be struggling with this. Do you have to learn lines in a different way now than when you were younger?

HAGEN: No, no. It takes me longer to learn lines because I learn them correctly, and not because my memory's gone. When people memorize lines mechanically they're learning them wrong anyway. I can do that very quickly. People say, "I'm a fast study." I say, "So am I, if I just want the mechanics." But I know that to learn the content of what I'm talking about, and have the words become inevitable through my connection with their meaning, takes a long time.

TG: You're known as a great teacher as well as a great actor, and you've written a couple of books about acting. You write that there are hundreds of different people within you who surface in day-to-day life. You recommend that actors find the person within them that's closest to the role they're playing.

HAGEN: Well, when you create a role, you are selecting from various aspects of your life and putting it together to create that new character. All that has to spring from your understanding of yourself, and that's what takes so long.

TG: There's a childhood experience that you've said has served you many times, including when you played Blanche in *A Streetcar Named Desire*. You were pelted with hard snowballs by kids in the neighborhood and were called an atheist. What is it about that scene that has stayed with you?

HAGEN: Well, it was a cold winter night. I was hounded through the streets by children with snowballs. That's terrifying. I've never forgotten it. It was like being in hell.

TG: What do you summon up from that experience for a role?

HAGEN: I don't know.

TG: Are there life experiences that are so frightening, or rich, that you've drawn on them several times for roles? Does the experience lose its power if you use it over and over again?

HAGEN: No. As a matter of fact, that experience might wear out if I've talked about it a lot. If you don't talk about it, it stays useful. When you explain to an audience, to a colleague who's working with you, what sources you're using, your secret is gone. They look at you with that knowledge of what you're using, and judge it. And you can't use it anymore.

TG: That's interesting. So you won't talk about these things with the people you're performing with?

HAGEN: No, no.

TG: But you'll talk about it with your students?

HAGEN: No, not when I'm using it in an immediate role. I'd give them examples like the snowball. That's used up for me because I've talked about it a lot.

TG: In one of your books on acting, you talk about how an actor can't be inert onstage. You say an actor has to find out what it is that he's doing when he thinks he's doing nothing, so that he can do it convincingly onstage. Have you thought about that a lot, what it is you're doing when you're doing nothing?

HAGEN: I'm going to interrupt you right now.

TG: Go ahead.

HAGEN: Everything you are discussing you have read—it interests you. Are you an actor?

TG: No, I'm not.

HAGEN: Then it's none of your business. Now, let me explain to you why. It may interest you, it may fascinate you. You see, I feel that in the theater everybody thinks they connect—everybody is fascinated about another human being onstage. If it's convincing, they usually are sure that they could do it, too, which is not true at all. If you would go to a violinist, you would not ask him about his bowing arm, about his elbow position, about his phrasing. And if he told you, you wouldn't know what he was talking about, and you would be bored. It is not the secrets, but the craft itself. You wouldn't ask a scientist because you wouldn't know what he was talking about. I feel an audience should learn to respect acting as a craft in the same way. If I do explain it, it might titillate you, you might understand a little of it, but the real impact or import of it, you would not get. I don't say that to offend you, I just believe that with all my heart.

TG: I totally respect what you're saying, but I beg to differ on a couple of things. For example, I *would* be asking the violinist about his phrasing and the bend of his arm.

HAGEN: Why? Do you play violin?

TG: No.

HAGEN: Then I think you might ask him, but I think the violinist would look at you like you were nuts. And I think you are.

TG: As someone very interested in the craft of art, I have found that if the violinist talks to me about his or her phrasing, it might help me hear things in music that I didn't hear before. I find that understanding more about craft is not only interesting in its own right but helps me perceive things that I didn't perceive before.

HAGEN: That's a very valid point, and maybe I'm just in reaction to so many people who asked these questions. The misunderstanding of the layman in terms of acting technique is so profound that I think I've pretty much had it in my life with that.

TG: Another reason why I'd be interested in hearing your thoughts about acting—though I respect you for not wanting to talk about this—is that I think good actors have great insights into the body and how the body communicates, how the voice communicates. Great actors are great observers of other people, and they have insight into how people think and move.

HAGEN: That's true. I believe that the body, as an instrument of communication, is all-powerful. The biggest influence in my life for that training came from modern dance, without being balletic or dancerish myself. But it very strongly influenced me. However, very fine actors often cannot define what it is they're doing. Laurette Taylor could not tell you what she was doing. She was an intuitive, instinctive great performer.

I found in my own work that very often when I couldn't explain something, it was because I didn't understand it myself. When I couldn't articulate it, it was because it was fuzzy in my own head. Now I do know that though I can do it, nevertheless, I may not be able to communicate it to someone else.

TG: Perhaps you'll let me ask you about the voice, since I use my voice professionally, speaking on the radio.

HAGEN: Yes.

TG: You've recommended singing lessons for people who aren't planning to sing professionally but who are going to be speaking onstage. What have you learned about your voice from studying singing?

HAGEN: It has the same effect on the voice as modern dance has on the body of the actor. Modern dance gives a sense of alignment, a sense of awareness of the body in space. In the same way, singing prepares the vocal instrument—the diaphragm, the whole tone of the voice in the head. Now, listen to yourself when you talk. Do you understand what I mean? The self-consciousness. When it makes you listen to how your voice sounds, you're going to be a bad actor. Your voice has to be there for you to serve you when the time comes.

TG: Right. So you're not worrying about how you're doing your lines.

HAGEN: Exactly.

TG: You're learning about the sound and the physicality of your voice.

HAGEN: Exactly. It's there from the singing. The instrument is ready. It's primed.

November 4, 1998

USE THE DISADVANTAGE

Michael Caine

*Michael Caine is the least pyrotechnical, the least showoffy of
actors. He has prodigious ease on the screen; it's only
afterward that you realize how difficult what he was doing is.*
Pauline Kael, *The New Yorker*, November 14, 1983

Michael Caine has appeared in more than six dozen films, including *The Ipcress File*, *Alfie*, *The Wrong Box*, *Get Carter*,
Sleuth, *Dressed to Kill*, *Educating Rita*, *Hannah and Her Sisters*, *Mona
Lisa*, *Dirty Rotten Scoundrels*, *The Cider House Rules*, and *The Quiet
American*. Who doesn't recognize his face by this point? But maybe
because I work in radio, I'm fascinated by actors' voices—and Caine's
is one of the most interesting. So that's where I started when I spoke
with him after the publication of his autobiography, in 1992.

TERRY GROSS: You've said that an actor's eyes are his most
important asset, and that his voice is the second most valuable
thing he has to work with. You have one of the most distinctive
voices in film. How did you realize your own voice was an asset?

MICHAEL CAINE: Well, I realized it when I first went into the theater. My natural voice—having a Cockney accent for a start—was difficult. But also, it's where the voice is placed, and Cockney's naturally right up in the throat. It's rather like John Major, our prime minister. He talks like that. The trick was to bring my voice down to the diaphragm. My first wife taught me how to do that in about twenty minutes. It was the most important thing that ever happened to me with my voice—it was placed. The second thing was that I never went to the normal diction lessons. British actors always spoke exactly the same because they all learned how to speak at the Royal Academy of Dramatic Art. What happened to me is I worked on my own voice, because I was never a trained actor. I came out of it with a voice that was correctly placed by accident, and a very, very individual accent. My accent is so individual that people who don't recognize me by sight, the minute I open my mouth, they know who I am.

TG: **Absolutely. So what did your wife tell you in that twenty minutes?**

CAINE: It is very difficult to do on radio because she put her hand on my throat. What I'm doing is I'm putting my hand on my throat, and if you were to talk like that with your hands on your windpipe, you'd find it all very tight, very, very tight. Then she gradually moved down to the top of my chest, felt the vibration, and said, "Hit the vibration." She put her hand on my chest and said, "Make the vibration hit there." So my voice came down. Then she brought it down a little further, and I hit the vibration there. Then she brought it right down to the bottom, which is the diaphragm. It was just a case of making her hand vibrate as she brought her hand down.

TG: **When you decided to work on your accent, what did you do?**

CAINE: Well, I didn't do anything, really, because I went into repertory, which means that I used to do a play a week for fifty weeks a year. So I was always playing someone different. And in England, we have a lot of regional accents, lots of class accents. I could do almost any accent. What I did was I kept my own voice. What altered my voice tremendously was becoming a movie actor in the United States when *Alfie* was released here. I'd never been to America when *Alfie* was made, and I didn't expect the film to come over here, but the first inkling I got that it was going to be released in America was when they said, "You've got to do 125 loops"—which means lines of dialogue which are on a tape loop—"to make it more understandable to the American ear." So I did 125 American loops. If you listen to the American version of *Alfie,* it sounds as though I can't do a Cockney accent, because I keep getting it wrong. But it was deliberate. I very quickly realized that it wasn't the rhythm of the voice that worried the Americans, it was the speed. The British speak very, very quickly and in a very clipped way. We cut off the end of words. And we talk terribly, terribly quickly.

GROSS: **Did your Cockney accent stand in your way when you were starting to make movies? England has a more rigid class system than America.**

CAINE: Yeah. Well, you have a class system here, but you can't tell it by people's accents. In England you can. I can listen to a person for three minutes, and I'll tell you how much his house costs, how much he earns, what sort of car he drives. The only drawback with a Cockney accent was nobody would put you into Shakespeare because, you know, you have to learn how to speak in verse and iambic pentameters. But even that I did. I played Horatio to Christopher Plummer's *Hamlet* on television and got away with it. When I came into the theater in England, there were no leading parts written for my natural accent. I always had to put on another accent. In actual fact, it did hold me back a bit for a while.

GROSS: **In *Mona Lisa* you played a crime boss, and Bob Hoskins played a character who works under you. You were really intimidating him in the film. You use your voice in a way that shows authority, and the willingness to intimidate and, if necessary, hurt somebody. Would you speak about the acting techniques you used to achieve that effect?**

CAINE: Authority is shown not only by voice but by movement. And the first thing in authority is you never move. If you look at aristocracy and other powerful people, they move very little because everybody is waiting on their every word, wish, or command. And their voice is very, very slow because everybody will wait no matter how long it takes for them to say what they are going to say. What you have to add in this case, where I played a gangster, would be menace. A gangster accent is a working-class Cockney accent. But there is a cheerful chirpy working-class accent, "Hello, lads. Let's all go down the pub," for that sort of chirpy Cockney lad, cheerful little soul. Then there's another one which is very drawn out. And it's very flat. I grew up with gangsters like this. They will say, "I like you." There's absolutely no emotion in the voice whatsoever. It's like an icicle. They say, "I think you're one of the nicest fellows I've ever met. I really do. I really think you're very nice." When you know you're in trouble with a Cockney gangster, he'll say something like, "Well, who's been naughty then?" Now, that question means you're probably going to get kneecapped to the floor. The voice just flattens right out.

GROSS: **If you demonstrate your character's power and authority by not moving a lot, does that mean you don't blink, either?**

CAINE: That's a trick for actors on film. I think the first place I heard it was Marlene Dietrich. If you blink on camera, it signifies weakness. If you look in the mirror yourself, and just stare and start saying things to yourself, you'll see how powerful it is. If you just blink once in the middle of it, you'll see how it all dissipates. It just dissipates the whole thing. Of course, if you're on a movie screen, you have to remember when you blink, each eyelid is somewhere between two to seven feet wide in a close-up.

GROSS: **How do you learn to not blink? It's hard to stop blinking. Your eyes start to hurt. You can do it for a little bit, but after a while it's a real strain.**

CAINE: When I was a young lad, I found a book in the public library, *How to Teach Yourself Film Acting.* The first thing it said is, "You must not blink." So I walked around this working-class district of London without blinking. I looked like an early serial killer. I'm sure I frightened the life out of people because I used to have long conversations and never blink. I would watch people getting hypnotized. They would walk away from a simple conversation with me, quite flummoxed as to what actually went on.

GROSS: You were born in the charity ward of the hospital. Your father was a porter at the fish market, your mother a cleaning woman. You spent several years in an apartment that had no electricity.

CAINE: Yeah. Well, I never lived in a house that had electricity until I was twelve years old, which was in 1948.

TG: What did your friends think of your ambition to act?

CAINE: Oh, they thought it was completely ridiculous. I was treated with absolute contempt by everybody, or ridicule.

GROSS: Why ridicule?

CAINE: Well, for a start, people of my class, in that society, never went into show business. And the male members of my family would regard any male going into show business or acting as being homosexual or a possible homosexual. There was a tremendous gay inference. When I said to my father I was going to be an actor, it was the equivalent of telling him I was a homosexual, as far as he was concerned.

TG: While studying acting, did you feel that you had to do things to prove your manhood?

CAINE: No. I was already doing those things, but my father didn't know about it.

TG: I think I get what you are saying.

CAINE: Yes, I really had to prove it to him. I married very young. I sometimes think that was an effort to prove to him that I wasn't gay. I had a daughter when I was twenty-two. Of course, with his simple-minded way of looking at it, he was wrong again, because the fact that I was married, and had a baby, meant to him that I was definitely not a homosexual. He had a very simplistic view of the world. I mean, he was a very, very tough man. It's very hard to get across just how tough he was. He actually thought that any man who ate chicken was gay.

TG: **Chicken? Why?**

CAINE: Because of this red meat thing. Real men ate red meat, and he thought that chicken was sissy food.

TG: **Did he ever see you in a performance or see your movies?**

CAINE: No. No, he died when I was completely out of work, completely broke. He died of cancer when he was fifty-six years old. One of my great regrets in my life is that his last memory of me was as a complete nothing, a disaster and failure. But at least he knew I wasn't gay because I had a wife and child.

TG: **In your master class acting video, you say that most screen tests reveal the actor's fear. Do you have an example from your own career?**

CAINE: My screen test which showed fear was for *Zulu*. I did it on a Friday morning. I saw the director, Cy Endfield, at a party on a Saturday night, and he ignored me all evening. So I thought, "Oh, well, he's seen the test. That's gone." Just as he was leaving, about midnight, he came over to me and said, "That was the worst screen test I've ever seen in my life." I said, "Oh. Well, that's fine." Then he said, "You've got the part." So I said, "Well, if it was such a bad screen test, why are you giving me the part?" He said, "Because we can't find anybody else, and we leave on Monday." That was how I got into *Zulu*.

But the test was terrifying for me. You know what happens. All your life you think, "I think I would work on-screen." There is something magical that happens on-screen. If your personality, or your talent, or whatever it is, works on-screen, then something happens. Then when you get the screen test, you find out without a doubt whether this something is there or not. No matter how good or bad an actor you are, you can't fake that. The camera either likes you or it doesn't. There's nothing you can do about it. That's what terrified me about my screen test. I was going to see whether I had anything. Well, Cy told me later that, although the acting was appalling and the notes were dreadful, he saw something else and that's why he gave me the part.

TG: **Did you ever see that screen test?**

CAINE: No. I think they burned it.

TG: **Since you obviously learned the craft of film acting by making movies, how did you pick up everything that you know now, like where to look when the camera's looking at you? Did you pick that up after watching yourself?**

CAINE: No. I never watch myself. I never see rushes. I see the finished film once just to see how it turned out and who goofed, including me. Film is listening, reaction, and behavior. That's what film acting is. It shouldn't be called film acting at all because it's not acting. Acting is what you do onstage, as far as I'm concerned. People behave. Normally what you do is you listen, and you react, and then you behave. That's all it is. When people say to me, "Well, what actors did you watch to learn how to act in movies?" I say, "Well, I didn't. What I watch is documentaries, or people on the subway, to see how they react to things."

The only actors that I ever watched for acting lessons were minimalist actors like Jean Gabin, the French actor, and someone who is remarkably similar to him, Spencer Tracy.

TG: **If you didn't spend a lot of time watching yourself, how did you learn techniques like where to look when the camera is looking at you?**

CAINE: I learned by watching where the camera was. The thing is when you play a part, you are playing it with another actor, and you look in their eyes. When you are acting, you suddenly go, "Well, how do I look into this person's eyes?" Now, during your lifetime, you've looked into hundreds of people's eyes—every time you speak to someone. But you can't remember how you did it. What you do is you only look into one eye, because if you look into two eyes, you'd go crosseyed. The one eye you look into is the one that is nearest the camera.

That throws the one eye that you're not using straight into the lens. That's how you do that.

TG: **How'd you learn that?**

CAINE: I figured it out myself, actually. I figured out a lot of stuff myself. You get a feeling in movies when you play someone that the actor should disappear. People should only see the person. It's a self-defeating thing in a way, because half the time people see me, and they say, "Well, he's only playing himself." It's because I've made the actor disappear. That's where you come down to behavior and the camera. You come down to the absolute minimum thing to do for the camera to pick up. That's what is fascinating about film acting, because the camera always finds it.

TG: **Let's talk about your early years.**

CAINE: I first started to act when I was around ten, in school plays. But, of course, at my age, I was the first generation of actors who first saw movie actors, not theater actors.

TG: **That left you with a different kind of role model.**

CAINE: My heroes were James Cagney, Humphrey Bogart, and Spencer Tracy; not John Gielgud and Laurence Olivier, who were the big theater stars when I grew up in England.

TG: **Did that help you overcome issues of class? It would have been hard for you to aspire to be an actor with an upper-class accent, and do the Royal Academy of Dramatic Arts thing.**

CAINE: Absolutely. In American movies you had working-class heroes. You rarely had working-class heroes in British movies. It was always about the aristocracy. I identified more with American movies and American actors than I ever did with British ones, because I thought that the American actors were of the same class I was. Whereas I absolutely knew from their accents and their demeanor that the British actors I was watching were not of the same class at all. People like me did not become actors in England.

TG: **Did you feel a stylistic connection to American actors, too?**

CAINE: All the time. The naturalistic way of playing, right through from Stanislavsky and the Method. I went for that as a young man rather than the very British theatrical declamatory fashion of acting. I was always much happier in movies than I ever was in the theater.

TG: **You made seventy-three films in thirty years. Some people have criticized you for not being discriminating enough in the movies that you chose to make. What have been your criteria for deciding which roles to take?**

CAINE: Well, nobody asked me to make anything for thirty years. So my first criteria was if they asked me at all. Then I had to learn how to act in films, so I made as many films as possible, as fast as possible, in order to learn how to do it, because I'd never done any. I didn't have a gradual workup. I was suddenly a leading man. I was fighting for my life, along with all the other movie stars in the world. I had to give a performance. So I did a lot of stuff. I remember after *Anatomy of a Murder,* Otto Preminger asked me to do a picture. I thought, "Here's this great Hollywood director asking me to do a picture"—a dreadful picture called *Hurry Sundown.* I would have almost done it without reading the script. I mean, I did read the script. I didn't understand it. I didn't even understand Otto Preminger because he had a thick German accent. But I was just so complimented that this great Hollywood director had asked me to do this film, I went and did it.

I was never like Paul Newman, where every new great script that came out came to me first. I was a foreign actor. I was never offered the great American parts. Eventually I had to make a career out of what all the American stars didn't want, which was usually flawed characters. It still happens. British actors always get flawed people to play. The last three Academy Awards have been British actors: Daniel Day-Lewis, *My Left Foot,* a flawed person; Jeremy Irons, he played Claus von Bulow, a man accused of murdering his wife, a flawed person; Anthony Hopkins, a cannibal—God knows, a terribly flawed person. These are all parts that great American stars, I'm sure, turned down and said, "My audience will not allow me to do this." And they quite rightfully did so. We are stars by default in America in a funny way.

TG: You got your Academy Award for *Hannah and Her Sisters,* playing a character married to a character played by Mia Farrow, but you are having an affair with your wife's sister. A flawed person?

CAINE: Again, always flawed. I played a transvestite, a psychopathic killer, in *Dressed to Kill.* I've played all sorts of weird characters. I can't see Clint Eastwood doing *Dressed to Kill,* dressed as a woman going around killing people. I did it, and I'm just as tall as he is.

TG: I get the impression from your book that you don't like doing love scenes very much.

CAINE: No, because if you're a very good actor and you play a murderer, my wife will see the picture and she'll say, "I thought that was brilliant. You were so convincing as a murderer." Right. I'm a very good actor, and I played a very good part as a murderer. My wife thinks it's fabulous. If I put the same amount of sincerity, skill, and dexterity into a love scene, she says to me, "Was there anything going on between you two?" So you can't win. If you're a good actor, you look as though you love the woman. It's very difficult for someone who loves you to watch that. I don't like doing them. Love scenes often obviously involve a lot of kissing and cuddling and sometimes nudity, and I hate it all. It gets in the way of everything. I couldn't do a nude scene. I've looked as though I was nude. But I never take my shorts off.

TG: Have you turned down movies because you didn't want to do a nude scene?

CAINE: Yeah. I turned down *Women in Love*—the movie Ken Russell directed where Oliver Reed and Alan Bates wrestled.

TG: Because of the nude wrestling scene?

CAINE: Well, for a start, I wouldn't appear stark naked in anything. And I couldn't imagine wrestling a naked guy. I thought, "Well, supposing I like this, I'll be in trouble."

TG: It sounds like your father's influence coming back again.

CAINE: Well, my dad would be spinning in his grave if I were rolling around on the ground with Alan Bates with no clothes on. I thought, "The hell with it."

TG: Do you think your father's fear of homosexuality stuck with you?

CAINE: No. I don't have any fear of homosexuality. He didn't have a fear of homosexuality. He had a fear of me being a homosexual. There was no chance of him being one. He wasn't worried about himself. He was worried about me. I'm not worried about me. But you know, there was tremendous homophobia in those days.

TG: You've described yourself as a very unneurotic person. Do you think that that's affected your approach to acting?

CAINE: Most actors would hold up a picture and say, "Look at me." I get rid of all that baggage by holding up a mirror and saying, "Look at you." What I'm doing is I'm playing you, not me. Therefore, I can watch from afar. I watch for the neuroses, or the behavior in people, that I can reflect.

TG: You still do that now?

CAINE: All the time. If you see a performance, even if you're a woman, you should say, "How does he know that about me? How does he know that's the way I would have reacted?"

TG: One more thing. You've said the eyes are the most important part of an actor. But you were born with an eye problem called ablepharia, which puffs the eyelids?

CAINE: Yes.

TG: **Did that make you self-conscious about your eyes? Did it make acting more difficult for you?**

CAINE: Yeah. In school they used to call me snake eyes because I have eyes like a cobra. They used to call me cod's eyes as well, until I grew to six feet tall; then nobody called me cod's eyes. But when I got into the movies, it came out as kind of dreamy and sexy. They could use makeup on them and you get a sort of dreamy quality. There was an old theater producer who said, "Use the disadvantage. Always use the disadvantage." So I used that. A lot of things worked for me like that in my life.

TG: **What else?**

CAINE: Well, I was rehearsing a play, and there was a scene that went on before me, then I had to come in the door. They rehearsed the scene, and one of the actors had thrown a chair at the other one. It landed right in front of the door where I came in. I opened the door and then rather lamely, I said to the producer who was sitting out in the stalls, "Well, look, I can't get in. There's a chair in my way." He said, "Well, use the difficulty." So I said, "What do you mean, use the difficulty?" He said, "Well, if it's a drama, pick it up and smash it. If it's a comedy, fall over it." This was a line for me for life: Always use the difficulty.

November 17, 1992

RIGHT IN THE GUT

Mickey Spillane

The original cycle of Mike Hammer novels, beginning with I,
the Jury *(1947) and culminating in* Kiss Me, Deadly
*(1952), made [Mickey Spillane] a genuine superstar of fiction
writing. Hammer sold more books than Sam Spade and
Philip Marlowe put together: In 1953, New American
Library boasted that "over 15,000,000 copies of his books
have been published in Signet editions."*

*So, Spillane's triumph represented the triumph of the
paperbacks as well. They were on the limit of the
permissible—far beyond movies and television and radio. In
that respect, their only real competition was the girlie
magazines then beginning to make their impact.*

Geoffrey O'Brien, *Hardboiled America: The Lurid Years of Paperbacks*

I spoke with Mickey Spillane in 1989, shortly after the publication
of *The Killing Man,* in which he brought back his tough-guy detective, Mike Hammer, after a twenty-year hiatus. I'm frequently
asked if I have regrets about follow-up questions I failed to ask.
Here's one: I should have asked Spillane if Mike Hammer was his
way of compensating for that girlish haircut his mother made him
wear.

TERRY GROSS: How has your Mike Hammer character changed over the forty-year span you've been writing about him?

MICKEY SPILLANE: Oh, he doesn't change. Mike Hammer is a state of mind. There has never been a physical description of Mike Hammer.

TG: Why?

SPILLANE: Because this way, every man can put himself into Mike's shoes.

TG: Does this mean that in your mind's eye, he's you?

SPILLANE: No. He is not me. I don't go out researching bullets anymore. Those days are gone for me. I am a spectator sportsman now. But I like to say a writer of fiction is really a professional liar. You write these things and people believe it. Mike Hammer gets more mail than I do. Strange, isn't it?

TG: When you started writing the Mike Hammer novels, did you have a sense of what you wanted to do different from the other detective novels that you'd read?

SPILLANE: Yes, sure. The first book was a psychological drama and had a big, sensual ending. Nobody had written one like this before. I came out with it, and it was interpreted in various ways and run down by the critics as being lurid and whatnot. But it sold.

TG: The scene at the end of that first Mike Hammer novel, I, the Jury, is probably the most famous scene you wrote.

SPILLANE: Well, it's the one that is remembered. They said it was a sensual scene. Mike's got a premise in life. He is going to kill the person who killed his friend, in the same way—by shooting that person in the gut. Now, at the end of the story he is facedown with the woman that he loves [the killer]. She knows what he wants to do. She has to get him away from this attitude. She starts to unrobe. She takes her clothes off, piece by piece. There are descriptions of her getting down to the point where she is nude. Then she leans over, and while she is about to kiss him, she is really reaching for a gun behind his head. If he's true to his premise, he'll stay alive. If he is not true to it, she is going to kill him. Watch what he does. He stays true. He shoots her right in the gut. She is a psychiatrist, but she couldn't understand that. And she says to him, "How could you?" He says, "It was easy." And that was the end of the story.

TG: "It was easy" is probably your most famous line. Was it unusual at the time for the private eye to kill a woman at the end of a book?

SPILLANE: Well, they didn't use to do it. In those days, women were held up on a pedestal. I knocked this one off. I've only killed two women in any of my stories.

TG: Why did you want to be the first to kill off a female character?

SPILLANE: Listen, women can be as deadly as men can, anytime. Just refer to your newspapers. It was fun doing it to them.

TG: Mike Hammer says that "in the end the people have their justice. They get it through guys like me once in a while." You have made Hammer into the guy who's going to get justice outside of the law.

SPILLANE: That's right. He can do things other people can't do.

TG: Were there any editorial limits or censorship restrictions on how much sex and violence you could use in the book and still be mass-marketed?

SPILLANE: Well, editors do funny things. When I wrote *One Lonely Night,* Mike Hammer killed off two hundred people with a machine gun, and kept reloading and shooting. It was a Commie nest, a real deadly area, and he shot two hundred people. The editor said, "Oh, that's too much blood." So they knocked it down to a hundred people.

TG: Mike Hammer is a violent guy. Have you been exposed to violence? I know that you were in World War II. Were you in combat?

SPILLANE: No, I didn't have to be. I was exposed to violence when I was a little kid. When I was seven years old, I lived in this crazy neighborhood. My mother wanted a girl, and let my hair grow long. I had what you call a Buster Brown haircut. The kids would get me by my hair, hold me down, and beat the garbage out of me. I got my mother's scissors out one day, and I cut all my hair off. That's why I've got a crew cut now in my seventies. Nobody's been able to grab me by the hair since.

But mostly, I had a nice upbringing. I got into sports, did all kinds of normal things. Violence, per se, is not in my backyard. I've been exposed to it. I've done a lot of police work and reporting; I've seen these things happen and been involved in some of it. I don't take pleasure in any of it, believe me.

TG: Once you were with the police on the bust of a narcotics ring and you took a bullet. When you were shot, how did it compare with how you imagined it, when you had characters shot in your books?

SPILLANE: Well, it was a little bit screwy because I was standing behind a whole bunch of tomato paste. There was a slogan for this tomato paste, "Who put those six big tomatoes in the itty-bitty cans?" The bullet went through the cans, got everybody splashed with tomato paste, and everybody else thought they'd all been shot, too.

TG: How bizarre. With tomato sauce all over, were you still able to figure out right away where the actual wound was?

SPILLANE: Yeah. You know right where that is. But you're not considering that right away, because you're going, "Has everybody got clobbered?" It wasn't deadly, I can tell you that. And you know, it was hard to get the tomato sauce off.

TG: Is this sensation of being shot something you've recalled for writing?

SPILLANE: No. No, you're better off if you use your imagination. You can do things with fiction that nobody would ever believe. Words are great. You can say things that you've never experienced and make them sound real.

TG: You once played Mike Hammer in the film *The Girl Hunters*. What did it feel like to be him on-screen?

SPILLANE: Beautiful. I had a great deal of fun with that because not only was I acting, I was a part of the production work. I had written the script. I was in charge of casting. I am not all that tall, like some of these big six-footers. I'm five foot eight, and I didn't want to look like a little shrimp on-screen, and I didn't want to wear high heels. I didn't want anybody walking in trenches or walking on "apples." I wouldn't hire anybody if they came above my eyes. It's easy to find short actors. So I was able to swagger through the picture. I had a good time making that picture. I didn't forget the words, because I had written them.

TG: I recently learned that you are a Jehovah's Witness.

SPILLANE: Oh, I've been a Jehovah's Witness since 1951.

TG: What surprised me was that, although I know you are not your character, Hammer is such a loner it's hard to imagine you belonging to an organized religion.

SPILLANE: Well, I am not going to discuss it with you now, but next time when a Jehovah's Witness knocks on your door, call them in. They will tell you all about it. Religion is a strange thing. I believe what I believe.

TG: Have the Witnesses ever objected to your books?

SPILLANE: No. I don't think they read them, and I don't blame them. This is a job with me. I don't write for any express purpose, like passing messages around. It's strictly a job. I try to keep them fairly contemporary and fairly clean.

TG: I also recently learned that you collect Blue Willow pottery, which is a surprising hobby for a hard-boiled guy.

SPILLANE: Well, at one time Blue Willow was just cheap kitchenware for farm ladies all over the country, but it was excellently made. It was great chinaware, cheap, very cheap. I like it. It's useful. It's pretty-looking, and it reminds me of my childhood because we had it at home.

TG: Well, speaking of your childhood, your father was a bartender in Brooklyn. Did you hang out at that bar?

SPILLANE: No. I would never hang out in a bar, because I don't like the atmosphere. Nobody goes into a bar to get sober, and it's a trouble spot. It's a place where people go when they don't want to go home. I don't hang around in those places. I never did.

November 22, 1989

You Will Not Find the Word "Lesbian"

Ann Bannon

When I was young, Bannon's books let me imagine myself into her New York City neighborhoods of short-haired, dark-eyed butch women and stubborn, tightlipped secretaries with hearts ready to be broken. I would have dated Beebo, no question. . . .

Dorothy Allison, author of *Bastard Out of Carolina,* Salon.com, June 10, 1999

Ann Bannon is the pen name for one of the most popular and highly regarded writers of lesbian pulp fiction—the author of the novels *Odd Girl Out, I Am a Woman, Women in the Shadows, Journey to a Woman,* and *Beebo Brinker,* published between 1957 and 1962. For contemporary readers, the character Beebo Brinker has come to personify the 1950s "bar butch and her ongoing search for true love," according to *The Bloomsbury Guide to Women's Literature.*

A wife and mother when she wrote these books, Bannon subsequently returned to college, earned a Ph.D. in language and linguistics, and served as a dean of a California state university during a time when being outed as the author of a series of lesbian novels—and possibly a lesbian—might have abruptly ended her academic career. Even though she's retired now, she's still uncomfortable about disclosing her real name when making public appearances as Ann Bannon. In fact, she managed to keep her identity a complete secret until the feminist publisher Naiad Press tracked her down in the mid-1980s, while preparing to republish her books.

I interviewed Ann Bannon in 1999, following the publication of *Strange Sisters: The Art of Lesbian Pulp Fiction 1949–1969*, an anthology to which she contributed a foreword. One of the things I learned is that even now she prefers not to discuss her sexual orientation.

TERRY GROSS: **What inspired you to write your first lesbian novel?**

ANN BANNON: Reading a few of them myself. I had the experience that so many women have written about, of going into a drugstore and furtively poking around the paperback books. One of them was by a young New York writer who was writing under the name of Vin Packer. Her books were contemporary and college-based, very new, but it aroused a lot of intense feelings in me. It was very hard to buy them, let me tell you. It is scary to walk up to a drugstore counter with your arms full of lesbian paperbacks and survive the stare from the clerk, pull yourself together, buy them, and walk out with your head held high. And then figure out where to stash them when you get home.

But as I read them, I came to think, "I can do this, I can write about this." I had absolutely no experience, but I had the feelings and I had the drive, and I knew I could write. I had an old typewriter that had been through fire, flood, and earthquake, and I set it up. I was a newlywed, and occasionally my husband would look over my shoulder and say, "What is that?" I typed on, looking neither to the left or the right. Within a few months, I had a manuscript. But being nervous, uncertain, very new to this, and very young—twenty-one—and since I didn't know any publishers or agents, I sent this book to Vin Packer. I said, "Is there any possibility you can help me out?" She said, "Come to New York, bring your manuscript. I'll introduce you to my editor."

TG: **What happened when you met the editor?**

BANNON: He was a jolly Irishman, very savvy in paperback publishing, very clever and successful. I walked in with this massive manuscript. It was about five inches thick. He read it very quickly and said, "Take this thing home and rewrite it, and concentrate on the two young women." Well, I had written a college novel in which I had a standard college romance, but I also had two young girls who were roommates. In the course of the story, they had become very intense about one another, to the point of actually physically exploring each other and making love. But at the end, one of the two opted for the classic college romance and married the fraternity boy. The editor said, "Throw that out. Your story is the two girls." That threw me for a loop, because I really thought I had been very subtle about all this, and that somehow that would go unnoticed, and the traditional romance would be the part that everybody would like. So I pulled up my socks. I went to Philadelphia, and I rewrote the book around two young women named Beth and Laura, and brought it back much slimmed down and with the two young women as the heart of the story. The editor, Dick Carroll, said, "This is it."

TG: **This was the novel *Odd Girl Out*?**

BANNON: Yes, in which, by the way, you will not find the word "lesbian," because I didn't know it.

TG: **I have a copy of the Gold Medal paperback in front of me, and it says, "*Odd Girl Out*, a confession of a shocking and forbidden love." Is that how you thought of it?**

BANNON: No. I thought it was a little bit unusual, but I didn't think of it as shocking or—well, forbidden. I did feel that it was rare and odd. I hadn't quite gotten to the point of provoking a reaction in enough people to realize how far afield I had gone with this. Nobody in my family knew what I was doing, except that my husband occasionally would peek over my shoulder and see that I was writing. But no one was more stunned than he that I had actually sold the book. I don't think he ever read any of them, to tell you the truth. So I didn't have any feedback. I didn't know any lesbians.

TG: **You were a newlywed when you wrote *Odd Girl Out*. Your heart was in this lesbian novel you were writing, but you were newly married to a guy. So it must have been a confusing time for you.**

BANNON: Yes, indeed, it was. It was a long marriage, too. I felt that I owed that to my husband, and we did have two children. My mother had soldiered on through difficult times. Her mother had soldiered on. I thought that was how one carried the flag for womanhood; you had to do these things. But it was bewildering. I think I must have known from the age of six, when I fell in love with the Statue of Liberty, that I wasn't going to be like ordinary kids. It gives you a clue. I've had a lifelong conviction that you live between your ears, that that's where all the fun stuff is.

TG: **You mean, in your imagination?**

BANNON: Exactly. I think that may be the key to a lot of creative work that people do, that somehow there's a life up there that's so private it's hard to articulate, or hard to share. In that case you find another way to express it. Sometimes it comes out as a long narrative in your head. I would retreat to my own internal storytelling when life got a little overwhelming, which it frequently did.

TG: **These pulps were sold, in part, by having lurid or very suggestive covers. After writing a novel and envisioning what the characters looked like, what was it like to then see the covers that the art directors put on the books? Describe one or two of the covers from your novels.**

BANNON: Oh, heavens. Well, it was a dismaying experience at first, until I came to realize that the lesbians who were looking for these books had learned to read the covers symbolically or ironically. If there were two women on the cover—particularly if one was blond and one was brunette, and even more if one was standing up and one was lying down—that was a code. You could read that as a possible lesbian novel. It would only take a few words of come-on, such as "twilight love" or "strange love" or "society rejects me"—these code phrases—and you had struck pay dirt. That was the kind of thing you learned to look for. After a while, you got past resentment of the total inappropriateness of the women on the covers, and you welcomed them, because you knew that they were a way of making the covers, let's say, salable.

TG: The covers of your books are reprinted in the new book *Strange Sisters*. Let me read one. This is the original cover for your book *Beebo Brinker,* and it says, "Lost, lonely, boyishly appealing, this is Beebo Brinker, who never really knew what she wanted until she came to Greenwich Village and found a love that smolders in the shadows of the twilight world."

BANNON: That captures it all.

TG: So you've got "smoldering in the shadows," "the twilight world," "boyishly." Oh, and she's wearing a skirted suit and sensible shoes, she's holding a wicker valise, and standing on the corner of Gay Street. There's a sign pointing "One Way."

BANNON: Yes. It was pretty ham-handed symbolism. They left nothing to chance. Of course, Beebo, as pictured there, if she came eyeball to eyeball with *my* Beebo, would have turned around and run screaming down Gay Street in the wrong direction.

TG: Why? What did you imagine your Beebo looking like?

BANNON: I imagined her in jeans and a blazer and a turtleneck, with her hair short. A big girl. I mean, she'd been working on the farm all her life, pitching hay bales and riding horses, and was not somebody with a model-slim figure, wearing bobby socks. And even the sensible shoes don't cut it. I think the editors sat the artists down and said, "Now, we want a pretty, young woman, and it's okay if she looks a little bit like a tomboy. But don't go too far overboard, because we really have two constituencies for these books. One's the women, and they'll buy it anyway. The other is the men, and that's who we have to appeal to. The guys want to find a woman who would be titillating to watch

making love to another woman." That was the guiding artistic princi-
ple, if it can be called that, which underlay the cover art.

TG: While you were writing these lesbian pulp novels, you were
married, you got your Ph.D. in linguistics from Stanford
University, and you were raising two children. Was your divorce
at all related to these books, or to your fantasy life related to the
books?

BANNON: I suppose, underlying it all, you have to say yes. I was never
the person in marriage that I believed myself to be, and I had to strike
out and find out who I was. It was interesting when the books were
reissued by Naiad Press. I was a little abashed. My position at that
time was as associate dean at a university. I thought, "Uh-oh, here
goes my job." But in fact, everybody was wonderful. All over campus,
little lavender flags popped out of foxholes and people said, "Good for
you"—particularly over in the PE department. It was a watershed
time in my life. The marriage ended, and I assumed an identity that
was more me.

TG: What have women said that they learned from your books
when they read them in the fifties or sixties?

BANNON: The big thing was "Thank God, I'm not the only one." That's
how isolated people were then. But also that it's okay to open up a little bit. It can be healthy. It can be a warm, generous, wonderful way
to spend your life.

TG: Were you able to believe that about yourself?

BANNON: You know, it's funny, Terry, I think what I did to myself in
that long-term marriage, and long-term career, was to learn to live so
well in my own fantasy that I never truly got out of it. That's not to say
I haven't reached out and tried. I have. It just never has taken. I have
friends who laughingly call me "the Ice Queen." I am not the Ice
Queen. I'm just someone who may have, in a sense, hurt herself, or
limited herself, by being so tremendously good at creating a life internally. I do it wonderfully, if I may say so myself. It's satisfying to me. I
live by myself, I have loads of wonderful friends, straight and gay. I

love them all; I depend on them all. But I don't have a gift for partnership in the real world, or I just haven't found the partner. I don't know.

TG: Your books are on the same shelves with all the pulps—the erotic novels and the crime novels of the period. Did you feel comfortable in that literary environment?

BANNON: At first I felt somewhat embarrassed and self-conscious about it. I thought, "This isn't worthy of me," and I really wasn't sure how to take it. But then my mother began reading my books, and she said, "Sweetheart, good for you, this is great. I would never have thought this would have been your subject." But she said, "I'm proud of you." I thought, "Well, dang! If my mother is okay with it, bless her heart—she was the most proper, lovely Victorian mother you can imagine—I'm okay, it's all right to be who you are."

TG: Well, Ann Bannon, I want to thank you very much for talking with us. How does it feel to be called Ann Bannon? Should I be calling you by your real name?

BANNON: Oh, no, no, please. Ann Bannon.

December 8, 1999

WE ALL DIE

Walter Mosley

*Mosley has never been a traditional crime novelist; rather, he
writes to serve a cultural agenda, and for him the mystery is
less a whodunit than a vehicle for exploring a way of life. On
the most basic level this exploration is racial: Easy is a black
man in a white man's world, and his every action requires a
delicate dance with convention, with the rigid social order of
L.A. in the 1940s, 1950s, and early 1960s—a landscape
characterized by racist cops and housing covenants and the
small, daily degradations of living on the color line.*

David L. Ulin, *The Atlantic Monthly,* July/August 2002

I recorded this interview with Walter Mosley following the publication of *Black Betty,* the fourth in his popular series of novels featur-
ing the private eye Easy Rawlins. The first book in the series was *Devil
in a Blue Dress,* published in 1990; in it, Rawlins had just returned
home to Watts and white racism after fighting in World War II. *Black
Betty* brings Easy into the early 1960s. President Kennedy and the
Reverend Martin Luther King, Jr., have given him a sense of hope,
but his day-to-day life in West Los Angeles remains pretty grim.

TERRY GROSS: **Easy's best friend, Mouse, gets into trouble in
each mystery. How would you describe Mouse?**

WALTER MOSLEY: I see Mouse as the hero of the world that Easy is talking about. He's a sociopath. He's very violent. He's willing to kill people, and it doesn't affect him. Easy is the hero of these books because these books are about him. But in the world Easy lives in, Mouse is really the hero. He's the man who's willing to stand up and fight and not be pushed down for any reason. Not for a political motive, but just because he's crazy. He's been driven crazy by the world he lives in.

TG: Did you ever know men like Mouse?

MOSLEY: Actually, I based Mouse on a friend of my father's—a man who used to hijack liquor trucks and bring cases of liquor to our house when I was a kid. And he would come over and say, "Well, Roy, why don't you keep these bottles of liquor for a week, and I'll come back and get them later." When he would come back, of course, my father would have drunk a couple of bottles. So the guy would say, "Well, you'll have to pay me for those bottles now." Finally, he was in a crap game in a barbershop in downtown L.A., and he murdered a guy. The guy owed him a dime, and he didn't want to pay it. So he killed him. He's in jail now.

TG: Did you grow up thinking, "How can a guy kill somebody over a dime?"

MOSLEY: Well, actually, I understood that. You know, if it's not worth it to kill somebody over a dime, is it worth it to kill somebody over a million dollars?

If you don't have a dime, or if you come from a place where you have to fight for everything that you have, then you just fight. It's a natural reflex, because when you stop fighting, that's when you're going to lose.

TG: Why do you think an insult can incite somebody to murder?

MOSLEY: If you're living in a neighborhood where your rep is the only thing that you have, and if people feel that they can insult you, and push you around, well, then, you're going to lose everything. You have to learn to fight for things that seem ridiculous from an external point of view. But internally, they make more sense.

The life that Mouse was living, and the life that Easy is very close to, is a thing where you have to fight over everything. You stop discriminating between when you fight and when you don't fight. You just are always willing to fight.

TG: There's an opening quote in *Black Betty* before the narrative of the book begins. It's headed "Ghetto Pedagogy." Would you read it and tell us where it comes from?

MOSLEY: This is a conversation I had with my father when I was a little boy.

> *Ghetto Pedagogy*
> *Dad?*
> *Yes?*
> *Why do black men always kill each other?*
> Long pause. *Practicing.*

TG: When your father said "practice," what did that mean to you?

MOSLEY: There's a lot of anger and rage in the black community, but at that time, black people couldn't exercise that rage on the people outside the community who had caused it—so they took it out on each other. In a way, it was getting ready for something that might not ever happen. But certainly it's getting ready for something.

TG: Were you exposed to much violence when you were growing up?

MOSLEY: I don't think there was as much violence when I was a child as there is now. However, there was a lot of violence in everyday life, a lot of anger, a lot of rage, a lot of despair. I feel that I react more to psychological violence than physical violence. Physical violence is kind of easy to avoid. But there's a psychological violence in everyday life that black people, and poor people in general, experience in America.

TG: **What was the psychological violence you were most exposed to when you were young?**

MOSLEY: People who were angry all the time, people who were upset all the time, people who felt that other people were trying to take advantage of them—sometimes they were right and sometimes they were wrong. Confrontations about everything—about how much something cost, about where you were going.

I remember coming out of a restaurant with my father and my mother when I was about twelve. There was valet parking, and so my father comes out, and he gives the guy his ticket. Then another guy comes out after us, a white guy. He gives the parking guy the ticket. The valet goes directly to get the white guy's car and brings it back. My father goes up to the valet, and he says in a very loud voice, "Well, listen, you know, I want you to understand, I'm not going to give you a tip. And I'm not giving you a tip because you went and got that man's car before you got my car. But I was first." I was twelve. I was very embarrassed by this whole thing. But my father was angry. He needed to express that. I think that went on an awful lot when I was a child.

TG: **Do you think he was right in doing that?**

MOSLEY: Oh, yeah. Absolutely. No question about it.

TG: **Is it hard to grow up surrounded by so much anger, seeing slights all around you, and not wind up obsessed with victimization?**

MOSLEY: One of the things that Easy experiences in the books is that sometimes when he's expecting a slight, it doesn't happen. And sometimes when he least expects it, it does happen. Sometimes it's not from white people—it's from black people. It's very hard to figure out where you stand in the world.

It's hard not to feel you're a victim, especially when you are, in certain ways. But then you have to understand that we're all victims. And that your job is to live your life and to survive, not to worry about what somebody next to you has or doesn't have, or what they're thinking.

TG: Your father grew up in the segregated South. Did he tell you stories about the violence he was exposed to there?

MOSLEY: One day my father sat me down and told me about every person he'd ever seen die. It was just amazing. Little children killing each other—black children—black people killing white people, white people killing black people, everybody killing each other, people being hung, people dying because there was not proper protection on their jobs. Then he went to World War II. And he talked about all the people that he saw die in World War II. He worked in statistics, so he typed up the names of all the Americans who had died. After that, he came back to the South and found that most of his old friends who didn't go to war had also died—in these petty and stupid little fights and arguments, and from disease. So he moved to Los Angeles. It took my father a long time to tell me about all of these deaths. At the end of it he said, "So then, Walter, I came to L.A., and I knew I was finally free. I was in a land where these kind of things weren't going to happen anymore." He sits down in a diner, and the guy next to him has a heart attack, keels over, and falls on my father and dies. It was a good way to end it because it was a funny story. But he was trying to tell me there's segregation, there's violence because of racism, and from ignorance and poverty—but also, we all die.

TG: Did your mother also come from the South?

MOSLEY: My mother came from New York City. She is Jewish, from Eastern European stock. Her father was a doctor and very dominant in a lot of ways. She needed to get away from him and that family. My father needed to get away from Jim Crow. They were both people looking for new lives, new ways. You notice in L.A. that everybody is looking for a new life.

TG: Some white people who have married black people have been in the absurd situation of finding that their families have disowned them for marrying a black person—

MOSLEY: And black people, too.

TG: **Did anything like that happen on either side of your family?**

MOSLEY: Well, it did to some degree. And it was very funny. The matriarch of my father's side of the family liked my mother, so she could never be completely ostracized. She got along with her, invited her over, and would do things. But some of the family didn't like her. That kind of wore off after a while, and they got along.

On my mother's side of the family, my grandfather just didn't understand. Even though he was a doctor, he didn't really think that black people and white people were the same species—not only not the same race, but the same species.

A very funny thing happened. Once he came to visit to see his grandson because my mother had demanded it. He was taciturn the whole time, and then went back East. In the meantime, my father built a whole house in our backyard, floored it, walled it, plumbed it, wired it. Did everything. My grandfather came back, and he saw this house, and saw that my father had built it. In a funny way, my father proved that he was better than my grandfather, because my grandfather would have loved to do something like that, and couldn't. After that, my grandfather really liked him. It was a very "country thing," you know, because my grandfather was from a rural background, too. They got along great after that.

TG: **On the whole, did both families get along?**

MOSLEY: Oh, yeah. When I was thirteen, I couldn't have a bar mitzvah, so I had a big party. We invited both sides of the family over. My aunt Fanny, and my uncle Hiram, and my godfather, Hollister P. Fontano, and the Douglas family. Hollister, who was six foot five, and the jokester on my father's side of the family, and Hiram, who was only four foot nine, and the jokester on the other side, would stand in a corner, telling each other jokes. It was wonderful.

TG: **Sense of place is central in your fiction. L.A. is treated almost as a character in your Easy Rawlins series. How did you happen to choose Greenwich Village as the place you want to live?**

MOSLEY: Well, you know, it's interesting. There are a lot of reasons, social reasons. One, it's a pretty safe place to live. It's nice. It's easy. Different kinds of people live there. Asians, Hispanics, blacks, whites, straight people, gay people. But also, the classes live together. One of the wonderful things about Manhattan that's different than L.A. and other places in the country is that it's not separated by class so much. You could have somebody who's living in a rent-controlled apartment—an old Italian lady, maybe ninety years old—and next door, Charles Kuralt. Down the street, Roy Lichtenstein lives. I like that.

May 26, 1994

A FAMILY COURTESY

Mario Puzo

Santino, never let anyone outside the family know what you are thinking.

Don Corleone to Sonny Corleone, *The Godfather*, Mario Puzo

Mario Puzo not only wrote the 1969 novel *The Godfather* and co-wrote the screenplays for all three *Godfather* movies with the director Francis Ford Coppola, he invented the term that Mafia dons now use to describe themselves. He wrote so convincingly about Italian American crime families that people frequently assumed he was somehow "connected" himself, but this was something he vehemently denied. Puzo, who also received screenplay credit for his work on *Earthquake, The Cotton Club,* and the first two *Superman* movies, died of heart failure in 1999, at the age of seventy-eight. I spoke with him three years earlier, following the publication of *The Last Don,* which (together with the subsequent *Omerta*) he considered part of the *Godfather* saga.

TERRY GROSS: How did the Mafia become the theme of so much of your work?

MARIO PUZO: In my second novel, *The Fortunate Pilgrim,* I had a minor character that was a Mafia leader. Everybody said, "Gee, you should have had more of that character." It's really just telling stories I heard in my childhood about people in the neighborhood.

TG: What neighborhood was that?

PUZO: Hell's Kitchen in New York.

TG: Who did you hear the stories from?

PUZO: Oh, members of my family. You know, like the rug-stealing scene and the keeping of the guns from the police. That happened in the family.

TG: Tell the story the way it was told to you.

PUZO: Well, this guy threw his guns across the airshaft, you know, the space between apartments. My mother took the guns and held them for him. When he came and got his guns, he said, "Would you like a rug?"

She sent my brother, who's older than me, over to get the rug. But my brother didn't realize the guy was stealing the rug until he took out his gun when the cop came. That story is almost entirely in the book and in the movie.

TG: How did your mother feel about protecting this guy's guns?

PUZO: Oh, in those days, when I was a very little kid, that was thought of as nothing. He was a neighbor and he wanted you to do it, and you did it because you were afraid of him; because you hoped that he would help you out.

TG: Do you think your mother looked at the mob figures in your neighborhood as people who could protect your family, or as people who were more likely to harm your family?

PUZO: No, protect. For instance, the business about the dog being committed to stay in the apartment—that happened in my family. My mother didn't want to get rid of the dog, so she went to the local guy of respect. I don't even think they thought of them as criminals. They were people who had influence—the way you would go down to your congressman, for instance.

TG: **So tell the dog story.**

PUZO: Like it happened in the movie: the landlord wanted my mother to get rid of the dog, and she didn't want to get rid of the dog. He was going to kick her out and the local whatever he was, I never really understood what he was, told the landlord not to do it. And the landlord didn't do it.

TG: **Did she owe anything in return?**

PUZO: No, she was the cousin, or the niece of somebody, who knew the Mafia guy. You know, one of those family things. A family courtesy.

TG: **Did she do anything to pay respect to the local organized crime figures who controlled the neighborhood?**

PUZO: Well, you have to remember that those figures are usually related by blood and were members of a family, so you gave them presents. If you had a family member who was powerful, you made sure that you gave a present at Christmas or a special occasion. Which was not regarded as a payoff in any way.

For instance, my parents grew up in Italy, and since they were mostly illiterate, when they had a letter that had to be read they would go to the local priest to have the priest read it for them. But they would automatically bring a gift. They'd bring three or four eggs, a chicken, or something like that. It's a whole different relationship.

It wasn't a bribe; it's a mark of respect. It's not like they said, "You got to give me a piece of chicken," or "You got to give me an egg, and I'll read it for you." It was just understood. In the same way, the local neighborhood guys that had influence, you gave them presents.

TG: **How did you envision your character Don Corleone when you first created him?**

PUZO: He was like a brother who was much older than you, who would always protect you, who would always stick up for you. He was somebody who was a protector.

TG: When Marlon Brando was cast in the film, and you saw Marlon Brando inhabit the character, did your idea of Don Corleone change?

PUZO: No. No, I'm the guy that picked Brando.

TG: You picked Brando?

PUZO: Oh, sure. I wrote him a letter, and he called me up, and we had a chat. Then I tried to get Paramount to take him and they refused. When the director, Francis Coppola, came on the picture, he managed to talk Paramount into letting Brando play the role. But it was my idea to cast Brando, which caused me a lot of trouble before it finally got done.

TG: What did you say in your letter to Marlon Brando when you were inviting him to play the part?

PUZO: It was something like, "Help, they're going to kill me. I think they're going to cast Danny Thomas as the Godfather!"

TG: Danny Thomas? Wow!

PUZO: Yeah. Well, Danny Thomas was very rich off television, and I read an item that he was going to buy Paramount Pictures so he could play the Godfather. That scared me so much I wrote a letter to Brando. He gave me very good advice. He said, "No studio will hire me. Wait until you get a director and then talk to the director." And he was quite right. When I talked to the studio they swore they would never hire Brando.

TG: Why were they so opposed to the idea?

PUZO: Well, Brando had built up what to them was a terrible reputation for being a troublemaker on his *Mutiny on the Bounty*, where he cost them a lot of money. He was always a rebel. And his movies had been flops.

TG: **Did he cause any trouble for you on the set?**

PUZO: I was never on the set, but they tell me he was perfect. Every actor just loved the idea of working with Brando; he was their idol.

TG: **What were the difficulties of adapting your first *Godfather* novel into a screenplay?**

PUZO: It was a cinch.

TG: **Yeah?**

PUZO: Yeah. I mean, it was a cinch because it was the first time I had ever written a screenplay, so I didn't know what I was doing. And it came out right. The story I tell is that after having won two Academy Awards for the first two *Godfathers*, I went out and bought a book on screenwriting because I figured I'd better learn what it's about. The first chapter of the book said, "Study *Godfather I* as the model of a screenplay." So I was stuck with the book.

TG: **It's interesting to me that the characters who wield power are very euphemistic in their language. They could be giving you the message that they're going to kill you unless you follow their orders, but they say it in the nicest way; killing would never be mentioned. Everything is between the lines, beneath the surface. What made you write the dialogue for these powerful, violent people in that coded way?**

PUZO: Well, it does come from the way the Sicilian Mafia operated. In fact, there was a funny story that an Englishman came to live in Sicily and he got a kidnapping note, because they liked to collect the money for kidnapping you before they kidnapped you—so they didn't have to go to the bother of kidnapping you. That was the way they operated. But the Sicilian Mafia wrote this Englishman such a flowery note that he really didn't understand what they were saying. He had to get an interpreter. He thought they were paying him some sort of compliment. He didn't realize they wanted like fifty grand off him before they kidnapped him. So it saved everybody the trouble of going through the kidnapping. But it was very flowery: "Your eminence, we love you. We'll do anything. If you're having trouble give us a call." You know, and meanwhile, "Just send us fifty grand and you'll never have any trouble with anybody."

But that's how they talked. That's where I got it from, you know. That horse's head thing was strictly from Sicilian folklore, only they nailed the head of your favorite dog to your door as the first warning if you didn't pay the money. They were great believers in collecting money before doing the job.

TG: **The most famous line you came up with was about making "an offer you can't refuse." Does that line have its roots in mob lore?**

PUZO: No, I made it up. I wrote memos on how we could plant that line because I was sure it would become a famous line. I recognized that it would become one of those lines that people would always be using. That was carefully constructed.

TG: **Did you come up with the expression "Godfather"?**

PUZO: Yeah. That was an accident. Of course, before I used it no Mafia man ever used the word "Godfather" in that sense. Nobody used it. In Italian family culture, when you're a little kid, you call the friends of your parents "godfather" and "godmother" the way in American culture you call family friends "aunt" and "uncle," even though they're not your aunt and uncle. That was the only way in which it was used, except in a religious sense. So I remembered it, and the more I used it in the book, the more it became what it was. Now the Mafia uses it. Everybody uses it.

TG: **You've said that your parents were nearly illiterate. How did you become a reader and a writer? Were your parents proud of you for being able to read and write?**

PUZO: No. I wrote a line someplace where my mother regarded my library card with the same horror that present-day mothers look at their sons' heroin needles. Reading didn't help you make a living, you know.

TG: **What did your mother think you should be doing instead of reading?**

PUZO: Oh, you know, a good clerical job indoors. If you could avoid hard labor, that was the big thing.

TG: How do you react to criticism from those Italians who complain that Italians are always depicted as mob figures in American popular culture? And how do you respond to people who criticize the *Godfather* movies for being so violent, and for having increased the amount of violence in American popular culture?

PUZO: It sounds like some of my relatives. But to me it's a completely irrelevant thing. For one thing, there was a time when Italians ran crime in America. So I'm not maligning them in any way. In fact, I present them as very lovable people that have to make a living— unfortunately, in a way that society doesn't approve. But also, I know that most Italians that I grew up with were so law-abiding that getting a traffic ticket was terrible.

TG: Your novels and the *Godfather* movies have had a huge impact on American popular culture. What do you think it is about the stories that make people connect with them in such a powerful way?

PUZO: Well, it's a story with warm personal family feeling, and I think it's everybody's wish to have somebody they could go to who would correct all their injustices without the problems of going to court, hiring a lawyer. You know, somebody fixing up your world for you.

TG: And if you crossed them, you'd be dead.

PUZO: But that's okay, because why would you want to cross them if they did everything for you?

TG: Of course, but there is always a bloodbath.

PUZO: People are not perfect.

July 25, 1996

MAKE SENSE OF
IT LATER

George Clinton

Funk at its creative peak in the mid '70s was embodied in one man, George Clinton, who proffered an aggressively vulgar, brilliantly literate version. . . .

Ken Tucker, *Rock of Ages: The Rolling Stone History of Rock and Roll*

George Clinton may have been the most influential figure in black pop between James Brown and the first deejays and rappers. He's also one of the most flamboyant of pop musicians and one of the most eccentric, even though his career started off conventionally enough, with "(I Wanna) Testify," a 1967 soul hit by his vocal group, the Parliaments. It was in the early 1970s that Clinton's genius fully emerged, when he created the Parliament-Funkadelic sound, an oddball brand of funk that drew inspiration from all sorts of things—acid rock, psychedelia, glam, even old science-fiction movies and comic books. Adopting the alter ego "Dr. Funkenstein," he sometimes made his stage entrance from a flying saucer.

Did I remember to mention that Clinton is eccentric? When we booked an interview with him for *Fresh Air* in 1989, he didn't have a home telephone. So how was his publicist going to be able to leave the customary day-before reminder? We were skeptical, but we needn't have worried. Clinton showed up in the studio early and in a fine mood, greeting me in a manner that might have puzzled anyone unfamiliar with his 1982 hit, "Atomic Dog."

GEORGE CLINTON: Woof, woof, woof. Yeah. I just got de-flead and got the ticks off of me. I've got my doggie bag. And I'm gonna get my rabies shots and I'll be ready for them. How you doing, baby?

TERRY GROSS: **Okay. Your new album, *The Cinderella Theory*, is your first new recording in over five years. What got you back in the studio?**

CLINTON: Oh, I got tired of laying up, being the old dog, and not learning new tricks. I said, "Let me get back out there," 'cause when rap started to get heavy like it is now, I said, "That's an old trick right there. I can do that." So here I am, back out here talking, still.

TG: **How do you feel when a rapper uses one of your rhythm tracks on one of his records?**

CLINTON: I love it. The ones they use too long, they pay. The rest of them keeps us alive. I mean, like "Me, Myself and I." That particular one brought my whole thing back to life. Plus they paid good. The main thing is that it brings you back to life, if you know how to use it. They did it with James Brown, too. I learned from him not to get upset. I figured out a way to benefit from it. So I sample my record back over theirs.

TG: **What was the first music you heard that made you want to make music yourself?**

CLINTON: Oh, wow. I could almost tell you precisely what it was. It was "Why Do Fools Fall in Love?"

TG: **Frankie Lymon.**

CLINTON: Frankie Lymon and the Teenagers. I was about thirteen. I started the Parliaments in '56, right around the same time. And the

Spaniels, of course. "Goodnite, Sweetheart, Goodnite." A lot of people remember that one. But I remember some of their earlier doo-wop records. They were the ones that actually made me want to really get into it. Plus, in Newark, New Jersey, where I grew up, everybody either sang or boxed or played ball. I tried boxing. That wasn't happening. I played ball. I had a baseball team, and they kicked me off my own team. So then I got my group together and that's been working pretty good ever since.

TG: At the same time that you were singing with your group, the Parliaments, you were also running a hair salon. Right?

CLINTON: That was later on. I started the Parliaments, say '56. About '59 I was working at a barbershop processing hair that would go right along with the doo-wops. You know, you get your hair done, and then go down the corner and sing all day and night.

TG: How were you wearing your hair at that time, when you were in the barbershop conking other people's hair?

CLINTON: Conked, too. How did you know that phrase? You ain't supposed to know that phrase. That's an inside phrase. Conk is a real old one. That's what it was, though. I was wearing my hair the same way. As a matter of fact, there's pictures around with my hair slicked, looking good, waves—make you seasick to look at my head. But it all worked real good for us because everybody in the band worked in the barbershop at that time. And we all did each other's hair.

TG: Was being stylish very important to you then?

CLINTON: Style has always been important. That's why I think we are able to survive. I can see styles coming long before they get here. And I can pretty much tell what goes with a style. So as I see it approaching, I try to jump into it early.

At a barbershop, you had all kinds of styles you could relate to. Styles fit faces or fit the time—Easter or Christmas. You had a variety of styles to appreciate. So I transferred that into music. My whole life has been one big style after another, and it all look like, "Wow, he's been that all his life." I forget that I have hair like I've got hair now [long, multicolored dreadlocks]. When I see somebody looking, I don't get upset 'cause that's what I do it for—the attention.

TG: When you had your first hit, "(I Wanna) Testify," in 1967, you were working for Jobete, the publishing company of Motown Records. I understand there was a lot you didn't like about the Motown style—everybody in the group dressing alike and doing the same steps.

CLINTON: Well, not that we didn't like it. We loved it. But we just couldn't see ourselves overcoming the Temptations or the Pips. The criteria at that time was height, and the Temptations all were six feet. And we were like five foot six, five foot two. We was all over the place. It wasn't uniform. The routines and things we had perfect. And the suits, of course, we had perfect. The styles was perfect. But there was no way to outdo the Pips with the routine. And the Temptations had the perfect image. There was just no way for us to overcome the competition within the company. Plus it was hard to keep the ties alike or shirts clean. That was the hardest part of all. So it was convenient when we realized that hippies and rock 'n' roll and blues was the exact opposite of what we had been into all our life. We changed our whole thing and went that way. We could do this having fun. We'd wear the clothes bag as opposed to the suit. We'd take the suit out and throw it down and cut holes in the clothes bag and put it on. And it became just a big joke at first. But the music was always very soulful, churchy, like *Maggot Brain,* psychedelic. Nobody had seen black groups doing psychedelic. They used to call us "The Temptations on acid" or "James Brown on acid." But it always worked.

TG: Were you doing a lot of acid yourself during that period? And if so, what effect did psychedelics have on your performances?

CLINTON: Well, at that particular time everybody did acid. And I did my share and two or three other people's share. At the time I wasn't into analyzing it as being the thing that helped us. But once it was over I realized, okay, it did break me out of that mold of the streets of New York, New Jersey—the rat race that tends to make you feel like

"I've got to do it to them before they do it to me." We was growing up into that and that's what we would have been.

TG: **Since your music was inspired both by soul and funk but also by acid rock, was it ever hard to get accepted by both black and white audiences?**

CLINTON: We was too black for most white audiences because there was so many of us. They could take Jimi Hendrix and a couple of white guys. But here you had ten guys up there acting like they were all from Newark. And we were. But it was all in fun. I think that one audience kept us alive; then the other kept us alive. There was a cult following of *Maggot Brain* fans—white fans—from Boston, Toronto, parts of Michigan, and Cleveland. We had a good audience in all the colleges. And then towards '71 and *America Eats Its Young,* a lot of the black audience started showing up. By the time we did *Cosmic Slop,* it was really both black and white, but one wouldn't come to the other's show. So we still had to do different places.

TG: **Since you've done some barking for us already on the show, let's talk about your hit "Atomic Dog."**

CLINTON: Yeah. You all better get your doggie bags out now and get your ticks out of there. Okay.

TG: **How did this record come together?**

CLINTON: Basically, we were off the road for a couple of years. It was my first solo album and I was trying new things. "Atomic Dog" was just the kind of life I probably was living at the moment. I don't know intellectually what made me do it. But I think we was getting all dogged out by the record companies about our whole lifestyle, or whatever was going on in the streets. Since we weren't working, you tend to get back into all of the party things. I think I probably was dogging myself out at the time. But I was walking to the studio one day and just started singing. I didn't even know what I was thinking about. That's the way it came. Most of our songs come like that. We make sense out of it later.

Somebody come along and say, "Did you mean so-and-so and so-and-so?" And if it sound really hip, I say, "Yeah. That's what I mean."

TG: **How did you start moving from singing to producing and doing these really far-out rhythm tracks? I know you produced the Parliaments' records, but producing really became your specialty.**

CLINTON: I realized that it was going to take more than one group to survive. I think if you have a number of outlets for your stuff, when one style is saying that you're over with, another one will be saying, "Ah, this is the new thing." So we not only did Parliament-Funkadelic, we did Bootsy, the Horny Horns—everybody that was in the band. They gave me a lot of different outlets, because so many members in the band would have liked to have their own group but didn't want the hassles.

TG: **You not only have a lot of different bands that you've created and produced, you also have several alter egos—like Dr. Funkenstein.**

CLINTON: Oh, yeah. Dr. Funkenstein, Mr. Wiggles, Sir Nose—

TG: **How did you create Sir Nose D'Void of Funk, your character who refuses to dance?**

CLINTON: That voice—I was actually imitating one of the guys that used to work in the barbershop, or used to come to the barbershop all the time. All the girls liked him. He was real cool. But as far as I was concerned, he was crazy. I mean, the dude stabs his car. When I told him, six or seven years ago, that I had been imitating him with that voice, it tickled him. He remembered those things. For most of the voices I usually use a character out of the barbershop, because the thing in the barbershop is to get up and tell lies. "When I saw Sugar Ray fight Joe Louis in '27"—those are the kind of things that always happened in barbershops. I found that they worked good on record. So a lot of the characters were based on people who I know. Dr. Funkenstein was like an FM disc jockey. Those kind of [rhyming] jocks is missing off of radio now. I figured, I'll put this type of thing on the *Mothership Connection*. It was the right thing at that time. Most rappers tell me now that they learned rapping from the *Mothership Connection* album.

TG: I think you're almost fifty now.

CLINTON: Just got to forty-eight.

TG: **Do you ever worry that as you get older you'll have to change your image and tone down the extravagance and sexual innuendos in your performances?**

CLINTON: That changed a long time ago, the sexual innuendos. In-you-out-doz. I wouldn't go to the front stage and flirt with the thirteen-year-old girls. But I would still probably say something really funky or dirty. You can always change that to fit whatever age. I don't worry about that. As long as I don't be walking around looking like this with no possible way of hit records. I told everybody around me that if I have no possible way of hit records, make sure I get rid of this Baby Jane look. You hip to Baby Jane, right? As long as I got some kind of reason to think that I got a record coming out, I don't mind looking different or weird or whatever, 'cause to me it's only a style. But if it don't look like I'm ever gonna put a record out, I told everybody, "Remind me to cut this hair off my head."

TG: **When we were setting up this interview with you, we found out that you don't have a telephone. I couldn't imagine why.**

CLINTON: I haven't had one for about ten years. The Mothership can get in touch with you if it needs to be in touch. You don't really realize how much you don't need a lot of things. I know most people think I'm crazy for real. But the majority of things that you depend on as lifeblood is not really that.

August 8, 1989

BOOTZILLA TWENTY-SEVEN HOURS A DAY

Bootsy Collins

Clinton and Collins became funk's Lennon-McCartney. . . .
Bootsy was an instrumental force on the P-Funk recordings of
1974–76 (Let's Take It to the Stage, Mothership
Connection, Chocolate City, Clones of Dr. Funkenstein)*,*
but was still eager to express his own vision.
AllThingsDeep.com

Before teaming up with George Clinton in Parliament-Funkadelic, Bootsy Collins helped push funk in a new direction by supplying a superheavy bass line to James Brown's 1970 hit "Get Up I Feel Like Being Like a Sex Machine." In the mid-1970s, while continuing to collaborate with Clinton, Collins formed Bootsy's Rubber Band, a spin-off group focused on his colorful stage persona, "Bootzilla" (he wore oversized, star-shaped eyeglasses proportioned to the name). For all of that, he's surprisingly down-to-earth in conversation. I recorded this interview with him in 1994, following the release of *Back in the Day*, a best-of collection, and *Blasters of the Universe*, his first new album in six years.

TERRY GROSS: You were still in your teens when you joined James Brown's band, at the height of its popularity, during the "Sex

Machine" era. Is it true that James Brown flew your band down to play a job with him because his band had walked out?

BOOTSY COLLINS: Yeah, but they hadn't walked out yet. They were still there. They were our heroes, and when we walked in, it's like, how do you cross the strike line, man? We felt really strange because we felt closer to the band than anyone else, and here we are walking in and getting ready to do their gig. We didn't realize that until we got there. We thought James just wanted us to do a gig with him. We didn't know we was coming in and replacing the old band.

TG: Did you feel you had to ask permission or apologize?

COLLINS: That was pretty much the feeling, because we really respected these guys. Fred Wesley, Maceo, Melvin—the drummer, Clyde. These were our idols. And man, to walk in and do their gig, it was like, "Wow, who are we?"

TG: I went back to James Brown's autobiography, *The Godfather of Soul*, to see what he had to say about you.

COLLINS: Oh, God.

TG: He writes, "I think Bootsy learned a lot from me. When I met him he was playing a lot of bass—the ifs, the ands, and the buts. I got him to see the importance of the *one* in funk—the downbeat at the beginning of every bar. I got him to key in on the dynamic parts of the one instead of playing all around it. Then he could do all of his stuff in the right places—*after* the one."

COLLINS: That's absolutely correct, yeah, absolutely correct.

TG: Was it hard to make the adjustment to playing on the "one"?

COLLINS: No, because I knew he knew something. And whatever he knew, I wanted to find out, because he had the tightest band in the land.

TG: Had you been playing on "two" and "four" before?

COLLINS: Actually, I started playing with a guitar. When I picked up the bass, it was like, "Oh, you mean I've got to play on the dominant note. Oh. Okay." It was all brand-new to me, but by James telling me that, it all made sense. And once I started hearing it, it was like, "Oh, and then I can still do this. And I can still do that." So it was a groove. It was really a groove.

TG: **How did your image and what you wore onstage change when you started playing with James Brown?**

COLLINS: Ooh. That's good. What I wore onstage. Oh, man. Well, those were the days in the sixties—kids were coming up front and wearing bleached jeans and T-shirts, and Afros, and the granny glasses. We was all freaking out. Then here we are. We're flying with James Brown—we're in the army now. It was good for the fact that it brought us off of the street. We had been out there doing what everybody else was doing—acting crazy, throwing firebombs, and doing everything. But we put everything else in the backseat because this is what we wanted to play, even though we wanted to dress crazy. We didn't know how crazy we wanted to dress, but we didn't want to wear suits. We knew that.

TG: **So you were wearing matching suits onstage while everybody else was wearing jeans and tie-dyed T-shirts?**

COLLINS: Yeah. While this movement was going on—the peace, the love—here we are, getting stuck with wearing suits and patent leather shoes. If you wanted to be with James, that's what you had to do.

TG: **You left James Brown after just a couple of years. What was the turning point that made you think it was time to leave?**

COLLINS: You just want to do things the way you want to do them onstage. And here we were just standing up there being the tightest band in the land. You couldn't jump out in the audience and freak out, and act crazy, and that's what we wanted to do. We wanted to have a low-down hoedown, a drip-until-you're-wet type party.

TG: **Shortly after you left James Brown, you met George Clinton. Did you think Clinton was taking James Brown's music to the next step?**

COLLINS: Not really. When I got with George, I wasn't even thinking like that. I was just looking at George as a way that I could really expound on what I wanted to do, because George had an open-door looseness that I could relate to. And he said, "Okay, if you help me with Parliament-Funkadelic, writing songs and playing in the band, then one day, at the same time, you can do your own band."

TG: **George Clinton is pretty outrageous onstage. What did that bring out in you?**

COLLINS: Well, George gave me what any young kid would need, and that's encouragement. Whether the world was saying you're doing something right or cool, or not, George said—*"cool."* I already felt it was cool, but for him to say that, and for him to be who he was—he was the craziest man in the universe, and that's who I wanted to be. He gave me the opportunity I needed.

TG: **Would you talk a bit about the stage persona you created for yourself?**

COLLINS: Well, I'd always dreamed of that kind of stuff in school, you know, the twinkle, twinkle little stars, and reaching for the stars, and one day maybe playing a guitar that's made out of a star, and maybe seeing through stars. When I got with George, I figured that this was the opportune time to make that a reality. That's when I went in search of people to make the glasses and make the basses and, you know, have a star-fulfilled type of thing going on.

TG: **Describe the glasses, and how you got them made for you.**

COLLINS: Ah, well, the same people that made Elton John's glasses out in California. I think they felt sorry for me. I was kind of wimpy and off the streets, and I had this lowly, humble thing going on. They said, "Come on in, kid. What you need?" I said, "Well, I need some star glasses," and they laughed at me at first. I drew them out a little bit. And they said, "Okay, okay. How much money you got to spend, kid?" I said, "Well, actually, none." They laughed at me again, but I think they really did feel sorry for me. They got me a pair up for about a hundred dollars. They were prescriptions, too. But the next time I went to get some star glasses, they charged me maybe triple. But it was cool.

TG: **When you started wearing those really, really big glasses, were those prescription, too?**

COLLINS: Yeah. All of them were prescriptions. Definitely. It was pretty good for me because I could really see the audience. Before then, I couldn't actually see what was happening out there. All I could do was hear them. And I knew they were out there, but I couldn't see what the funk was going on. But now I can.

TG: **When you got a band of your own, what were the pressures of having to take care of business, and make sure people showed up for gigs and were not too high to perform?**

COLLINS: It was pretty strange, because it was a ghetto-level thing with me before. We always rode around in cars—maybe eight, nine people in the car—and equipment. I was out here to enjoy people and have a big old party, and beer to go. I never really looked at having to take care of people until I got with George and we started Bootsy's Rubber Band. When it hit me, it was like—*whoa*. I started having to take care of this truck, and rent sound gear, and make sure everybody was there. Everybody's babies is hungry, and I had to be responsible for everybody. It was a whole other ball game. I just had to grow up.

TG: **Did you hate that aspect of the work?**

COLLINS: Yeah. I pretty much did, because it took me away from what I actually came out there to do.

TG: **Music.**

COLLINS: Yeah. Yeah, I hated it, but at the same time, I was in it. I was at the point where Jimi was at, and where Sly Stone was at. You don't know what the heck to do because there's no books on it.

TG: **So what did you do?**

COLLINS: I just stopped playing music, and everybody thought I was crazy. And I thought I was crazy, too, because at that point we was doing stadium dates. I was making like a hundred grand per stadium and couldn't nobody understand why I stopped.

TG: **How long did you drop out of the music business?**

COLLINS: I would say a good six years before I even thought about messing back with it.

TG: **So what's your plan now?**

COLLINS: I'm just going to do what I got to do. And when I come off the stage, that cat stays on the stage. I go back to the farm with the rest of the aliens. It's just a way of life. You have to separate it. I never knew that. I always wanted to be Bootsy and Bootzilla twenty-seven hours a day. It's like Bugs Bunny, man. Don't he get a chance to not be Bugs Bunny? No! So I had to come up with ideas of how to do this—how to be on like a light, and then turn myself off when I got to be off.

TG: **What do you think about rap performers who've sampled your music on their records? Do you consider it robbery or homage?**

COLLINS: I guess they kind of kept the funk alive, you know, because the new kids didn't have a clue about us at first. Then the rappers came on with the zapping the funk, and getting it out. My hat is off to them because they kept it alive. It gave me an opportunity to come back around a second time. A lot of people don't get that chance.

TG: **Do you think some of the rappers initially heard your records through their parents?**

COLLINS: Yeah. Definitely. As a matter of fact, Ice Cube was telling me he wanted to come to one of our shows when he was around ten years old, and his momma wouldn't let him. He was wired. I mean, he was really upset he couldn't make it. But he was telling me about that, and it was like, wow, man. The parents passed the records down. That's where they picked up on it.

TG: **One of your new records is dedicated in part to all your friends in the kitchens and jails across the world doing hard time.**

COLLINS: Yeah. When I was playing these big coliseums and big time—everything was going groovy, groovy, great—everybody just kind of related to me out of the kitchens of the Holiday Inns and the Ramadas. I always went back, signed autographs. I never forgot that, because I used to work in the kitchen myself when I was coming up. When I was eleven years old, I'd go get a job. I told them I was sixteen. I told a little white lie every now and then. By me being tall, they thought I was sixteen or eighteen. "Yeah, you can have the job." And then they'd take me there and work me to death, put me under the stoves. I'd be cleaning under the stove, but it was a groove, because I finally got me a radio. And that's pretty much what started it off.

TG: **You also dedicate the album to people in jails. A lot of your fans or people you know?**

COLLINS: People I know. I came up the same way. Everybody around me was going to jail. The only thing that kept me out of jail was the music. That's what kept me out.

October 10, 1994

DISSONANCE

Nick Hornby

What really matters is what you like, not what you are
like. . . . It's no good pretending that any relationship has a
future if your record collections disagree violently, or if your
favorite films wouldn't even speak to each other if they met at
a party.

Nick Hornby, *High Fidelity*

I recorded my first interview with the British writer Nick Hornby in 1995, following the publication of his funny and knowing novel *High Fidelity*. Rob, the novel's narrator, a used-record-store-owner, defines himself by his taste in music, movies, and books, and judges other people by theirs (usually finding them wanting). This rang a bell with me, because I, too, am frequently guilty of administering what Danny Miller, *Fresh Air*'s executive producer, and I call "the taste test." Taste is part of what attracts two people to each other, and often it's what drives them apart. But taste can be puzzling. Take Sam Phillips, for example. Who could be hipper than the man who discovered Elvis Presley and Johnny Cash? Yet when we talked on *Fresh Air*, he told me he was a fan of Arthur Fiedler. "Fiedler was so crazy," Phillips said. "I love him, man. He was scared of nothing. Give him a drink before he went out onstage, a half a pint, and you can forget it, honey. You were going to have fun with music." So you never know.

TERRY GROSS: **Do you size people up by their favorite recordings and movies like Rob does in *High Fidelity*?**

NICK HORNBY: I'm always very interested in other people's stuff, and I guess it's something that I want to know fairly quickly. But I don't think I'm alone in this, a lot of men are like that. They'd rather cut to the chase in conversation and just get people to list things.

TG: Rob is always drawing up top-five lists, like his top five Elvis Costello records, or top five American films. Do you think it's the impulse to create lists that is particularly male, or do you think the entire obsession with taste is male?

HORNBY: I think the quantifying aspect is very important.

TG: **I confess, I am baffled when people get together who don't share the same taste. I mean, if somebody is obsessed with movies and starts a relationship with someone who doesn't like to go to the movies, you wonder, are their inner lives compatible?**

HORNBY: Yes, I would say that they probably aren't. I think it probably gets easier as you get older to form relationships and to find points of contact that aren't based on taste. But at the times when one is form-ing relationships, these things are very important.

TG: **Film critic Pauline Kael once wrote that she broke up with someone after they saw *West Side Story* together, because he loved the film and she detested it, and she just couldn't imagine seeing him after that. Have you ever been through something like that?**

HORNBY: No, but a friend has quite recently. They had an argument because the woman described a TV movie as a great film. You could feel the doubt in his voice, from a very early stage thereafter, and it didn't last long.

TG: The main character, Rob, in *High Fidelity* owns a record store called Championship Vinyl. Why don't you describe what it's like?

HORNBY: Well, it's a rather seedy secondhand store for collectors, and it sells all vinyl. When I imagined it in my head, it's just racks full of vinyl. It's empty most of the time, so the three guys who work there spend most of their time arguing with each other, and they don't make a lot of sales.

It sells the pop music canon. If Harold Bloom has a canon, these guys have a canon. It's kind of R&B, New Wave, sixties rock—all the music that rock critics would approve of.

TG: Plus a little ska.

HORNBY: Oh, yes, yes.

TG: Some of the customers in this record store are people who virtually have no life outside of looking for rare singles. About one customer, the main character thinks, "I can't imagine telling him anything of a remotely personal nature—that I had a mother and father, say, or that I'd been to school when I was younger—I reckon he'd just blush, and stammer, and ask if I'd heard the new Lemonheads album."

Do you know people like that who seem to have no life outside of book or record stores?

HORNBY: Yes, well, the thing that interests me about people like the characters in the book is that what they listen to all the time is incredibly emotive, and yet they're very anal. There's this great dissonance between the music and its consumers.

TG: Where does your character fit in to that?

HORNBY: The central character is emerging from an obsession with pop music. His thirty-fifth birthday takes place during the narrative of the book, and he's beginning to think that it's about time he did something else, but he's not sure what that might be. He's in between two camps, which is quite an uncomfortable place to be.

TG: Back in 1973, one of his girlfriends had a list of top five recording artists that included Carly Simon, Carole King, James Taylor, Cat Stevens, and Elton John. The main character thinks, "I can imagine what sort of person she became—a nice person." How did you choose that list for this early girlfriend?

HORNBY: I guess that was pretty much a composite of the record collections that I saw in girlfriends' bedrooms in the mid-seventies. One of those artists was always represented in any collection that I saw.

TG: I think it's true that many men want to be the mentor in a relationship, so they'll seek out a woman who's younger, or less experienced or less educated.

HORNBY: Yes, I think it's very representative and very common male behavior. In *High Fidelity,* Rob Fleming spends a lot of his time making compilation tapes for women that he meets. In a rather unpleasant way, it's like dogs and lampposts; it's marking out your territory. Virgin ears are very important to that kind of man.

TG: Tell us more about the compilation tapes your character Rob Fleming makes and how he uses them.

HORNBY: Well, they are a means of seduction. He meets Laura, who's the other central character in the book, at a club where he's a deejay, and he offers to make her a compilation tape of the music that she's been listening to, and dancing to, in this club. It becomes very important that he has introduced her to all sorts of things. Later on, he meets somebody else, and he finds himself making a tape for her, too. Laura sees him and knows exactly what he's doing.

TG: I have to tell you, I've always found that male urge to mentor a girlfriend kind of irritating.

HORNBY: Yes, I should think it is, actually.

TG: Yes, it's somebody who doesn't want an equal, someone who doesn't want to share an interest, but wants to teach it.

HORNBY: Yes, you're trying to turn the other person into a female version of yourself, which kind of defeats the point of the relationship.

TG: Exactly. Now, what about *your* top five singles of all time? Do you have such a list?

HORNBY: I guess the permanent number one is Marvin Gaye's "Let's Get It On," which I think is the greatest piece of pop music ever made. The four after that change periodically, but there's always something like "Hey Jude" in there, and I have a residual fondness for "Maggie May," Rod Stewart, so that those three are always there, or thereabouts.

TG: Do people expect that your choices will be more obscure than that?

HORNBY: Yeah, but I've gone through the obscure stage. In fact, the records that you tend to end up listening to when you've been listening to pop music for twenty years are the great ones, and the great ones tend to be the famous ones.

TG: Your main character not only divides pop culture into top-five lists, he divides up his life that way, too. The book starts, "My desert island, all-time, top five most memorable split-ups in chronological order." Then he lists the five women, or girls, who left him during his formative years. Did you ever find yourself doing that in real life? Or is this just an extreme you invented for your character?

HORNBY: This is something I invented for the character, yes. I tend to try and forget as quickly as possible.

TG: When you were writing this book, did you have to do any research, so to speak? Did you hang out at a record store or observe certain people you felt were close to the characters that you created for your book? Or did you already know all this stuff inside out?

HORNBY: I think really I knew this stuff inside out. There's some stuff about women's underwear in there—

TG: Oh, I was just going to mention that. That's a really funny part. This is a character who is really disappointed because he finally figures out that women save their best, sexy lingerie for Saturday nights when they expect to actually be sleeping with someone. But when you move in with the woman, you see her tattered, torn undies hanging up to dry on the radiators.

HORNBY: Yes, that was something that obviously came from bitter experience. But I did check it out with a lot of women friends, and so my one piece of research was to ask women about their underwear.

TG: Did they concur?

HORNBY: Yes, they did. I'm getting a nod here from the studio [at the BBC in London].

TG: From your engineer?

HORNBY: Yes, that's right.

TG: I'll move off the subject of underwear for a moment. So just how big is your record collection?

HORNBY: Well, I guess I have seven hundred or eight hundred vinyl albums and a few hundred CDs, and quite a few tapes as well. I've gotten to the stage where I have most things I want.

TG: Well, that's actually pretty modest by collecting standards.

HORNBY: Yes, I'm not really a collector, and I have ditched loads of stuff as I've gotten older, which Rob Fleming, the guy in the book, would never do. He'd never get rid of anything, because he uses his records as a kind of autobiography, whereas I practiced a sort of Stalinist rewriting of history.

TG: What do you mean?

HORNBY: Well, I sold all the dodgy heavy metal albums, all the Black Sabbath records I bought when I was sixteen, and they're now no longer to be found in my record collection.

TG: Did you ever have to divide up a record collection after living with somebody?

HORNBY: No, I've always kept things very separate.

TG: How do you file your records? Just alphabetized straightforwardly?

HORNBY: Alphabetized, but with the first names first, so Bob Dylan would be under "B."

TG: What?

HORNBY: Yes.

TG: Why?

HORNBY: Because I've always found this problem with certain artists and groups, like the J. Geils Band. If you walk into a record store, you never know whether to go to "J" or "G." And it's firmly under "J" in my collection. I think it makes sense.

TG: Uh-huh. Well, I guess this answers the Sun Ra question.

HORNBY: Absolutely, yes. And I recommend it to all your listeners.

TG: Have you ever wanted to call a moratorium on taste, so that for a day, nobody would have any taste? And you wouldn't be thinking, "Well, what do they really like and what does that say about them? And what do I really like and what does that say about me?"

HORNBY: Yes, I think it is a terribly burdensome thing, but those habits are so deeply ingrained that it's very hard not to judge. But it would be nice. John Lennon should sing a song about it.

> *Imagine there's no Quentin Tarantino.*
> *It's easy if you try.*

September 26, 1995

As a postscript to the High Fidelity *interview, here are a few questions and answers from a later talk with Hornby in which I learned more about a part of his life that has nothing to do with his record collection. This is from 1998, when Hornby came on* Fresh Air *to talk about his novel* About a Boy.

TG: **Your book *About a Boy* tells the story of a single guy who's been avoiding committed relationships, yet in spite of himself becomes a father figure to a teenage boy. I read in one of the reviews of your book that you have a son who is autistic. You must have been totally unprepared to have an autistic child, who will be very different from whatever expectations you had when you first learned you were going to become a father.**

HORNBY: Yeah. Especially if you make your living out of words, the kind of basic expectation you have as a parent is that whatever else, you're going to be able to talk to your kid. My kid doesn't talk, so that was a huge readjustment.

TG: **You probably also had fantasies about being a pop culture mentor to your child—teaching him about your favorite books and records and movies.**

HORNBY: I can kind of do that. My son really likes music, and he watches a lot of videos, although he watches the same four videos over and over again. But that's not such a big deal, really. I'm sure that he will respond to music in some form or another. I think that we just have to be inventive in the ways that we relate.

TG: **I know you're separated from his mother. How much time do you spend with your son now?**

HORNBY: I see him every day. I live and work around the corner, so I give him his bath every day and I give him lunch a couple of times a week, when he's not at school. I spend weekends with him. It's not very much less than it ever was.

TG: It's hard to answer questions like this without being false—but how do you think you've been changed by having a son who is autistic and being exposed to a completely different way of relating to the world?

HORNBY: That is a very hard question to answer. I think that it's made me tougher in some ways. When I first started writing, the writing took off quite quickly with my first book. It's easy to get overwhelmed in those circumstances. You end up doing what people want you to do, and it's hard to say no to things.

But the moment that Danny was diagnosed, it became much easier to keep time for myself and to almost hide behind him. You can afford to be much tougher with people as a result of something like that.

TG: What do you mean "tougher with people"?

HORNBY: It's very easy for me now to tell people to shove off, if they get in my face or want to take up time, because the time is for Danny. And money is for Danny as well.

It makes me feel better about earning. I've earned quite well over the last few years. That makes you feel kind of weird at first, because you think, "What's all this for?" But now I know what it's for.

May 20, 1998

IN THE JUNKYARDS

Grandmaster Flash

Grand Wizard Theodore may have introduced scratching but
Flash is certainly the man who made it matter.
"Punchphrasing"—playing a quick burst from a record on one
turntable while it continues on the other—and "break
spinning"—alternately spinning both records backward to repeat
the same phrase over and over—are credited to Flash. Moreover,
Flash was a showman. . . . Crowd-pleasing tricks associated
with hip hop, such as spinning with his back to the turntables
and using his feet to mix, first flowered from Flash's imagination.
Nelson George, *Hip Hop America*

Grandmaster Flash was one of the first and most influential hip-hop deejays. His description of the many hours he spent hidden away in his bedroom rewiring old turntables as a teenager makes him sound a little bit like a nerd, not a spiritual ancestor to the rappers we see grabbing their crotches and boasting about their guns and bitches on MTV today. That's one reason I liked him so much when I interviewed him in 2002.

TERRY GROSS: I'm interested in how you started mixing music, using two turntables or more. Was this something you started doing at home or in clubs as a deejay?

GRANDMASTER FLASH: My love for vinyl and for the turntables probably started off when I was a toddler. Growing up at home, I was pretty fortunate to be around a montage of music. My sisters were into Tito Puente, Joe Bataan. My father was into Dizzy Gillespie, Miles Davis, Cab Calloway. My mother was into Ella Fitzgerald, Lena Horne. And one sister was into the Michael Jackson sound.

I grew up listening to quite a bit of vinyl, and my love for it came about when I was old enough to start looking into turntables and stuff of that nature. It was a negative experience—I say negative, meaning I used to take apart electrical items in my mother's house, including turntables, just to figure out how they work, and why they work. My intention was to put it back together properly. But I just could not do it. I had this thing where I had to know how the inside of a turntable worked. How the inside of a radio worked, and my father's stereo. That's probably where it really started.

TG: **You started using turntables as if they were instruments to change the music that you were listening to, as opposed to simply playing the music. How did you come up with this idea?**

FLASH: Well, I watched a lot of deejays in my early teens, and my great positive influences—I'm talking about DJ Kool and DJ Jones— inspired me to do what I did.

They would just play the music, and I felt like I could take the most exciting part of a record, which we call the break, and extend that—because a lot of these songs were obscure funk tunes where the break section was maybe only ten seconds long. From a frustrated point of view, I had this thought that if I could just come up with a system—a way of taking duplicate copies of the record, with two turntables and a mixer—I could extend that five- or ten-second break seamlessly and make it ten minutes long if I wanted to.

And, you know, my thoughts manifested into creating an art form called the Quick Mix Theory, which is actually taking a passage of music, or two duplicate copies of vinyl, and moving the disc back and forth and repeating a section of the passage, between duplicate copies of the record. That's where it started.

TG: So you'd have two copies of the same record each cued to the same place on separate turntables. After playing the short break on the first turntable, you'd play that same break on the second turntable. While the second turntable was playing, you'd cue the first turntable back to the same spot on the record, preparing to play it again so you could hear that break over and over.

FLASH: Exactly. That was called the Clock Theory, yeah.

TG: Some people say that you were able to look at the grooves of a vinyl record and know exactly where the rhythm was that you wanted to play. Could you actually see the right spot to drop the needle in the grooves?

FLASH: Well, I was pretty decent at it. That was called "needle drops." My first student, Grand Wizard Theodore, was probably the best at that. But what I came up with is what I call the Clock Theory. The Clock Theory was where you would place the needles down on both copies of the vinyl, and when one ended, you would push in the next fader, but while that record was playing, you would spin the other record back one or two revolutions to the top of that break. Then you would do it all again. So it was like push, spin back, push, spin back.

This made it an assured way of being able to get back to the beginning of the break section without actually having to pull the needle up. Once I picked the needle up, I could always get close to the right spot, but it was never really exact. So, if it was, like, a twelve-inch LP from Atlantic Records, and if the break began, let's just say, at the top of the A-side, I would put Magic Marker right there. That would be my clock of where I had to bring the record back one or two revolutions, to the top of the break. I would do this with two copies of the same record, back and forth, back and forth. Picking up the needle was no longer an issue. Creating the Clock Theory, which all deejays use today, where they mark the album at a certain point, is one of my contributions to the art of the deejay mix.

TG: In order to play these turntables as instruments, and to get them to do exactly what you wanted, did you have to spend a lot of time at home practicing?

FLASH: Yeah. I was looking for something. At this time, there was no point of reference, no blueprint around. So I was constantly at it, yes, but I was looking for something. And as I was looking, I would run into obstacles, so I had to start coming up with different techniques—to deal with things like torque versus inertia for turntables.

You can buy a turntable, or a mixer, or a needle now that's suited for whatever you want it to do. But at this particular time, in the seventies, this stuff didn't exist. I had to actually come up with the science and the terminologies. Now, with turntables, I came up with this thing called the torque factor. The torque factor is based on how long it takes from the state of inertia when you press that power switch, before that platter comes up to speed. If that platter takes more than a turn to be up to speed, then the torque of that motor wasn't very good.

In my search, I went through a countless amount of turntables. I had to actually create the electrical items first before even coming up with the Quick Mix Theory. I had to go look at needles and I learned that needles come in two classifications. One is the elliptical. The other is the conical. And conical, although it doesn't sound as good, stood in the grooves better because it was shaped like a nail versus like an elliptical stylus that was built like a backwards J. As soon as you would bring the disc back, the elliptical stylus would fall out of the groove. So, you know, all these things had to come into play before I was able to even start doing any cuttings, scratching, whatever the case may be.

TG: **You must have been pretty obsessive at that time, taking apart turntables, shopping for just the right needle, and designing variations on the technology to get what you needed.**

FLASH: Well, I probably was more frustrated than anything. There was so much stuff I had to buy. A lot of it was trial and error. Trying to get my hands on the right needle, I had to go through countless needles. I had to go through countless turntables and find the right mixer. Then it didn't have a system where I could prehear the music in my headphones, so I had to create something called the Peekaboo System. I had to actually jury-rig these things.

My frustration fueled the fire to keep me staying at this. I was throwing away my teenage years, you know, when you're feeling your oats and you want to go hang out with the girls and go to the parties. I think I probably lived either in the junkyards—going through abandoned stereo equipment or going through abandoned cars, and taking out the speakers and the radios—or I lived in my room searching for something in my frustration.

TG: **Did you have the money to buy the stereo equipment you needed?**

FLASH: No. That's why I had to go into backyards and look for stuff, and go through abandoned cars or ask people who might have been throwing away stuff. But at this point in time, I still didn't know what these internal parts was. So I was tearing up all this stuff inside my mother's house and became like public enemy number one with my sisters. Then my mother decided to send me to school.

TG: **What kind of school?**

FLASH: Samuel Gompers Vocational and Technical High School. That's where I started to understand, like, what is a resistor, what is a capacitor, what is AC versus DC, what is a transformer, what's a push-pull circuit, what's a dial rectifier, and what's an ohm meter, what's an oscilloscope, what's a wave?

I started actually understanding. So now when I tore into something I had somewhat of an idea of what it was, or what it did. All these things helped me to jury-rig this Peekaboo System. It helped me to put together the system so that I could start getting this concept out of my head, so to speak.

TG: **Once you perfected your technique and started working parties and clubs, what was it like for you to see the reaction of the crowds to this thing that you had been working on alone in your home for so long?**

FLASH: Well, I guess after maybe a three-year period, when I finally came up with it, I showed my partners, Disko B and EZ Mike. Actually, as I was creating it, they were the only ones that I would allow to come into my room and watch me do this. The first time that I de-

cided that I would show this to the public, it was an outdoor dance—
a block party, we called it. You can come into the park for free and
party. My theory was if I play the climactic part of duplicate copies of
a record—so there'd be like maybe ten or fifteen duplicates back-to-
back, seamlessly, on time—I should have the neighborhood park in
an uproar. When I got the exact opposite, it was kind of painful. It
didn't work according to what I thought it would. People just stood
there quiet. I'm talking about hundreds of people. They didn't get
loud and they didn't party.

TG: **Why not?**

FLASH: I don't know. I'm not sure what it was at that time, because I
had all the equations sort of set. I watched certain deejays play these
songs I picked from the beginning, and I knew that a particular part
is where the audience went wild. So I figured, "Let me just go to the
parts of these songs and just do them one behind the other," but it
was just extremely quiet. It turned out that the real factor of the matter is vocal entertainment was needed to accompany this new way of
deejaying. I made the first attempt, and I was totally horrible at trying to rap with my mix. It was really too much to do at one time because you're constantly taking records on, taking them off, putting
them on. I was horrible at it. Then what I would do is put a microphone out on the other side of the table and anyone that thought that
they can verbalize to this newfound science of mixing—please feel
free.

　　Everybody failed except for this one person who probably was
the savior of my esteem. His name was Keith Wiggins. He was my
first MC. He went by the name of Cowboy. Cowboy reminded me of
a ringmaster at the circus. He had a very commanding voice. He
came up with a verbalization like, you know, "Throw your hands in the
air," "Say ho, say party," and this and that. That was the perfect diver-
sionary tactic to get people off of looking at me, and to look at him,
and do what he says do, while I go through a series of breaks—you
know, just playing one behind another seamlessly to the beat.

July 8, 2002

ALIVE IN A COFFIN

Paul Schrader

Schrader thinks that movies are obligated to grapple with life's pulpy profundities—sex, politics, madness, violence, the eternal wrestling match between the sacred and the profane.
John Powers, *LA Weekly*, October 17, 2002

Paul Schrader was brought up in a strict Dutch Calvinist home in which movies were forbidden. As a screenwriter and a director, he's been responsible for movies you could imagine his parents using to justify their hard line. Schrader wrote screenplays for three of Martin Scorsese's films: *Taxi Driver, Raging Bull*, and *The Last Temptation of Christ*. Among the films he's written and directed—all obsessed with questions of sin and salvation—are *Blue Collar* (cowritten by his brother, Leonard), *Hardcore, American Gigolo, Light of Day, Patty Hearst, The Comfort of Strangers, Light Sleeper*, and *Affliction*.

Taxi Driver has a special place in the history of *Fresh Air* (as you may have noticed, we never pass up an opportunity to play music from Bernard Herrmann's score). Both Danny Miller, our longtime executive producer, and I love *Taxi Driver*. Danny came to work on *Fresh Air* in 1978, when he was still in college and we were still a local show. Not long after, Cybill Shepherd was in Philadelphia to sing at a small jazz club, and we booked her for an in-studio interview. Because we had no transportation budget then, it fell to Danny to drive her from her hotel in his dented, barely functioning '67 Dodge. He still talks about seeing her framed in his rearview mirror, just like Travis sees Betsy in the final scene of *Taxi Driver*. This could be why Danny decided to stay on at *Fresh Air*—I can say for sure it wasn't the money.

Fresh Air had become a national show by the time I finally got to talk with Schrader about *Taxi Driver* and his other films in 1988, following the release of *Patty Hearst*. (There's more about *Taxi Driver* in my interviews with Jodie Foster and Albert Brooks.)

TERRY GROSS: **When you were growing up in Grand Rapids, Michigan, you planned to become a minister. Your family followed the teachings of the Calvinist Church so strictly that you didn't even enter a movie theater until you were seventeen, because there was a church ban against seeing movies.**

PAUL SCHRADER: Well, it banned what they called worldly amusements, which included things like card playing, smoking and drinking, dancing, and theater attendance. This came out of Prohibition days; the ban was instituted in 1928. Once, as a child, I rather impassionedly queried my mother about this. I think I wanted to see some Disney film. She said to me, "It doesn't matter. The quality of the film doesn't matter. It's the industry that is evil." That was the position.

TG: **Did you have a sense of what you were missing?**

SCHRADER: No. I'm actually very happy about having missed all those things.

TG: **No. Really? Why?**

SCHRADER: Because you are imprinted as an artist or as a person by how you come to a specific field. I came to films as a college student. The first films I saw, or paid serious attention to, were the films by Bergman, Buñuel, Antonioni, and Bresson. That was my original imprinting in films. My peers and coevals were imprinted with Westerns and Disney films. When they say, "I want to make the movies that I loved when I was a child," they think about those films. When I say that, I think about the films I first came to love. I came to films as an adult, and then later learned to love them as a child. So it has given me a unique perspective and a unique place in this business. I've never really worried about anyone doing what I'm doing because no one has my perspective.

TG: **What's the first film you saw and what effect did it have on you?**

SCHRADER: Actually, the first film was a Disney film, *The Absent-Minded Professor*. I snuck into the balcony and I started to watch this, and I was wondering what all this fuss was about. Then about a year later, a friend of mine took me to see *Wild in the Country* with Elvis Presley and Tuesday Weld. I sat there and I realized, "Ah-ha. This is why they don't want me to go. Here's the problem."

TG: **What effect did seeing *Wild in the Country* have on you?**

SCHRADER: I developed a mad crush on Tuesday Weld.

TG: **Did that make you feel bad?**

SCHRADER: No. It made me want to see more movies.

TG: **So what made you so passionate about movies?**

SCHRADER: It was a very luxurious forbidden fruit. Not only could you be a rebel and do something that upset your elders but you could also wear the mantle of respectability while you were doing it. It was like having your cake and eating it, too. It was a rare opportunity to be a rebel without having to do things like break into cars.

TG: **Was there still a little voice in the back of your mind that said, "This might damage me in some way?" While you were watching a movie did you ever feel that it was having a harmful effect on you?**

SCHRADER: No. I've a pretty solid sense of who I am. I mean, there are movies that are damaging, there are movies that I would not watch, and that I would not want other people to watch. Society does have the right to protect itself against certain forms of violence or pornography.

TG: What kind of movie wouldn't you watch?

SCHRADER: Child porn. I wouldn't watch violent sex. I would not watch amoral violence, violence that is graphic just to titillate. It's debasing. I don't want to sound like a censor. But at a certain point, everyone has to make their own decisions.

TG: There are some people, I'm sure, who would have liked to censor parts of *Taxi Driver*.

SCHRADER: Yes. I don't think that kind of censorship is in any way appropriate. The problem with censorship is that it's a case-by-case situation. Certain things you just say, "Well, this is too much."

TG: When you started to go to the movies, did you feel hopeless about catching up? Everybody else had grown up with movies and you hadn't.

SCHRADER: I came in as a film critic, and I went to UCLA Film School. My first year in Los Angeles I kept a notebook and I averaged twenty-two films a week for that year. This was before videocassettes. So I was jockeying from one little university cinema to the next. All I did for about two years was get caught up.

TG: Though you had intended to be a minister, you became a film critic, then a screenwriter and director. Why had you wanted to be a minister?

SCHRADER: It was part and parcel of the background. Ministers were the most respected figures. And I've always had this proselytizing urge to go out and communicate and convert. So it was natural.

TG: Did you channel that urge into movies?

SCHRADER: Well, I think it's pretty obvious.

TG: One of your movies, *Hardcore*, is about a father from a background similar to yours; he's a Calvinist in Grand Rapids.

His daughter runs away to the city and starts working in pornographic movies. When you left home to work in movies, did your parents feel like the father in this movie? Even though the movies you worked on were not pornographic, do you think your parents might have had such a negative attitude toward movies that they perceived your work as hard-core?

SCHRADER: I suspect they may well have. They've had to make some hard compromises over the years. My mother's dead, but my father has had to compromise in order to keep his family relationship.

TG: Did they ever break the ban to see any of your movies?

SCHRADER: I believe so. But it's not a subject that comes up.

TG: After leaving Grand Rapids, did ordinary secular life, or life in the film world, seem exotic to you?

SCHRADER: Yeah. People who come to Hollywood talk about how tough it was. Before I moved to New York, I was in Los Angeles fourteen years. Strangely enough, it never seemed that tough to me, because I had come from a background where people were not just trying to tell you how to behave, they were trying to tell you how to think. You had to fight off the mind control aspect of it. I got to Hollywood and I said, "These people don't care how I think. They just want me to behave in a certain way. This is no problem." So I didn't see it as that difficult.

TG: To what extent have you kept religion in your life?

SCHRADER: I'm Episcopalian now. I've moved to the less strict side of the aisle. But the imprinting you have as a young adult is part of your permanent makeup.

TG: Your screenplay *Taxi Driver* is about a lonely and alienated psychopathic taxi driver. You've described the taxi as the perfect metaphor for loneliness—a man driving around the city in a steel coffin. His alienation erupts into a bloody killing spree at the end of the movie, which he thinks of in heroic terms. He thinks he's helping to clean the city of the pimps and the filth.

SCHRADER: What's interesting is that in the film, he fixates on two women, one he can have, and one he can't. Of course, he wants the one he can't have, and doesn't want the one he can. Out of this dilemma, he decides to kill the father figure of the good girl—a politician. When that fails, he kills the father figure of the bad girl, the prostitute. In his mind there's really not much difference. They're both these competing father figures. In the mind of society, of course, he becomes the hero because one of them [the one he kills] was a pimp and not a politician.

TG: This has a Freudian sound to it. Were you in Freudian analysis at the time?

SCHRADER: No, subsequently.

TG: In the film, the taxi driver, Travis Bickle, keeps a journal—which of course you wrote. The tone of writing in that seems so perfect for the character. Lines like, "Thank God for the rain which has helped wash away the garbage and the trash off the sidewalk. . . . All the animals come out at night—whores, skunkpussies, buggers, queens, fairies, dopers, junkies. Sick, venal. Someday a real rain will come along and wash all this scum off the streets."

SCHRADER: I love the line "I don't believe that one should devote his life to morbid self-attention," which of course is what this character does. Every moment of the day.

TG: Oh. Precisely. The next line is just the most perfect line about alienation I've heard: "I believe that somebody should become a person like other people." How did you know the tone of voice to get for this? It seems just right.

SCHRADER: Well, I wrote that script in ten days in two drafts. It jumped out of my head like an animal. It was really a *cri de coeur,* a cry from my heart. I'd fallen into a difficult period in Los Angeles, where I was living in my car and just sort of driving around and having a lot of trouble sleeping. Finally, I got a pain in my stomach that turned out to be an ulcer and I went into the hospital. While I was talking to a nurse in emergency, I realized I hadn't spoken to anyone in several weeks. In the hospital, I realized that that's what I was. I was like a taxi driver. I was like this person floating around in this car. Then I got out of the hospital and I wrote that script, like I said, in ten days.

TG: Did driving around in that car, almost living in it, increase your sense of detachment and alienation?

SCHRADER: Yeah. Particularly in Los Angeles, you know, you really do feel like you are alive in a coffin.

TG: Back to the tone of *Taxi Driver*, there's something almost biblical or apocalyptic about it. "Someday a real rain will come along and wash all this scum off the streets."

SCHRADER: Yeah, that was my first real script. I'd done one thing before. I didn't know how you were supposed to write scripts yet.

TG: Had you studied the journals of people who had become assassins or murderers?

SCHRADER: No, I was actually surprised. Arthur Bremer's journal came out after I had written the script. I read it and I was very surprised to find that the voice was almost identical. I think the reason that some psychopathic people have attached themselves to this film is because the voice is absolutely authentic.

TG: Did it scare you that you were able to so authentically and so intuitively capture a psychopathic voice?

SCHRADER: It scared me that I was in that place at that time. The person who wrote that script is long gone. I don't even know if I would recognize him if I saw him.

TG: What was your reaction when you heard that John Hinckley said that he had seen *Taxi Driver* and he wanted to impress Jodie Foster by attempting to assassinate the president?

SCHRADER: I was in New Orleans at the time scouting locations, and it came over the radio that this kid had tried to kill Reagan. And he was from Colorado, sort of a white-bread kid. I said to the person sitting next to me, "It's one of those *Taxi Driver* kids." I got back to the hotel, and the FBI was waiting for me. In fact, it was one of those *Taxi Driver* kids. The film didn't create them. They existed before the film and after the film. It's actually sort of rare that they attach themselves to a good film. More likely they attach themselves to things like advertising.

TG: When you were growing up you were always warned about the danger of films. Did that come back to you in the wake of this experience?

SCHRADER: No.

TG: Three of your films, *Taxi Driver*, *Hardcore*, and *American Gigolo*, are set, in part, in the sex trades. What's your interest here?

SCHRADER: It was a lot of adolescent acting out. I came from a rather puritanical background. So, at a certain age, you've got to trash the candy store.

TG: Is that what you saw yourself as doing?

SCHRADER: Yeah.

TG: When you started directing, what was the most difficult thing for you to learn?

SCHRADER: A visual logic. I came from a background that believed ideas exist in the province of words. If you had something to say, you used words to say it. It took me a long while to understand that images were also ideas and that they were not synonymous with words. The image of a fork is not the same as the word *fork*. It sounds rather simple, but I tell you, it took me a long time to figure it out.

TG: How did you learn to think visually?

SCHRADER: I fell under the tutelage of a wonderful architect named Charles Eames, and that played a very important role in understanding the poetry and the logic of imagery.

TG: You've also said that you had to learn how to avoid being too literary when you were writing screenplays. You've said, "I don't think a movie should have too many good lines, at most five great lines and ten good ones. The rest should be absolutely ordinary and banal."

SCHRADER: You can overwrite a movie—unless that is your intention, unless language is the subject matter of the film, such as in a David Mamet production. But if you are trying to convey a quotidian, a daily reality, then you've got to restrain yourself from getting excessive in that area.

TG: Pauline Kael, the film critic, was one of the people who influenced you when you were first making movies. She encouraged you to be a film critic instead of going into the ministry. She helped you get into film school, and then you decided to write screenplays instead of writing criticism. What's it like for you now when she reviews one of your movies?

SCHRADER: We had a falling out a number of years ago. Basically she thinks I should have stayed a writer and never become a director. For some reason, she has not reviewed the last three or four of my films, which is actually fine with me. I regard it as a favor because I do not think those reviews would be good.

TG: Why don't you think they'd be good?

SCHRADER: Like I said, I don't think she feels I should be a director. She thinks it's all right for a writer to be cerebral, but not a director.

TG: You said that you are no longer the same person who wrote *Taxi Driver*. At that time, you were motivated by certain demons, by alienation, by loneliness. You're now married. You're a father. I figure loneliness wouldn't have the same pull on you that it did then. Are there different things that motivate you now when you are writing, or different demons that drive you?

SCHRADER: Yes. Certainly. You miss those old demons, boy, because those are powerful engines and they really drive you hard. It was actually easier to write then, because you had no choice. You were just trying to keep the demons from swallowing you up. Today it's a little more difficult. You have to use your imaginative powers and your creative skills to a greater degree.

TG: Several of your films, like *Patty Hearst* and *Hardcore*, are about leaving the family and breaking away, either voluntarily or involuntarily, from what your life has been. When you left your home and broke away from the church, was that a wrenching experience for you?

SCHRADER: No. No, it was more like the way a bullet must feel when it's finally discharged from a gun.

TG: Do you want to explain that?

SCHRADER: Well, I'd been waiting a long time to get out of there and I came out with a *bang*. I took off and didn't look back.

September 8, 1988

Another of my interviews with Paul Schrader was in 2002, following the release of Auto Focus, *his film based on the life of Bob Crane, the sexually obsessed star of the TV series* Hogan's Heroes, *who was murdered in an Arizona hotel room in 1978. As you'll read, there were still things I wanted to know about his early life. And I still wasn't finished asking about* Taxi Driver.

TG: How do you see the character of Bob Crane connecting with other characters you've made movies about, like Travis in *Taxi Driver,* or the character in *American Gigolo,* or the father in *Hardcore*?

SCHRADER: I think that beginning with Travis, the first script I wrote, or in *Affliction,* a more recent movie, you have a person who is acting at cross-purposes. Bob Crane is saying, "I'm a one-woman man, I'm a family man," and all the while this tail is growing out of his backside.

Usually when I make this kind of character, at some point, at the end, they have a brief moment where they "get it," because essentially they're clueless and they're out of sync. And all of a sudden they "get it" for a moment. Wade Whitehouse in *Affliction* gets the fact that he has to kill his father. But Bob Crane never gets it. He's as clueless on the day he dies as he was on the day we meet him.

TG: **Yes, the Bob Crane character in your movie is delusional, he's clueless, he thinks he's happily indulging in sex, not realizing the depth that he's sinking to, but he also narrates the movie. What are the tricky issues you have to deal with when the main character is narrating his or her own story but is clueless about what's really happening to their life?**

SCHRADER: You've just touched on something that I really love doing, which is the unreliable narrator, because narration works sort of like intravenous feeding. You're getting nourishment but you don't taste it, so it seeps into your consciousness and therefore you assume that your narrator is reliable. When he's unreliable, it creates a nice little frisson between what you're seeing and what you're hearing. It goes back to *Taxi Driver*, my first script, where you have an unreliable narrator who's telling you how the world works and you are seeing that world and it isn't working the way he was telling you it worked. Again, it's the same with Mr. Crane. The narration does a number of things. It helps you expositionally because you're covering fifteen years, and it allows you to hear how this man thinks, but it also creates an odd dislocation between what you're hearing and what you're seeing.

TG: **Have you thought a lot about how a sexual drive can get so out of control?**

SCHRADER: Well, I don't know whether it's sex, per se, or it's just addictive behavior. Part of his sexual addiction was a kind of cataloging. When he was a family man with young children, he used to catalog all the games they played. When he became the home-porn freak, he cataloged all the women. There was something going on there that was beyond simple, sexual release. It was an obsessive-compulsive addictive force that was blotting out or replacing some other insecurity. Sex becomes problematic when it becomes counterproductive to your life.

TG: There's a scene early on in the movie where Bob Crane meets with a priest. He's still holding on to the fiction of his life, and the priest says, "It's not easy to resist temptation. You must remove yourself from the occasion of sin." Those lines made me think of your film *The Last Temptation of Christ*, of course. But I also thought about *your* life. In your family even dancing and going to the movies was forbidden. When you broke away from that life, where so much that we would consider ordinary and commonplace was forbidden, was it easy to swing to the opposite extreme and overindulge in all those things that had been forbidden?

SCHRADER: No, I don't think so. I had a Calvinist background and that ethic is hard to escape—this sense that you are put on this earth for a reason. There is moral certainty—at the end of your life you will be called to account. Even when you leave that world, those elements still stay with you. So even though I became so-called liberated and lived in Los Angeles, my primary drive was the work and to do things that I felt would be worthy of my talents.

TG: In the book *Schrader on Schrader,* in which you are interviewed and some of your early work is reprinted, you say that when you were writing *Taxi Driver,* you were enamored of guns, you were suicidal, you were drinking heavily, and you were obsessed with pornography. Would you talk about that obsession with pornography and how, if at all, it figures into the new movie, *Auto Focus*?

SCHRADER: Well, I was wandering. In Los Angeles, where I was living, the pussycat theaters were open all night long. It was kind of a loner's paradise. And it is such a strong visual world that it is like a narcotic. It blurs and blasts all the other pain out of your life. That was the function for me, more than any overheated prurience.

TG: You said that you didn't go to extremes after leaving the Calvinist religion, but you must have felt like you were doing something very taboo when you were going to strip clubs.

SCHRADER: Well, I don't think anything's taboo.

TG: No, but you came up in a world where that was taboo.

SCHRADER: Once you leave a closed community, like Grand Rapids, Michigan, was at that time, you fall off the edge of the table. When you return home, they don't ask you where you've been and, in my case, they don't pay attention to your career. It's almost like you've walked through a doorway into another world. You're still bringing your old world with you, but then a lot of the reference points are simply gone.

TG: I want to just get back to that quote in which you said that when you were writing *Taxi Driver*, you were very enamored of guns and you were suicidal. You owned a gun then. Was the gun for possible suicide or for self-protection?

SCHRADER: Again, you're talking about blotting out a certain level of emotional pain and just the fantasy that you can end your life is a palliative and an anesthetic. So that drifted around in the back of my consciousness for a number of years, in greater and lesser degrees. Then I got married and had a daughter. Shortly after she was born I was lying in bed and I realized all the suicidal fantasies were gone. They were just gone, and I had suddenly been jolted into a reality where I realized how selfish and silly all these fantasies were and that I could proceed now without them. Although when I told this story to a friend he said, "Don't worry. They come back."

TG: Wasn't that reassuring. But I imagine you've used some of those old fantasies for your characters.

SCHRADER: The secret of the creative life is how to feel at ease with your own embarrassment. We're all in the dirty-laundry business and we're being paid to take risks and look silly. Race car drivers get paid to risk their lives in a more concrete way; we get paid to risk our lives in an emotional way.

TG: Since writing and directing a film is such risky business, do you have to banish the film critic in you when you're working on a movie so that the critical part of your mind doesn't paralyze the creative process?

SCHRADER: Yeah, absolutely. The analogy I like to draw is that the film critic is like a medical examiner. He gets the cadaver on a table, he opens it up and tries to figure out how it lived or why it died. The filmmaker is like a pregnant mother who is just simply trying to nourish this thing, and trying to make sure that it is not stillborn. You have to keep the medical examiner out of the delivery room, because he will get in there and he will kill that baby.

October 14, 2002

A DIFFICULT PLACE
TO GROW UP

Jodie Foster

*No one can accuse Jodie Foster of going for the flashy
glamour-girl roles. . . . She is a beautiful woman, but there
has been little pretty about her work. Not since she was twelve
and tugged at Robert De Niro's fly, saying "So how you wanna
make it?"*

Gerri Hirshey, *Rolling Stone,* March 21, 1991

As promised, here's another interview that gave me a chance to ask
about *Taxi Driver.* My friend Carrie Rickey, a film critic for *The
Philadelphia Inquirer,* recently pointed out to me that Jodie Foster
has been one of the very few child movie actresses to go on to a successful screen career as an adult. While making the transition, Foster
somehow also found time to graduate from Yale. She's won two Os-
cars, for her performances in *The Accused* (1988) and *The Silence of
the Lambs* (1991), and directed *Little Man Tate* (1991) and *Home for
the Holidays* (1995). I interviewed her in 2002, following the release
of *The Dangerous Lives of Altar Boys,* which she produced. We talked
about her performance as a very strict nun in that movie, of course,
but I could hardly wait to ask her what it was like playing an underage
prostitute in *Taxi Driver* when she was just a kid herself.

TERRY GROSS: You play a nun in *The Dangerous Lives of Altar Boys*. Were you around nuns in church or in school when you were growing up? I'm not even sure you went to school.

JODIE FOSTER: Oh, I went to school all right.

TG: Did you? I thought you might have had private tutors.

FOSTER: No, I went to a very strict French school. Everything was in French. It was not a Catholic school. I've been exposed to no religion whatsoever. I'm probably one of the few people that was raised as a true atheist, which, of course, makes me terribly interested in everything religious.

TG: Your mother was an atheist?

FOSTER: No, my mom was an ex-Catholic. She had gone to high school in a convent and came from a Catholic family. I suppose that sparked some interest with me.

TG: In *The Dangerous Lives of Altar Boys,* you play a nun who thinks that the violent comic books that her students are reading and writing are very damaging. She means well, but she cuts off an important part of their fantasy lives because she really doesn't understand it. Now, here you are playing a nun who finds comic books disturbing, but at the age of twelve and a half you were starring in *Taxi Driver.*

FOSTER: Yes, I was a child actor.

TG: You were immersed in the type of fiction that some people would say poses a danger to young people who are exposed to it.

FOSTER: Right, that's true. I suppose some people would say that, and maybe to some young people it is. I've always felt that more information is better, as long as children know how to handle it emotionally.

TG: When you got the part in *Taxi Driver,* was your mother afraid of what you'd be exposed to, playing a child prostitute?

FOSTER: First of all, I had been an actress since I was three years old, so I had a long body of experience. And my mom took me to all sorts of movies, including R-rated movies. I grew up in Hollywood, so I was exposed to it all over the place. I knew the work of Martin Scorsese and knew what an artist he was and had seen *Mean Streets* and had done *Alice Doesn't Live Here Anymore* with him. I don't think it was that big a consideration. It was a consideration for the board of education, and at that time they really wanted to know that I would not be emotionally damaged by playing this part. My lawyers brought in a psychologist to decide, I suppose, decipher—after an hour of meeting me—whether I would be entirely damaged by the atmosphere.

TG: Well, how the heck did they figure that out? What do they do to test your psychological health?

FOSTER: I don't know. They asked me a lot of questions like "Do you like Chinese food?" Things like that. I have a very fond memory of my therapy session at twelve, and it really was pretty boring.

TG: In *Taxi Driver*, Travis Bickle, played by Robert De Niro, wants to rescue you from a life of prostitution. He's taken you on as a cause. You're a thirteen-year-old kid who's being sold by a pimp played by Harvey Keitel. De Niro goes to Keitel and buys some time with you, not to have sex, but to convince you to let him rescue you from this life. Then you are in a room with De Niro for the first time. He wants to get you out of prostitution. You want to give him his money's worth, because he just bought some time with you. At the end of this scene, you're unzipping De Niro's fly. Were you old enough to understand what this was about?

FOSTER: Yes. Twelve-year-olds are able to understand what's going on. We're all very blind to think that they don't. The way I approached my character was this: She was a runaway and was taking a lot of drugs and had really been under the influence of an older man. She'd probably run away from an oppressive family structure. Boy, I understood all that. I went to a private school where I wore a little gray skirt and I got straight A's and spoke foreign languages. I mean, I don't think I'm scarred.

TG: **I was going to ask you if you felt you walked away with any scars. Guess not.**

FOSTER: Well, no. In fact, I think in some ways it's good, if you know your child is ready, to show them the adult world when they're still open to having conversations about meaningful paths and what makes an unmeaningful life. If it's slightly younger than adolescence it's almost better.

TG: *Taxi Driver* **is such an extraordinary movie. I mean, it's near the top of so many people's lists, and so many of us have seen it over and over again. I'm thinking, though, at the age of twelve, to work with Scorsese and De Niro and Keitel, gee—**

FOSTER: It really changed my life. At that time I had made many more movies than either one of them had.

TG: **That's amazing.**

FOSTER: Yeah. But it never occurred to me that being an actor was ever going to be a satisfying career. It seemed dumb to me because you read the lines someone else wrote, and there was no building of the character. It wasn't until I met Robert De Niro and he took me under his wing, and sat down with me for hours at a time, that I understood that there was more to acting than just being a puppet.

TG: **I'd love to hear some of things he told you in those talks about acting.**

FOSTER: Mostly he would take me to these divey coffee shops, sometimes in Spanish Harlem and different parts of town he found. He didn't talk to me much; he just let me sit there. I realized that this was his way of teaching me, so I'd look around and I'd talk to people, and I'd go on my merry way. I'd read the newspaper occasionally. After a while he might bring in the script and we'd do the lines over and over and over again. Having been a child actor, of course, I knew my lines, so now I was really bored, because I'd have to do these lines over and over again with this adult.

By the end of our meetings, he would throw improvisation in, and that was a really good lesson. Suddenly I learned that improvisation was about knowing the text so well that you could deviate from it in a meaningful way, as if you had been living this conversation, and always find your way back to the text. That's a lesson that most young actors don't really get.

TG: **Do you think that he took you to those divey coffee shops so you'd see characters like the character you were playing?**

FOSTER: I think it was his way of getting me to feel comfortable with him. I don't think he really knew what he had in mind. You know, Robert De Niro then and Robert De Niro now are two very different guys. Then he was a guy who made one film every two years or three years; he immersed himself in the character. He barely ever slept when he was doing *Taxi Driver*. He was a mess. He was living the character of Travis Bickle, and so his method, in some ways, was just to live in that place and to try and drag me into it. You know, I'd made a lot of movies. I'd done a lot of TV shows. I did a lot of rolling of my eyes and thinking, "Well, this is a big waste of time." But by the end of it, I realized how important it was and how it had changed my characterization.

TG: **Did Martin Scorsese give you advice about your character or about working with the actors in the film?**

FOSTER: Well, he brought in a girl he had met who had had similar circumstances as the character; she was a very thin, very young girl who had some of the mannerisms that he wanted me to copy, and he pointed them out to me. That's pretty much all he did. Then he shot a lot of film and did a lot of takes. The one thing that I remember about him that I think is the most inspiring to me as a director is that he used to sit behind the camera—of course, back then there were no video monitors that directors could hide behind—and sometimes we'd do thirty takes, forty takes. Every take he would laugh, he would giggle and have to hold his mouth shut so that he wouldn't make noise. Not just the first or the second take, but every take. He enjoyed the performances so much that it was almost as if he was inside the actors' faces.

TG: I was surprised that Disney Studio cast you in *Freaky Friday*. After *Taxi Driver*, I can't believe that they wanted you in a Disney film, because—

FOSTER: I'm so happy that they did.

TG: Why do you say that?

FOSTER: It tells you how loyal Disney was. I had made many movies for Disney and it was a conscious choice by my mom. When she was ferreting out which film I would do next, she wanted to make sure that I would do different kinds of movies so that people wouldn't pigeonhole me as one type of character. She felt it was very important for me to do a teen film or a Disney film. And *Freaky Friday* was probably the first feminist movie out there for youngsters.

TG: In *Freaky Friday* you're quite the tomboy. You play hockey. You wear braces. Could you relate to this character? It was a movie about a suburban tomboy schoolgirl, and about as far away from the life of Iris in *Taxi Driver* as possible.

FOSTER: I don't think it was as big a stretch as you might think. I went to school, I didn't wear braces, but I certainly played a lot of sports and I was kind of a tomboy. My mom went out of her way to make sure that I could lead as normal a life as possible. You have to remember that I had been in the business since I was three years old, so normalcy, feeling like I fit in, was something I really had to fight for.

TG: You got your first break into the business when you were three. You were the Coppertone kid on TV commercials. Am I right about that?

FOSTER: That's right. The still photographs came out in the fifties, but I was in the first TV commercial that they did with a Coppertone girl in the sixties.

TG: Was your behind showing on the commercials like in the still photographs?

FOSTER: You know, they tried to get that dog to pull down my pants, but he just wouldn't do it. So instead, I stand in front of the billboard of the Coppertone girl, and the dog just keeps barking and barking at my pants, but he can't quite make it to my underwear.

TG: How did you get cast?

FOSTER: My brother was an actor, and he went in to do an interview, and my mom didn't want to leave me in the car because it was a bad neighborhood. Of course, in those days you did leave your children in the car quite a bit. I love my brother and followed him around and when people asked him questions, I volunteered my name and started flexing my muscles and running around. They changed the campaign and decided not to hire a little boy to be in the Coppertone commercial. They said, "Well, let's go find a little Coppertone girl and this girl will be it."

TG: Did you always want to act?

FOSTER: I don't ever remember wanting to be an actor, but then I don't remember a lot at three years old. But then I don't ever remember not being an actor. It's just something I've always done. There have been times in my life where I've questioned it, because I don't have that personality. You know, they're the kind of people that like to jump on the table and put a lamp shade on their head and do impressions and dance for Grandma. I have never been like that. In some ways, it has colored my performances. I have a strange style as an actor that's not quite as external, that's a little more internal than most actors you'll meet.

TG: Many kids who were child actors were damaged emotionally by their early acting experiences and feel like they've been cheated out of an essential part of their lives, or even that they were literally cheated financially by their own family, who squandered the money they made. You seem to have survived intact and with a great career in adulthood, as well. Why do you think you were able to avoid that damage?

FOSTER: Well, it is a difficult place to grow up in. There are responsibilities and stresses put upon you that are really meant for adults, and yet you have to figure out how to live them in a child's body, or in an adolescent's body. There are dynamics that are unnatural. I don't think that it is natural for a parent to have a place in a child's career. It's important for a kid who's becoming passionate about something as an artist to do it on their own and to rebel against their parents and not have their parents' approval be of day-to-day significance. And, financially, the melding of your parents' assets and your assets can be very damaging to young people.

But I have to say I got through it. It just depends on your personality. Some people can handle it, and some people can't. I feel enriched by the experience of having been able to travel and learn different languages and talk to adults on an equal basis at a young age, and having adult responsibilities and living up to them. I'm pleased that this is how I grew up.

TG: When you went to Yale, I remember it really made news. Everybody was wondering, "What's it going to be like for this young movie star to be a student at a university?" In retrospect, was it possible for you to be just a student?

FOSTER: It was a wonderful moment in my life. I'm so glad that I did that, and it was a big step. At that time no other young actors had done that—left their careers and said, "I'm going to get an education." But that had always been phenomenally important to me, and I never knew I would be an actor when I grew up. It was the farthest thing from my mind. I thought, "Oh, well, you know, I'll act for a few years until I'm sixteen or seventeen, and then that'll be it. No one will want me anymore," which is what everybody had told me would happen.

Going to Yale, I did think that I would have this anonymity. For the first time in my life, I actually felt that. I felt like I was living without any kind of scrutiny, without the eyes of everybody on me. Unfortunately, my freshman year, as you know, the assassination attempt on Ronald Reagan shattered that. Very quickly, I realized that people had been watching me all along. It became a mad media circus, and my life in college changed from then on. But then I moved off campus and had a new life in college, and things did die down somewhat. It truly was the best time in my life.

TG: Did you study acting when you were at Yale?

FOSTER: I studied no acting when I was at Yale. Not that I could have, because liberal arts education, in their minds, is not trade school. I didn't study any theater at all, though that was certainly available to me. I wanted to learn about literature. That was my passion. I had always loved reading, and I wanted to stay as far away from acting as I could, and even as far away from the real world as I could. I'd been paying taxes since I was three years old, and I just wanted to be in an ivory tower for once.

TG: Do you think studying literature has helped you in reading screenplays and evaluating them?

FOSTER: Oh, absolutely. Everything that you do as an actor is about reading. Everything you do as a director is about reading. It's about reading deeper, and reading between the lines, and perceiving more than just what's on the surface. The study of literature is just about looking deeper.

TG: As you mentioned, John Hinckley shot President Reagan during your freshman year at Yale. May I ask you a couple of questions about that or would you rather not go there?

FOSTER: Well, I'd rather not. You can ask them, but I'll just say, "Gosh, I don't really talk about that."

TG: People said Hinckley was probably inspired by *Taxi Driver*; therefore, *Taxi Driver* must be a bad movie, and we can't allow movies like that to be made again because they inspire killings. Did it ever test your faith in films, or in a certain type of violent film that you think is a good film even though there's violence in it?

FOSTER: Well, I love dramas, and I believe in dramas. Dramas are provocative and evocative, and they are the stuff that makes you think harder and deeper about who you are and about your role sociopolitically. I don't believe in censoring art. Movies that attack issues like violence and attack them dramatically are important to have out there. As I like to say, You can take a two-by-four and do one of two things. You can build a building or you can hit somebody over the head with it. It's up to the person to make a decision about what they're going to do.

I try and hope and believe that it's my responsibility as an artist to make movies that help make people better and not worse. I try my hardest—as mistargeted as it may sometimes be—to make sure that my films reflect that hope in me. Hopefully, it will inspire people to be better and not worse. But you just don't know what other people will do with that information.

June 17, 2002

I Never Told Jokes

Albert Brooks

It's not like he's using humor as a cushion to make life more palatable. He's using comedy to get further inside the pain.

James L. Brooks, director of *Broadcast News* and executive producer of *The Simpsons,* to Bill Zehme and Bonnie Schiffman, *Rolling Stone,* April 18, 1991

In the 1970s, while establishing himself as a stand-up comic, Albert Brooks also directed short films for *Saturday Night Live,* played a presidential campaign worker in *Taxi Driver,* and directed, starred in, and cowrote the film *Real Life.* Since then, he has directed and starred in *Modern Romance, Lost in America, Defending Your Life, Mother,* and *The Muse,* and also starred in *Broadcast News, My First Mister,* and *The In-Laws.* I spoke with him in 1997, just before the release of *Mother,* in which he plays a neurotic middle-aged man in the early stages of a divorce who blames all of his insecurities on his mother (played by Debbie Reynolds) and makes the big mistake of moving back in with her.

TERRY GROSS: **The classic Jewish mother in a lot of American fiction and movies is the critical, domineering, overprotective** mother. The mother in your movie *Mother* is critical, but she doesn't care quite enough about the son to be domineering and overprotective.

ALBERT BROOKS: Right. I think that there are two kinds of mothers on the planet, no matter what religion—they can be Catholics, Protestants, Jews, or atheists. Some think that everything their children do is perfect. The other kind of mothers—and this is about the other kind—are critical.

TG: Was your mother critical?

BROOKS: Well, I wouldn't call it critical. My mother has always been puzzled by why I am who I am. If there was one thing we didn't share, it was probably that she didn't get my sense of humor. Sense of humor is a very personal thing. You can love a child and still have no idea why other people are laughing at him. I must have done fifty *Tonight Shows* when Carson was hosting and the audience would laugh their heads off. My mother and I would always have the same conversation after every show. I would say, "Did you see it?" And she would say, "Oh, honey, it was wonderful. What did Johnny think?" And I would say, "Well, he liked it. But did you like it?" "No, of course, honey. But Johnny liked it?" So that was going to be the title of my autobiography, "What Did Johnny Think?"

TG: There are some very funny things about food in the new movie. Your character comes back to his mother's house and she saves a lot of food in the freezer, where it's guaranteed to taste really bad after a while. And she buys all those horrible store brands. In the movie, it's "Sweet Tooth Sherbet."

BROOKS: Yes, I made that up.

TG: Was this a problem at your home, too? That your mother would buy all the cheap brands?

BROOKS: We could afford anything, but she just didn't believe that there was any difference. Like Debbie says in the movie, "Honey, there's no difference. The man in the store told me it's just the label."

My mother probably has said that to me. Somewhere in the back of her mind, she felt that all food came from the same vat in Chicago and they just put on a different label. We had brands of food that looked like the real thing. Like the cookies—they were black with white in the middle, but the brand was "Soreos." It was one letter off.

There's a bit that I love in this movie. There's this sherbet that's been in the freezer for about sixteen years. You can't even see what it is anymore. In the movie, I say to my mother, "Look at this crap that sits on the top." And she's named this stuff. She says, "Oh no, honey. You have to look under the protective ice."

TG: Yeah, I love the "protective ice."

BROOKS: To this day, my mother has this Neapolitan ice cream. There aren't three colors anymore. It's blended into one color. The chocolate and vanilla and strawberry have long ago stopped being divided. They are all a light yellow.

TG: In your early work as a comic and in some of your early movie work, you made fun of a certain showbiz kind of comedy. Your father was a comic. You must have grown up with that kind of comedy.

BROOKS: Yeah. Well, my father died when I was eleven, but I still remember that it was okay to be funny. I watched somebody do it for a living. He was a radio comedian. He went under the name of "Parkyakarkus." He was a Greek dialect comedian, and that's the character he played. Even though he was off the air when I was born, we used to have those big sixteen-inch records of all the radio shows, and I would listen to them.

TG: How did your father, who I assume was Jewish—his name was Einstein—get to play a Greek dialect comic?

BROOKS: Well, during the forties when he was on the air, I think being an immigrant was a very popular thing. He was born in Boston and he worked in the advertising business. And he just did this character for fun. Then Eddie Cantor heard him once at a dinner and actually thought he was really Greek. Cantor talked to him slowly, like my father wouldn't understand him, "Would-you-like-to-come-to-New-York-and-be-on-my-show?" And my father said, "You can talk faster. I'm born in America."

TG: When you started doing comedy, your monologues were pretty autobiographical; they seemed to come out of who you were as a real person.

BROOKS: Right. I never told jokes. I don't think I've ever told a joke in my life.

TG: So this autobiographical approach was very different from what your father was doing. He didn't even play his own ethnic group, let alone talk about his life.

BROOKS: Absolutely. That's exactly right.

TG: Did you have any models for what you wanted to do—a more autobiographical approach?

BROOKS: When I was very young, I remember watching Jack Benny and thinking that this man had figured it all out. Jack Benny never told jokes. I mean, he would stare and people would laugh. His persona was so clear. The audience understood it so well. He was the world's great minimalist comedian.

TG: Is that what you were trying for? To do very little and have it be very effective?

BROOKS: Those old guys used to play themselves. This is not a new thing. George Burns and Jack Benny and Fred Allen—it was their lives we were laughing at. They didn't stand up there and say, "My wife is fat." There were other things to do.

But actually, the kind of stand-up comedy I did—I really hadn't seen before. I didn't have a role model. I was making fun of the institutions that were still going on. When I first started, I tried out everything I ever did on national television. There weren't any clubs to go to even if I wanted to. It was interesting because I would think up things in my house and drive down to NBC and do them on *The Dean Martin Show*.

At that point, if you were funny, the only thing people would ask you was "When are you going to Vegas?" That's all they associated with comedy. I tried to change that. I was trying to give dignity to the idea of doing stand-up because it had none. Everyone thought comedy was just sitting there with a big cigar and opening for Frank Sinatra.

TG: Early in your career, when you did stand-up on TV variety shows like *Dean Martin* and *Merv Griffin,* your contemporaries thought you were funny. But on the variety shows, you played to a predominantly older audience that often didn't know what to make of you. Give us an example of one of your early routines.

BROOKS: Well, the first thing I ever did was a ventriloquist act called "Danny and Dave," which was basically the world's worst ventriloquist. He was introduced as a real ventriloquist and his mouth moved more than the dummy. The dummy used to drink water while he would sing. I would do all of those ventriloquist tricks where I would try to smoke a cigarette. And I just threw the dummy on the floor to get him out of my hands so I could smoke. A lot of people got it and laughed, but a couple of people in the very beginning said, "That's the worst ventriloquist I've ever seen."

So when I did *Real Life,* I played a character called Albert Brooks, who was filming a family and trying to make it a sociological experiment. Half the reviews I got in America treated it as a real documentary. One critic said, "Why in God's name would a studio give this man money to do such an important experiment?"

I was stunned. I always thought everybody would figure it out. But they didn't. It took years to make a few people realize that this was thought out and that it wasn't just a bad act.

TG: It was like the whole world was on your mother's wavelength and not quite getting the jokes.

BROOKS: Yes—not the whole world, but a lot of people.

TG: You went from doing comedy on TV variety shows with an older audience to opening for rock acts like Neil Diamond and Richie Havens. It was one extreme to another.

BROOKS: Exactly. Everybody else does clubs and then gets on television. I did about five years of television before I ever performed in front of a live concert audience. The first time I ever performed live was in Mississippi with Neil Diamond. The previous year I had done fifteen shows on CBS with Merv Griffin.

Sometimes the live shows were fun, but opening for rock acts in the early seventies, I wouldn't wish that on anybody.

TG: **Why not?**

BROOKS: Well, it was way before comedy was in or even popular. Let's face it, these people took a lot of drugs and they wanted to hear the loudest music they could. I think there's an old Chinese adage that says, "Sixteen sleeping pills does not make for a good comedy audience." They took a lot of these downers and would sit there waiting for Sly and the Family Stone, and the disc jockey had to come out and tell them *I* was there.

TG: **Right, and you were going to come on and talk about things that made you neurotic and insecure—**

BROOKS: Stop right there. It doesn't matter. It's not the human voice they were waiting to hear. They wanted to hear these amplifiers turned up to a billion decibels. They wanted to be hurt, you know. I had some very rough experiences trying to get people to listen.

I remember once I did open for Sly and it was in Tacoma, Washington. The show was at eight o'clock and my phone rang at seven thirty in the motel, and it was his manager. At that time, it wasn't a secret, Sly was experimenting with Colombia's most famous product, and I don't mean the studio.

So the guy said to me, "Let me ask you something, Albert, how long do you do?" I said, "Well, you know, normally a half hour, but I'm a little worried about this audience—maybe twenty minutes." Now, we're in Tacoma, and he says, "What's the longest you can do?" I said: "Well, I don't know. Why?" He answered, "Well, Sly called and he's in Cincinnati."

He had missed the plane. I said, "What are you talking about? I gotta do three and a half hours? Look, you got the wrong guy here. I don't know if I should even go on." Actually I did go on, and I remember somebody threw a beer can and cut my leg.

TG: **Oh, geez.**

BROOKS: I got angry at the audience. I started to yell at them and say, "He's not even here, and I'm gonna go on Johnny Carson and tell them that you're horrible!" As if they would all stop and go "ooooh." Anyway, I just got out of town quickly. I ran off the stage. It was not fun.

TG: **See, you could have said you had two hours left and then taken questions from the audience for the next two hours.**

BROOKS: Oh, yeah, questions like, "How do you want to be killed? Fire or knife?" That would have been the question. No, it was bad. I'll tell you what I did do. I went to the back of the stage because all their equipment was there. And I started to play a bass note like the beginning of a Supremes song—*bom bom bom, bom-bom, ba-bom*. And they all quieted down. I tried to say very patiently, "He's not even here." But you know, they didn't care. They weren't in the mood to be polite and, as I say, I think drugs and comedy don't go well.

TG: **Well, how did you decide to go from comedy to movies?**

BROOKS: Really all I ever wanted to be was an actor. I never wanted to do comedy. I went to Carnegie-Mellon and I studied acting and at nineteen years old, I came back to Los Angeles and saw that I couldn't get any acting roles to save my life. Some people convinced me that if I did stand-up, I could get all the work in the world and that would get me into acting. It really didn't work that way. It just got me more stand-up.

TG: **Well, you did get a big break when NBC started *Saturday Night Live* and offered you a chance to create a series of shorts for the show. That led to your first acting job in *Taxi Driver*. What a great film to get started in. Did you realize how lucky you were when you got that role?**

BROOKS: Well, not until the president was shot. No. Then I thought, "Oh my God, this is historic." But who would ever know that that would turn out to be such a legendary movie?

TG: Well, in *Taxi Driver* you play a political campaigner working for a presidential candidate. You work in an office with Cybill Shepherd—

BROOKS: Yes, and there's a funny story with that.

TG: Oh, tell it.

BROOKS: Well, the part of the campaign worker wasn't written, so Marty Scorsese hired me and said, "You know, maybe you could figure out that part and work out the lines and everything." So we worked on it, and what you see in the movie was developed in a hotel room. I worked on lines and moves. He would tape it. And that's what would appear in the script.

When it was all over, Paul Schrader, the writer, said, "I want to thank you. That was the only character I really didn't know." And I said, "Really? You knew Travis Bickle and Harvey Keitel and all of the pimps and hookers, but a simple guy who works in an office, you couldn't figure out, huh?" So it was really a great experience.

TG: There's a scene where Robert De Niro as Travis Bickle, the taxi driver, is hanging around the campaign headquarters, just eyeing Cybill Shepherd, who he really wants to pick up. He comes in and tries to talk with her. And your character chases him out. Did you come up with the way to do that? And the lines to use?

BROOKS: Well, De Niro did something interesting, because in those days he was very "Method"—way before the restaurants. He wouldn't ever even talk to me. So that moment of uncomfortableness on-screen was extra-real. Of course, I thought it was just about Method acting. Then at the cast party, he wouldn't talk to me either. So, you know—he probably just didn't want to talk to me. But seriously, he wouldn't let me know him. I was trying to make conversation and say, "So, you having fun doing this?" And he would just walk away. At that moment in the movie where I had to figure out how to throw him out, it was extra-tense because I didn't know who the hell I was dealing with.

TG: **Tell us how your character, this very middle-class campaign worker who isn't a very physical person, deals with De Niro's character, Travis, who's a threatening, shadowy guy.**

BROOKS: Well, my character uses the police. He keeps saying, "There's police across the street. I'm gonna call the police." This guy I played is not going to get in a fistfight with the guy that Robert De Niro played. Immediately, De Niro goes into this karate position—and he's playing the world's most frightening man anyway. All my guy does is say, "There's police across the street. I'm calling the police. I'm calling the police." You know, getting police in there a lot.

TG: **Now, after your role in *Taxi Driver*, which direction did you want to head in—being an actor in other people's movies, playing characters who weren't necessarily like you at all, or directing your own movies and writing characters that were very close to your personality?**

BROOKS: If offers had started to come in, six a week, I probably would have just pursued acting only. I love to do that. But they didn't. It forced me into writing, and once you're going to write, then you have to do the whole deal, because writing is the blueprint. If I thought there was a director I could hand my stuff to and go home and go to sleep, I would, you know? Part of me is a lazy guy, but I think that if you don't do it yourself, especially in comedy, you'll never get it right. The nuances will be wrong. The casting will be bad. So, once I decided that I could sit down and write these movie scripts, the rest was just something that I had to do.

TG: **There's a line from *Broadcast News* that you're quite famous for. Your character says, "Wouldn't this be a wonderful world if insecurity and desperation made us more attractive?" Did you write that line?**

BROOKS: No, Jim Brooks wrote that line.

TG: It seems like you should have written it.

BROOKS: I'm not taking credit for it—because he might be listening.

TG: Right. Did that ring true to you?

BROOKS: You know, not really. I mean, I understand what you're saying, but I don't know. I don't feel that that's necessarily me.

TG: Mm-hmm. There must be a reason, though, why you gravitate toward playing or writing characters who are somehow motivated by their neuroses.

BROOKS: Well, because, you know, I never believed John Wayne. Movies are so fake. Listen, if an alien landed on Earth and went to our cinema, boy, wouldn't they be confused? They would think we're all police.

TG: One last question. Has your mother seen your new movie, *Mother*? Did she get the jokes?

BROOKS: Yes, she's seen it a few times now. The first thing she said was "You know, honey, I think one or two things are about us." I said, "One or two things? It's an hour and forty minutes." She said she liked this one the best. She praises me by using my other movies. She said, "I think this is going to be your most popular movie yet. In this one you don't have to die or drop out or—" I said, "I know. I get it. I understand what you're saying."

But you know something? She really did like this one. I can tell. I know my mother, and I think that she loved it.

December 19, 1996

BEAUTY GONE BERSERK

Divine

Deep down, he knew he was the most beautiful woman in the world, but how could he convince the rest of the blind fools on this earth?

John Waters, *Shock Value*

Divine was usually identified in the press as a 300-pound transvestite, but as you'll soon read, this wasn't how he saw himself. Divine was the actor most prominently featured in John Waters's early movies, and together they set new lows in bad taste. Divine first gained attention in Waters's cult classic *Pink Flamingos*, playing a woman who retains her title as "The Filthiest Person Alive" by eating a fresh dog turd. But in his subsequent movies for Waters, Divine showed that he was capable of doing more than grossing us out. Dressed in a skintight gown, he was a grotesque parody of glamour. But he played sympathetic female characters in *Polyester* and *Hairspray*, his last two films for Waters. In *Hairspray*, he played both the chubby heroine's beleaguered mother and (in one of his few roles as a man) the bigoted owner of a Baltimore television station. (Harvey Fierstein subsequently played the former of these roles on Broadway.)

I interviewed Divine in 1988, just before *Hairspray* opened in theaters. He died two weeks later, at the age of forty-two, after suffering a heart attack.

TERRY GROSS: **Over the years, you've played so many female roles, do you think it's given audiences and directors the wrong idea of who you are?**

DIVINE: Oh, definitely. It's the cliché Hollywood story of being typecast. I'm definitely, definitely a victim of that. I'm very lucky that I'm starting to come out of it. It's taken twenty years. I was screaming at people, "I'm not a transvestite. I'm not a drag queen. I'm a character actor." I never set out to play female roles. Fortunately, or unfortunately, they were the only things that were offered to me. These were lead roles—and they were written for me. It's just unbelievable to have that done. If you're a young actor, you don't go around turning down lead parts written specifically for you. I had no idea these roles were such strong characters that people would think female parts were all I could do.

TG: *Hairspray* **pays tribute to those great teased bouffant hairdos of the early sixties. I know John Waters really loves those old hairdos. You used to be a hairdresser, didn't you?**

DIVINE: Well, for a very short time. I'm glad I had that experience. It's come in very helpful now because when I'm on the road doing my club act, there aren't always hairdressers available. I end up having to do it myself, and I'm glad I know how to tease hair, because that's definitely the look they want. I told John that he doesn't have to go far from his front door to still see women that look just like that. When I was doing the film, it was very funny because the first day on the set, I walked down the street; no one looked at me twice. I walked right through the camera crew and past John and kept going. None of them looked at me. I came back and stood right in front of John. He did a double take. It was very funny. He said, "I can't believe it. That's perfect." I looked just like one of the girls on the street.

TG: **How did that make you feel?**

DIVINE: Oh, good. That was the best compliment. I mean, I did fit right in. And I looked exactly the way I was supposed to. With my size I'm so self-conscious about sticking out too much and being the largest person on the set. Except in a way that's the best thing, too. You're noticed more.

TG: Let's talk about the male character you played in *Hairspray*. He's the head of the TV studio and opposes the integration of the teen dance show. He's a villain. John Waters told me you got fitted for new teeth for this role.

DIVINE: Yeah, they wanted me to look completely different. The great part of being a character actor is to look like the character, and not yourself. That's why I never cared about looking glamorous as a woman. I always thought that set me apart from being a drag queen, because I certainly looked anything but glamorous as Edna Turnblad in *Hairspray,* with long, stringy hair. In the same way, they fitted me for big buckteeth that had decay on them. I have blue eyes, so they poked me in the eye every morning about fifteen times trying to get these brown contacts in. I wore a toupee with the kind of hairstyle that men who are balding wear—where they sweep it up from the bottom and over the top. It really doesn't cover anything up, but they think it does. You can see the skin in between the hair, and it's a real dark brown because they usually dye their hair. It was quite, quite hideous. With a little blue cord suit and suspenders.

TG: It's great. You had to put on as much makeup to do this male part as you did to do the female part.

DIVINE: Oh, it was more. It took much longer. I used to pray to be Edna again. And there were a couple of days when I had to be both. I was running around with Edna's wig on, and I've got great big teeth sticking out of my mouth. They'd say, "Wait a minute. Give us those teeth." After a while, you'd jump out of one to the other so fast you'd forget to take half the costume off.

TG: Did you love movies when you were growing up? What were some of your favorite films?

DIVINE: I've always had very macho taste in movies. My favorites when I was a kid were Knights of the Round Table movies and war movies. I still like a good war movie. I mean, like *Platoon*. And I like the *Rambo* movies and Sylvester Stallone. Charles Bronson is probably my favorite.

TG: **Did you also like glamour movies when you were growing up?**

DIVINE: Well, I liked anything with Elizabeth Taylor.

TG: **Did you like her better when she was thin or heavy?**

DIVINE: It didn't matter to me. Didn't matter. It was just more of her to look at when she got heavy. But she was still very beautiful. I finally met her one day, and I couldn't speak at all. After years of planning what I was going to say to her, I was, "Ah-ba-ah-ba-ah-ba." I don't drink, but I went and had a double scotch and came back and had a little conversation with her.

TG: **Did she know you?**

DIVINE: She knew of me. It was a party for her daughter Maria. And her hairdresser and makeup man were people that I'd used. They had told her all about me. So she wanted me at the party.

TG: **That's great that you used the same makeup man.**

DIVINE: Yeah. We look a lot alike.

TG: **John Waters has said that he always appreciates it when people who don't fit mainstream good looks take what they have and turn it into style, turn it into an advantage. Was that what you did when you were growing up? I think that you were always pretty heavy.**

DIVINE: Well, no, actually not. I was very much an introvert. I never really went out of the house until I was sixteen years old. I was very uptight about my weight and the way I looked, and always wanted to look like everyone else. Finally, my junior year, when I started hanging out with John, I got the confidence to go out. I always had a raincoat on. People probably thought I was a flasher, but I was just uptight about how fat I was. At the same time, I couldn't, or wouldn't, do anything about it. Finally, I went on a diet. My junior year I lost 80 pounds and went down to 140 my senior year. I was able to get dates and go to the prom and everything. It was strange. All of a sudden, people talked to me that wouldn't talk to me when I was fat. I thought, "Well, what's this all about?" It was a rude awakening, at a very young age.

TG: Was it liberating when you started playing these extravagant roles where your weight was an important part of the character? You were very theatrical about your size and the way you dressed.

DIVINE: Oh, yeah. Well, John did help me gain self-confidence. Working with him helped me give up trying to fit the mold that I think they put you in, especially here in America—that you've got to be thin; you've got to be under two hundred pounds.

TG: You and Waters had a lot of adventures together in the movies you made, in the parties you gave, and even shoplifting. But it seems to me, you were into a theatrical kind of juvenile delinquency as opposed to being real hoods. Is that right?

DIVINE: Oh, yeah. We weren't really bad. We were just bored, young teenagers from upper-middle-class families with nothing to do. The movies grew out of that situation, too. When we were making movies, we were locking each other in the trunks of our convertible cars and letting our friends out at the drive-in movies. We were drinking beer every now and then, which, I guess, could be one of the worst things we ever did. We were never into the heavy drug scenes or anything so bad that we would have to go to jail, except for the few bits of shoplifting. All the kids did it. There was a bit of peer pressure about it. But it wasn't an everyday occurrence. Basically we were good kids.

TG: How did the tough guys in the school treat you, the people who really were the hoods?

DIVINE: Oh. Well, they used to wait for me every day to beat me up after school to the point where I was quite black-and-blue and afraid to say anything because they had threatened my life. It was very bad. Finally, one day I had to go for a physical to the doctor. When I disrobed, it was quite obvious that something terrible was happening to me. I broke down after a lot of questioning and told him what the problem was. They called my parents, and when they saw what I looked like, they were quite hysterical. We had the police at the school, and the kids were expelled. It was quite an ugly situation, which made me even more unpopular with their friends. I had to go through the next two years of school with that stigma attached to me. But then, in my senior year, it was more or less all right. Up until then, it was quite hideous. I really hated school. I hated the whole situation.

TG: **Since you've become a famous actor, have you had a chance to see the guys who beat you up?**

DIVINE: I have. I've seen them in theaters that I've played.

TG: **Have you really?**

DIVINE: Yeah, and in different situations. I don't think they actually knew who I was. In a way, I had the last laugh. It didn't make me feel good, because I'm never the type of person to seek revenge.

TG: **You said that it was John Waters who helped give you your image. How did you decide on what your image would be?**

DIVINE: Well, at the time, Andy Warhol and others were making cult movies. They called them "underground films" then. They were just the equivalent of your independently made movies today—low budget. One name, "Viva," was very popular, so John decided to give me the name Divine. He said he thought I just was. We had a very heavy Catholic upbringing, so we went for sort of religious names. He wanted a 300-pound beauty as opposed to a 110-pound beauty. He wanted, as I've been called, an inflated Jayne Mansfield. So that's what he got. And also, I rather think he would say that the most beautiful woman in the world turns out to be a man. Everything is backwards. Divine is really a John Waters character. But then, Van Smith, a very good friend of ours who does all the makeup and costuming for John's movies, helped create the look for the character. He's the one who said, "Go in the bathroom, shave your head halfway back, and pluck all your eyebrows out." You've really got to trust people. I went in the bathroom and did this and came out and thought, "What have I done now?" Then he did my face in what he called "a beauty gone berserk." It was similar to Kabuki-type makeup.

TG: Oh, that's true isn't it?

DIVINE: Yeah. The work that he does is quite beautiful. Also we didn't want me to look like a normal everyday woman because I'm not a woman. We wanted a cartoon character of a woman.

TG: Had you dressed in drag before doing it for movies?

DIVINE: No, only a couple of times on Halloween. I was Martha Washington once.

TG: I want to ask you a question about the famous scene in *Pink Flamingos*. To prove how tasteless you are, you had to eat a fresh dog turd. You and John Waters both said that you did it to get attention, and the film really did get attention.

DIVINE: John came to me and said, "Well, would you do this?" And I said, "Oh. Sure." I thought he was kidding. A year later he said, "Okay. Now, tomorrow, you do the dog turd." Oh. Ho. This is great. He wasn't kidding. I mean, he said, "Well, listen, do you want to be famous? Or do you want to be completely forgotten about? It's going to do either one or the other for you. It's going to make you, or forget you. But your name will go down in movie history forever." I thought, "Well, what do I care?" you know. I was very young. I didn't really think about it until I had to follow that dog around for three hours. And finally, finally, it went. It was quite a hideous experience actually.

TG: Well, here's my question. Did you rush off to an emergency room afterwards?

DIVINE: Well, no. I went home.

TG: That's a silly question, but I'd be wondering about germs.

DIVINE: Well, I know. I had mouthwash and things like that. I brushed my teeth and gargled. Anyway, I went home. And I was sitting there. And the more I thought about it, the more I started to worry. I called the hospital. I'll never forget this. I didn't know what to tell them, because I was a bit old to run around eating dog feces. So I called and said, "Oh, hello. This is Mrs. Johnson. My son just ate dog doo-doo. What should I do?" And she said, "Well, how old is your son?" And I said, "Oh. He's twenty-four years old." Well, then the nurse said, "Some maniac's on the phone here. Her son's twenty-four and he's eating dog shit." She got back on the phone and said, "Well, why?" I had to tell her. I said that he was retarded and that we had a dog and he was in the backyard playing with the dog. The dog had gone to the bathroom and he had eaten the dog mess. She said, "Well, you just have to wash his mouth out, and feel his stomach every day because he could get a white worm." Every day I was feeling my stomach to see. Finally, one day it got hard, and I thought, "Oh my God. I've got it." But I had hysterical white worms. I didn't have anything. I was very lucky. But she suggested that I get rid of the dog.

TG: **Well, I know John Waters wants to do a sequel. You wouldn't go through that again for a sequel, would you?**

DIVINE: No. I said, "You want me to stand on an elephant the next time? Forget it." I decided to draw the line somewhere. So I said that was my last experience with animals, please.

February 23, 1988

POSTSCRIPT: Thirteen years after Divine's death, his mother, Frances Milstead, published the memoir *My Son Divine*.

KISSING AND
LICKING BOOTS

Mary Woronov

The cruelest of the Chelsea Girls—at least on film—was
Mary Woronov.
Wayne Koestenbaum, *Andy Warhol*

Like all of Andy Warhol's 1960s "superstars," Mary Woronov reinvented herself on joining his factory after dropping out of Cornell in 1964. Woronov was a butch temptress in *The Chelsea Girls* and other Warhol films. She toured with the Velvet Underground as part of Warhol's Exploding Plastic Inevitable, doing a quasi–S&M dance with the poet Gerard Malanga and a whip. I'm glad I didn't interview her back then, because being in Warhol's orbit meant staying in character offscreen as well as on. But she had long since dropped the pose by 1995, when she published *Swimming Underground: My Years in the Warhol Factory,* a memoir in which she looked back on her days as a member of the in crowd through the eyes of someone who was even then probably something of an outsider. Woronov is different from most of Warhol's scene makers in having had a postfactory career, appearing in such films as *Death Race 2000, Rock 'n' Roll High School,*

Eating Raoul, and *Scenes from the Class Struggle in Beverly Hills*. I talked with her shortly after the publication of her memoir.

TERRY GROSS: **What was your life like before you became part of the Warhol crowd?**

MARY WORONOV: It was a very fifties home life. I went to a private girls' school, my mother was a housewife, my father was a doctor, and everything was very Ozzie and Harriet. You know, very happy, but not very happy. When I got to Cornell my life changed radically. Suddenly, well, sex was around and there were people that took drugs. Shortly I met Gerard Malanga and went into the Andy Warhol factory.

TG: **Malanga was the one who introduced you to Warhol? How did you meet Malanga?**

WORONOV: Well, at Cornell I hung out with a very druggie crowd. They liked rock 'n' roll and they liked drugs. They considered themselves the inheritors of the Beat Generation. Gerard was a poet. He was a very well-connected person and I met him through a friend at Cornell. When I first saw him, he was totally dressed in black leather. He was carrying a whip. He had this gorgeous blond hair and necklaces. He was very unlike what I was accustomed to—you know, the regular Levi denim boy, sort of slouched with a lot of pimples.

TG: **Then you ran into Malanga again at the Warhol studio in New York. You were on a class trip from Cornell visiting artists' studios. What happened?**

WORONOV: We went to Warhol's studio, and Warhol's studio was totally unlike anyone else's studio. The other studios were white boxes with lots of light and paintings on the walls. At Warhol's there were no paintings on the walls. The walls were covered with tinfoil and it was dark, and it was weird. There was stuff all over the place. It was messy. It was very evil-looking and chaotic. There were always people hanging around. Obviously, people who weren't artists. They had nothing to do with art. They were just good-looking and very moody. I don't know, I was attracted.

TG: You became a dancer with the Warhol show, the Exploding Plastic Inevitable. You and Gerard Malanga used to dance as the Velvet Undergound performed?

WORONOV: Yes. Well, the first thing that I did with Warhol was a movie. I thought, "This is fine, I have a job. I'm going to do these movies for Warhol for which I'm not paid. What a great job." I was very naïve.

Barbara Rubin brought the Velvets in, and they would play. Gerard would get up onstage and start dancing. I was with him, so I would get up on the stage and start dancing, too. It evolved into this show. They put up a movie in back of the Velvets, and we danced in front. Then Andy started promoting it as the Exploding Plastic Inevitable.

TG: Would you describe the dances you and Malanga did to the Velvet Underground?

WORONOV: It's going to sound very strange. Both of us dressed in black leather, and both of us had whips. It was definitely rock 'n' roll dancing. It wasn't Martha Graham–ish at all. We would have black lights and those flickering strobe lights and crosses. Everybody there was very accustomed to "happenings," as they were called then. Gerard and I were very good together—we were very instinctive. We'd do all of these pretend S&M things while we were dancing.

TG: Like what?

WORONOV: Oh, he spent a lot of time on his knees, and he kissed the whip because one of the songs says to. It was very sexy.

TG: The song ["Venus in Furs"] also has a fetishistic line about leather boots. Did he lick your boots, too?

WORONOV: Yeah, a lot of kissing and licking of boots. As a matter of fact, he made a whole movie of it. I didn't get to talk in that movie, obviously. We were very young and just did things, and nobody said no.

TG: The Warhol road show of the Exploding Plastic Inevitable went to California, and it was a disaster. What happened, nobody came?

WORONOV: One night several people like Cher came. They all thumbed their noses at us, and then nobody came. Then they shut down the club, which was called the Trip. There was tremendous antagonism between the New York and L.A. scene.

L.A. was full of colorful, acid-full hippies—and we weren't like that. We dressed in black and white. We did not like free love. We liked S&M—perversion, too. We took amphetamines. They took LSD. They were loving and happy. We were intellectual, more about art.

TG: **Most of the people in the Warhol crowd had a persona, a pose of some sort. Did you have one?**

WORONOV: My pose at the time was unsexual. Gender-shifting into male. Very powerful, very threatening.

TG: **You describe your persona as asexual, yet the whip dance was very much a sexual turn-on. Make those two add up for me.**

WORONOV: Doing Warhol, one of the sexiest things was gender slipping. I think it's very sexy. In the beginning, the entire basis of Warhol's movies was the drag queens. They certainly represented gender slippage, and they were certainly very, very sexy. A lot of art is about gender slippage. That's what makes it interesting and attractive.

TG: **But you describe yourself as having an asexual pose. How is that sexy?**

WORONOV: I did not come on flirty. I would act tough and very masculine. To see such a pretty girl act masculine was a turn-on.

TG: **And you're about six feet tall, so you were imposing.**

WORONOV: Yes. Everybody posed. If you didn't pose, nobody saw you. It was a fight to get the biggest pose on. I mean, you can't be around all of those queens and not think about posing every minute of the day. It was a language.

TG: **Was it tiring after a while to live in a pose?**

WORONOV: No. Nothing was tiring. We were all on amphetamines.

TG: Was it mentally exhausting to have to stay in a pose all the time, or did you become the person?

WORONOV: No, you never became the person. Our poses were completely ridiculous. Half of those guys, when they got dressed up as girls, didn't do it like guys do it now. It was totally dumb. They'd have runs in their stockings and runs in their hair. It was about doing something that was obviously not working, but pretending it was working to such an extent that everybody buys it. It was fun.

TG: In your memoir, there is a very alarming scene describing a party you went to with other people from the Warhol crowd. One of the women there OD'd, someone stretched her out on the table, and the party continued. She was the centerpiece at the table.

WORONOV: Yes. We were so far gone that death didn't really enter into it. We weren't even thinking of her as a person.

TG: But she actually lived? She hadn't really died?

WORONOV: No, she hadn't. I didn't have that much experience with heroin. Apparently, you can look like you've gone under, and then you come back. I didn't even know she was shot with heroin. We all thought she was dead.

TG: At what point did you say to yourself, "It is not human to behave this way"?

WORONOV: When I stopped taking drugs.

TG: Were you shocked when you looked back on that?

WORONOV: No, because I can remember that I felt it was fine. I didn't really get in trouble. A lot of people got in trouble with drugs. They saw people get shot in the head and killed. I was really very protected.

TG: In the biography of Andy Warhol, Victor Bockris quoted this passage from Gerard Malanga's diary: "Mary was someone I invented, put a whip in her hand and spread her name around and made her a star, but she did not really show any interest and because of her passiveness allowed herself to be eclipsed by Ingrid Superstar. . . ." What do you make of that?

WORONOV: Gerard is right. He definitely invented me. He found me at Cornell, and when he brought me to New York, I was definitely someone different. But I wanted that invention. I really loved that whole scene. I wasn't interested in becoming a superstar. I was not interested in fighting for Edie Sedgwick's place. Fine, I would do a movie, but I was not interested in becoming a star. They loved girls to fight and to try and be stars. If Ingrid wanted to pretend she was a star, fine, go let her. I refused to go into that game, and Gerard was furious with me. I was the most talented, I was the one who understood what was happening. Even Andy said this to me. But I just didn't feel like fighting. I liked the queens. I liked the whole drug scene. I just wanted to do what I wanted to do. You know, if Andy sat down and four girls tried to sit next to him, I'd walk the other way.

TG: You write in your book that this was a period when you didn't like sex.

WORONOV: No, I hated it.

TG: I'm trying to figure out if I can ask you to explain why, on the radio. What do you think?

WORONOV: For one thing, my parents didn't get along the way I thought couples should get along, so I definitely was against marriage. I was very young, and I was furious at the thought that I should be happy just being a wife with a man. That really infuriated me. I had floating rage about that one. The other thing is that when I went to Cornell, I had been a virgin for a long time. Then I did not have a great experience. This apparently nice kid tried to go with me. I was just so mad and so angry that it didn't work out. Instead of being upset, I said, "Okay, we're just gonna make rules, and one of the rules is sex isn't in the game for me. I just don't want it. These other girls can go make fools of themselves, but for me it's out."

TG: It's interesting that during this period when you were very defiant about not having sex, you were doing this very provocative whip dance, turning yourself on and everybody else.

WORONOV: No, I think it was very normal, because you can't shut someone down when they're starting to peak with their hormones. I mean, I had to do something.

TG: So it all came out in the dance?

WORONOV: Yes, it came out in everything I did. Everything I touched. I was a walking joke. I was a fool, a young fool.

TG: During this whole period when you were part of the Warhol crowd and you were performing with the Velvet Underground, you were still living with your parents. So you'd go from this incredibly "out there" scene back to your parents' middle-class, nice home.

WORONOV: Yes, and lucky for me I did. Otherwise I'd be dead. In other words, when you get high, you have to come down. When you go out, you have to go home. I had no money. I had to stay there.

TG: Is this part of the reason why you survived, when so many of the Warhol people were casualties?

WORONOV: Absolutely.

TG: Do you have your parents to thank?

WORONOV: Oh, of course. My parents were great to me.

TG: Do you now think that your mother did the right thing in not objecting to your behavior?

WORONOV: Absolutely. Everybody has to go through a journey, so that you become someone else, so you can get your third eye, or whatever. That's the American way. And any kid knows that they have to prove themselves. Kids used to want to go to war. Well, this was my war. I met up with a stone wall because I went in with the wrong idea. But I had to go through it. If she had stopped me, I would have gone harder, much harder. I would have left home, and that wouldn't have been good.

TG: **What did you do with your life after leaving Warhol?**

WORONOV: For about half a year I just sat down and recovered. I had a tremendous addiction to get rid of.

TG: **And you got rid of it that quickly?**

WORONOV: Oh yeah, my family is really strange, you don't say anything. The first thing I did was get very fat. I just sat in my bedroom until that went away. That took a couple of months. Then, slowly but surely, I started being the "next person," and went on a date. My parents are the fifties. They never mentioned that I'd done something wrong. When I came back, and sat in my bedroom for about two months, they treated it as if everything was fine. Thank God, because I couldn't explain what was going on. All I knew was I needed to rest.

TG: **Do you know who you are now, and are you comfortable with that person?**

WORONOV: I am more comfortable with myself. I have gone through a lot of things, and once you go through these things, you know life isn't that bad. I still ask people what they think of me, or who I am to them, so I don't know everything, no. I do finally feel, because of this book, that I'm a good writer. I'm really proud of myself for the first time.

December 7, 1995

TO IRON A SHIRT

Joyce Johnson

Naturally we fell in love with men who were rebels. We fell very quickly, believing they would take us along on their journeys and adventures. We did not expect to be rebels all by ourselves . . .

Joyce Johnson, *Minor Characters*

Where do bookstores keep Joyce Johnson's *Minor Characters*? Beat Literature? I doubt very many of them keep it in Feminist Literature, even though I think that's where it belongs, because it has so much to say about gender expectations. *Minor Characters,* which won a National Book Critics Circle Award, details two years in Johnson's life when she was Jack Kerouac's lover. She and Kerouac met in 1957, on a blind date arranged by their mutual friend Allen Ginsberg. Johnson was twenty-one and working at a Manhattan literary agency; Kerouac was fourteen years older and not yet famous. But before the year was out, the publication of *On the Road* had transformed Kerouac into an unwilling symbol of the Beat Generation. For much of the time that Johnson and Kerouac were "together," they were geographically apart; she stayed behind while he traveled to San Francisco, Mexico City, Paris, and Tangier. Years later, looking back on herself as an impressionable young woman, she realized that she had become part of a rebel subculture that in one way was no different from the mainstream—men were heroes in their own adventure, and women were just minor characters.

Johnson has published several novels and worked for many years as a book editor. Her correspondence with Kerouac is collected in her *Door Wide Open: A Beat Love Affair in Letters, 1957–1958*. This interview is from 2000, when that book was published.

TERRY GROSS: **When you first met Jack Kerouac, you weren't attracted by his celebrity because he wasn't famous yet. What did you find attractive about him?**

JOYCE JOHNSON: He was the most unusual person I'd ever met. He had an incredible memory, he told great stories. He'd had amazing adventures. And he had a kind of sweetness and melancholy about him that was also very appealing. He had an ability to take pleasure in small things. You know, if I made him a bowl of Lipton's pea soup, I was a great cook. He totally charmed me when I met him.

TG: **You met Kerouac through Allen Ginsberg, and shortly after you met, he was off on his travels again. While he was having this big adventure traveling around the world, you were living in New York. Your adventure was having a relationship with him.**

JOHNSON: Absolutely. That was a big adventure for me. But also my adventure was being in New York and discovering all these very gifted people converging on downtown Manhattan: painters, poets, photographers, actors. It was a very, very good time to be in New York.

TG: **Although Kerouac sounds excited and invigorated in the first letter he sends you, soon after his letters start to sound more depressed. Let me ask you to read an excerpt of this March 1957 letter Kerouac wrote to you from Tangier.**

JOHNSON:

> *. . . not too interested in this oldworld scene, as tho I'd seen it before plenty . . . anyway in early April I'm off by myself to Paris, the others can join me later, to get cheap garret . . . then London, Dublin, Brittany . . . then I try to get job on freighter, work my way*

back this summer . . . I just dont seem interested, got too much to do in America, shouldna come at all of course . . . so I'll likely be seeing you in NY in July maybe . . . look forward to seeing you, lonely here, dont like whores anyway and no girls speak English . . .

TG: How did it make you feel to have him complaining about the whores?

JOHNSON: Well, it certainly made me feel weird. It was as though he had forgotten that I was his girlfriend; he sounded as though he was writing to one of his buddies. I didn't know what to make of it.

TG: You were always having to change your plans for him. For instance, he'd invite you to come and be with him in San Francisco and then he'd write and tell you he was leaving for Mexico. How did that affect you?

JOHNSON: It complicated my life immensely, and it was very disappointing because I wanted so much to travel myself. And I had to take steps in order to prepare myself to travel, such as giving up my job, or saving money, or giving up my apartment. I had a rather complicated summer of 1957, when I was thinking, first, that I would join Jack in San Francisco, and then later in Mexico City. I was particularly disappointed about not going to Mexico City. I began to realize that this was Jack, this was the way he was. It was almost impossible for him to make a plan and stick to it.

TG: You never met up with him in San Francisco or Mexico, but in the spring of '57, he did come and stay with you in New York for a few days. Would you read the letter you wrote to him a couple of months later? This is July of 1957.

JOHNSON: This letter was written to Jack after he had left San Francisco, gone to Orlando, Florida, with his mother, and then was preparing to go to Mexico City.

I remember walking with you at night through the Brooklyn docks and seeing the white steam rising from the ships against the black sky and how beautiful it was and I'd never seen it before—

imagine!—but if I'd walked through it with anyone else, I wouldn't have seen it either, because I wouldn't have felt safe in what my mother would categorically call "a bad neighborhood," I would have been thinking "Where's the subway?" and missed everything. But with you—I felt as though nothing could touch me, and if anything happened, the Hell with it. You don't know what narrow lives girls have, how few real adventures there are for them; misadventures, yes, like abortions and little men following them in subways, but seldom anything like seeing ships at night. So that's why we've all taken off like this, and that's also part of why I love you. Take care.

TG: Did Jack Kerouac understand your thoughts about how few adventures young women could have at the time? Did he comprehend the difference in gender?

JOHNSON: He did. One thing that was very important to me about our relationship was that he was very encouraging to me about my writing. He often told me that in order to be an important writer, I would have to expand my experience. He would counsel me to give up my job and take to the road like he did, which, of course, was impossible for me to do. The idea that I was going to go to Mexico City to meet him, for example, was to be a kind of educational experience for me. That's how he referred to it. He did have some notion of it, but I think he also didn't understand that a young girl like me couldn't just take to the road by herself. That sort of eluded him.

TG: While he was in Mexico in the summer of 1957, he wrote to you asking you to come visit him. You must have been happy to get that letter.

JOHNSON: Oh, I was thrilled to get that letter. I immediately gave up my job and bought a ticket on TWA, which I never used.

TG: Why?

JOHNSON: Why? Because the next I heard from Jack, he had gotten the Asiatic flu in Mexico City and was going back to Orlando, Florida. From there, he planned to come to New York in time for the publication of *On the Road*. He thought it might be interesting to be around for it. He had absolutely no notion of what awaited him.

TG: In fact, he was staying with you at your apartment the day that famous review by Gilbert Millstein came out in *The New York Times*. Would you describe what it was like to go with him to the newsstand at midnight and pick up this review that made him a star overnight?

JOHNSON: Well, it was nothing that Jack was prepared for. He could barely take it in. Millstein made him the spokesman for a whole generation and said that what F. Scott Fitzgerald had been to the Lost Generation, Kerouac would be to the Beat Generation. Jack kept reading it and shaking his head, saying, "Well, I think it's pretty good. What do you think?" I'd say, "Yeah, it's really good." Then the next day, the phone started ringing and never stopped.

TG: Not all the reviews were positive. The one Truman Capote wrote was pretty scathing.

JOHNSON: By and large, the reviews were hostile and humiliating; very insulting things were said about *On the Road*. Truman Capote said, "This isn't writing, this is typing." I can't think of any American writer other than Jack who endured such consistent abuse from critics and reviewers all through his career. It was very, very devastating for him.

TG: How did he take the bad reviews?

JOHNSON: They made him depressed. Of course, he had a tendency to be depressed. And the only way he seemed to be able to get himself through this period was to step up his drinking, which was already pretty heavy.

TG: Soon after that review in *The New York Times*, Jack left New York and you wrote a letter to your friend Elise. Would you read an excerpt from that letter?

JOHNSON:

> *I dig ironing his shirts, cooking for him, etc. It's funny—it's not at all romantic anymore, but it doesn't matter—I love him,*

don't mind playing Mama, since that's what he seems to want me to be. I may go down to see him in Orlando—I've gotten kind of a left-handed backwards invitation (his mother seems to want me to come?). There's no doubt in my mind anymore that Mama is the villain in the true classic Freudian sense.

TG: When you wrote "it's not that romantic anymore," what did you mean?

JOHNSON: I found myself in the position of almost having to take care of Jack, to get him through this whole experience that he was coping with so badly. It was an unfamiliar role for me. I was only twenty-one. I thought he would come out of it, but that's not what happened.

TG: You were in this unconventional relationship with Jack Kerouac, yet were expected to do very conventional things for him like cook and iron and take him home when he got too drunk. How did that make you feel?

JOHNSON: Well, you know, everything seemed so crazy. We were living such a strange life that it was almost a relief to iron a shirt. Everything that was quiet and familiar and homelike seemed exotic to me because the life we were living was so strange. It was a very anxious business, getting Kerouac home, up four flights of stairs. I was living in a brownstone at the time, on the fourth floor. That was anxious. So was fending off various admirers, especially other women.

TG: In one of your letters you wrote that there's no doubt that his mother is "the villain in the true classic Freudian sense." What did you mean by that?

JOHNSON: It became apparent to me that Jack had not separated from his mother. He was overly attached to her. You know, he planned to settle down and live with her, which was very hard for me to understand.

TG: Was it her trying to keep a hold on him, or was it him wanting to be with her?

JOHNSON: Well, it worked both ways. She wanted to keep him with her, so that any young woman who came into his life was considered the enemy, someone who had to be fended off or driven off. At the same time, she had always been a refuge for him during those years when he was broke and obscure, wandering around the United States virtually homeless. She provided a base for him, a place where he could come and crash, write another book, and keep his manuscripts and his letters. Without Jack's mother, we might have had fewer Kerouac novels. She was important to him in a good way, but her emotional hold on him was very crippling for Jack.

TG: Was Kerouac's personality any different when he was in his mother's presence?

JOHNSON: I only saw him in her presence once. This was in the summer of 1958, after Jack had bought her a house in Long Island and moved into it with her. He really seemed cowed by her. You know, she ruled the house. He was like a child in that house, who wasn't allowed to do this and wasn't allowed to do that. He retreated from the whole situation by drinking a lot.

TG: How did fame agree with him?

JOHNSON: Not very well at all. Part of the problem was that he didn't become famous the way he wanted to become famous. What he really dreamed of was having a real literary success that, for one thing, would have been much quieter. But instead, he found himself the spokesperson for the Beat Generation and this was not a role he felt at all comfortable with. It was something Allen Ginsberg could have played to the hilt. But Jack was not very good at facing the public. He was a shy, rather naïve guy. It was frightening for him, and it made him feel that he didn't know who he was anymore.

TG: You say that after he became famous there was a pack of predatory women that invaded your lives. What was it like watching all of these women flirting with Kerouac?

JOHNSON: Oh, of course I hated it. It made me furious. It was as though I didn't exist at all. Right in front of me, these women were throwing themselves at Jack. It was very unpleasant to watch.

TG: During this period, when he already had a drinking problem, everyone wanted to give him pills or buy him drinks. Did it get worse?

JOHNSON: It did. He felt he had to live up to an image that other people had of him. They didn't really expect to see someone like Jack Kerouac, who was a fairly quiet guy, kind of an observer. They expected to see someone very extroverted like the Dean Moriarty character in his novels. The only way he could approximate that character was to get very loaded.

TG: You grew up in a family where the only alcohol was Manischewitz Passover wine. Were there things you didn't understand about Jack's drinking?

JOHNSON: I couldn't understand his drinking at all. I thought that if Jack could just get through this period and settle down, and have a real home, he could straighten himself out. He kept wanting to stop drinking. He would make attempts, and we'd take the phone off the hook and stay shut up in the house for a week. He seemed a different person when he'd stop drinking for a while. Then his innate sweetness would come out.

TG: One time he came to New York to do a series of readings at the Village Vanguard. At the performance you saw he was very drunk. What happened?

JOHNSON: Well, this was one of his last performances after a week at the Vanguard. He came onstage with a bottle of Thunderbird in his hand and he turned his back on the audience and sort of bopped along with the musicians as though he'd forgotten where he was. Then when he read, his words were slurred. People in the audience got very restive. Some booed, some left. It was a humiliating performance.

TG: How did you and Kerouac break up?

JOHNSON: It was in October of 1958 and we went out to dinner with a bunch of artists we knew. Right before my eyes, Jack was flirting outrageously with a woman who I knew was very interested in him. I could see the handwriting on the wall. I'd seen this kind of thing one too many times. I couldn't stand it, so I asked Jack to come outside the restaurant with me. I told him that it was the end. I said to him, because it was the only thing I could think of, "You're nothing but a big bag of wind."

TG: What was his reaction when you told him you couldn't take it anymore?

JOHNSON: He said, "I told you. I don't like blondes. Unrequited love's a bore." We were shouting nonsense at each other, and then he stomped off into the restaurant and I went up the block, and that was it.

TG: So that was really it?

JOHNSON: That was it. It ended very abruptly.

TG: How did he describe you in *Desolation Angels*?

JOHNSON: As "middle class, sad, and looking for something."

TG: He also wrote, "perhaps the best love affair I ever had."

JOHNSON: Right. And he said, "I had me a companion there." That was important to Jack—the fact that we were both writers and we wrote to each other a lot about our writing. It was a novelty for him to have a woman in his life who was as interested in writing as he was.

TG: Kerouac's letters were published long after his death, and for the first time you were able to read what he wrote to his men friends about you. What surprised you about those letters?

JOHNSON: Oh, well, for example, he wrote to Neal Cassady, "I have a blond novelist following me from New York." I mean, I wasn't following him. He'd invited me. Then he said that there'd be orgies in San Francisco, which was a lot of nonsense.

TG: **Orgies with you?**

JOHNSON: Yeah. Yeah, you know, it was male boasting. He would write to his male friends that he'd just been in bed with three women. It was always three women. As I read the letters, I thought, "The same three women?" A lot of it was assuming a certain persona when he wrote to these guys. Most hurtful to me was a letter he wrote to Allen Ginsberg. This was around December 1957, and he had just been in contact with an old girlfriend of his and wanted to get back together with her. So he wrote to Allen that when Allen's friend Peter Orlovsky came back to New York, perhaps he could move in with me if he needed a place to stay, because Jack wanted to make it with this other woman. That was really ugly. Even though it was many, many years later, it still hurt when I read it.

TG: **It must have been strange to read these things years later.**

JOHNSON: Very strange. I mean, what an odd position to be in. One often doesn't know much about the people that one has loved.

TG: **You probably had to ask yourself: Which were the more honest letters, the ones he wrote to you? Or the ones he wrote to his men friends?**

JOHNSON: Exactly.

TG: **In your book *Door Wide Open*, you write that you've had to protect your memories from being swamped by Kerouac's legend. What parts of the legend don't fit with your memories?**

JOHNSON: The idea that Jack was such a free spirit, or that he was this great Buddhist. Although he did travel on the road, deep inside he wasn't free at all. He was knotted up and miserable, and so attached to his mother. Buddhism was something that was very important to Jack, and he looked to it to find solutions to what troubled him. But he really misused it, even though he had a profound intellectual understanding of it. He used Buddhism to rationalize all his problems.

He'd say, "What's the point of dealing with them, since we're all going to die anyway?"

TG: A few years ago there was a Gap campaign, "Kerouac wore khakis." What did you think of it?

JOHNSON: Well, one thing amused me very much. There was that picture of Jack wearing khakis in an old photo that had been taken for *Pageant Magazine*. A photographer had followed Jack and me around the Village for a night. I was airbrushed out of the photo, almost as though I had never existed.

TG: That's really funny. So you saw that photo—with your image erased—on the sides of buses and on billboards.

JOHNSON: That's right. I knew there was a ghost there.

TG: Oh, gosh. That's so perfect, because your first book was a memoir called *Minor Characters*. All about how women were relegated to the status of minor characters in the Beat story.

JOHNSON: Exactly.

July 19, 2000

So What?

Larry Rivers

*Rivers wedded representation with abstraction, parodied art
history, anticipated by a decade the concerns of both the Pop
and color-field painters and prophetically engaged in what
post-modernists might call appropriation and deconstruction.*
Carrie Rickey, *The New York Times*, August 12, 1990

*He helped change the course of American art in the '50s and
'60s, but his virtues as an artist always seemed inextricably
bound up with his vices, the combination producing work
that could be, by turns, exhilarating and appalling. . . . Mr.
Rivers had an omnivorous curiosity about life, sex, drugs,
politics, history and culture.*
Michael Kimmelman, *The New York Times*, August 16, 2002

The artist Larry Rivers died of liver cancer in 2002. I'd interviewed
him ten years earlier, following the publication of *What Did I Do?:
The Unauthorized Autobiography of Larry Rivers,* in which he revealed
at least as much about his sex life as he did about his art. Before the
interview, I told him the same thing I tell many of my guests: "If I ask
you anything too personal, just let me know, and I'll move on to something else." He assured me this wasn't very likely, before adding, "But
tell me this, should I use the word *penis* or *cock*?" I should have said,

"We'll both be better off if you use neither." Luckily, we managed to avoid that particular subject.

TERRY GROSS: **You wrote in your memoir that you don't have the faith in self that abstract painters need. What do you mean?**

LARRY RIVERS: I'm not the kind of painter who thinks, "Well, I did it, therefore it has to be good and has meaning." If I put down an orange and blue, and then a line through it, and a big square shape and things like that, I felt as if there was something necessary in carrying that off that I didn't have. I didn't believe in it. I didn't know what art was about, in a certain way. I still don't. I'm not trying to be cute. But I don't know exactly what it is about. I can only get at those things that interest me. I also have something in my nature that wants people, no matter who, to get something from the work—something.

TG: **Often when you paint a figure, there's a feature that's missing. For instance, you'll paint one eye, but the other eye is blank. It hasn't been painted at all. How did you start doing that?**

RIVERS: Well, there was a certain spontaneity in my work. In other words, no matter what I was doing, I wanted it to come off quickly, without too much trouble. Before that point, I had wanted things to look labored, as if hard work would be a reflection of good character.

You don't have to worry about where you place the first eye. You just put it down somewhere below a brow. But when you come to the second eye, you have to make calculations about how wide apart the eyes are. There's no way of putting in a second eye, making it realistic, without close judgment that slows you down, and makes your hand work from the knuckles instead of an arm movement.

I just left it out at first for those reasons. I didn't think it was necessary. There are other parts of the body missing, too, but people notice it in the face because the face is so clearly an image that we know all the parts of.

TG: **There's something else you've done throughout most of your career. You write on paintings. Sometimes the letters are** stenciled, sometimes handwritten. Sometimes parts of letters are missing or blurred. How did you start using words on paintings?

RIVERS: Don't forget, the cubists had the word *journal*—I mean, they would have a newspaper in their painting. In other words, I didn't do anything that new. But I was bolder about it and didn't hide it. In certain paintings, it's almost the point of the painting. I did these vocabulary lessons, which obviously are words and features, and I thought that there was something ironic in that. My hand is a very artistic one, in the sense that I make gestures with my paint that are loose and flowing, whereas a letter has sharp edges and it's much more definite than the painting. The combination of this very definite thing plus this loose, arty work with colors all over the place seemed to make me happy.

TG: You married quite young when your girlfriend got pregnant. She already had a son, but you didn't want a family. In fact, you wrote, "My life was not going to be about living. It was going to be about art." Did you feel trapped by having a family?

RIVERS: I guess so. Given my personality, I probably didn't even feel trapped. Nothing was going to stop me. I mean, I felt a little bit of something. Don't forget, I never gave my family up, and eventually, I really brought the children up myself. I brought up these boys and lived with my wife's mother. I just didn't live with the wife. So it's complicated. I was not going to be stopped from what I wanted to do, but at the same time, I wasn't going to abandon the boys, or their grandmother, and we lived together. And they were very helpful in many ways.

TG: Do you believe that it was necessary to be at least somewhat selfish in order to become an artist?

RIVERS: That's right. I modeled myself on my distorted notion of what Picasso was about. I thought that somewhere along the line I had heard that Picasso walked away from every relationship, and children. All that life was about was art. That model was of interest to me.

TG: Looking back, do you think that you behaved badly toward your family?

RIVERS: Some people might. I don't think I behaved badly. In one way, I was sort of selfish, but at the same time I provided for them. It's not very different from what most men are about. They go to offices eight, ten hours a day and they come home and say, "Don't bother me." They're looking at television or a newspaper, and they're drinking a beer, and the child walks in. They give them a two-minute kiss and maybe once a year they go somewhere for three weeks or something. I don't think life is that different for myself and other people.

TG: You lived with your mother-in-law for many years. You painted her naked a couple of times. She was an older woman, kind of heavy.

RIVERS: Yes. You mean the painting that's in the Whitney Museum. It's *Berdie Twice [Double Portrait of Berdie]*.

TG: Yes. Why did you want to paint your mother-in-law naked? It seems like a real taboo.

RIVERS: Well, she asked the same thing, "Why do you want to paint me?" She had the simple notion that an artist wants to paint beautiful things. She looked at herself, she didn't think she was beautiful. So I said, "Rembrandt painted older women." I thought that I had a very special opportunity. I was able to get someone that age, who was close to me, who I could really look at, and see what was going on.

I painted it to make a painting. But I couldn't help but be aware of what happens to the body. I was amazed that it looked that good. I'm talking about on a sexual level. She didn't really seem to me to be unattractive.

TG: When she was posing for you, were either of you uncomfortable?

RIVERS: I certainly wasn't uncomfortable. Maybe she was, the first few times. Then it was okay. It was her son-in-law, you know, and she thought, "Anything she could do to help." I told her, "Maybe we'll sell that painting." She thought she was posing for a good reason—a working-class woman who thought that we would make some money.

TG: **Did you?**

RIVERS: Did I? I think when I sold those paintings, they weren't very expensive. I made something, sure. But I wish I had a lot of them today. I would have made more.

TG: You also did a nude painting of your son Joe, when he was fourteen. In your book, he talks about what it was like to be painted by you. He wrote that he wanted to be immortalized in your painting, but he didn't want to hang around and pose nude for it.

RIVERS: Right.

TG: In the painting he's nude except for his socks. He says his pubic hair was just coming in.

RIVERS: Right.

TG: **The portrait was shown at the Southampton Gallery in Long Island, New York, and half of the high school from that area had "parental permission" to go to the gallery—**

RIVERS: In other words, in order to walk into that gallery, they had to have a note from their parents saying that they had permission to walk into that gallery. Go ahead.

TG: **Your son was very embarrassed. He was relieved when the police removed the painting. He says, to this day, he has a twinge of embarrassment when he sees it. Did you realize that at the age of fourteen it would be so embarrassing for him to have his nude portrait publicly displayed?**

RIVERS: No, no. It had all been very jolly, like in a lot of families that don't speak of the dark things. He may have felt that way, and maybe I even thought about it, but I didn't think it was too much to ask of a child, truthfully speaking. And, you know, he did it. He knew I was a painter, that's what I do, and that he would be useful. If he was embarrassed, I'm sorry. You know, so what?

TG: **How did you feel when the police removed the nude portrait of your son from the gallery?**

RIVERS: I wasn't surprised. I thought, "It's the United States of America and that's what they do." It followed a certain pattern. I actually got a hoot out of it. In other words, when do people get talked about? When they do something! No one heard of Mapplethorpe until everybody got into the act complaining that his work was horrible and pornographic. I was following a certain path of the avant-garde. You do a painting, there's a lot of clamor, it's taken down, and then it ends up in the history books. I must have thought all that.

TG: **You were very close with the poet Frank O'Hara. You were lovers for a while, even though you don't think of yourself as homosexual.**

RIVERS: That's right.

TG: **And you'd been married twice and—**

RIVERS: I was so straight, I could be homosexual.

TG: **You write that it was only when you started hanging out in homosexual circles that you began to think of yourself as sexually attractive. What was the connection?**

RIVERS: To feel sexually attractive is rather pleasant. I'm not saying that that's why I got interested in men, but there was that difference. Women didn't describe a guy as having a great ass or a great basket, like homosexual talk of the time. It brought me up to another sexual level. I, too, could be exciting to someone.

I really wanted it to be with women. They would go to bed with me, but I never got the feeling that they went to bed with me because I was sexually exciting. I don't know why. I mean, it's kind of silly. I feel like a baby now. I can't see how they could not have thought that I was attractive sexually. Why else would they go to bed with me? Probably they wanted to have sex with me. But I never interpreted it that way.

TG: **When you were younger, you were part of a circle of artists, musicians, and poets. There were artists' bars to hang out in. Is there anything like that in your life now?**

RIVERS: No. There's no place. You have personal friends. But I don't go to bars. It's embarrassing.

TG: **It's embarrassing because people know you?**

RIVERS: No, not because people know me. It's that I thought bars were a place to try to pick up someone, forgive me. It's the idea of sitting there with this notion in my mind, looking the way I do now and getting the "Mr. Rivers" treatment. I'm no longer a possibility for a liaison, but just some respected citizen. I think that it just doesn't work anymore. So I stay home and paint.

October 27, 1992

NOT TO THINK

Sonny Rollins

*Rollins's list of [early] associates . . . reads like a modern jazz
who's who: Charlie Parker, Thelonious Monk, Bud Powell,
Dizzy Gillespie, Miles Davis, Max Roach, Clifford Brown.
But simple cross-referencing of this sort fails to convey
Rollins's true significance. . . . When conjuring up an image
of the quintessential jazzman—heroic, inspired, mystical,
obsessed—as often as not, it is Rollins we picture, because no
other jazz instrumentalist better epitomizes the lonely
tightrope walk between spontaneity and organization implicit
in taking an improvised solo.*
Francis Davis, *In the Moment*

I share my husband's enthusiasm for Sonny Rollins—not just my favorite tenor saxophonist but one of my very favorite jazz musicians.
He has a reputation as someone who doesn't enjoy being interviewed,
yet he always seems to give a thoughtful answer to any reasonable
question that is put to him. He was certainly thoughtful with me
when I interviewed him in 1994. Maybe because he listens to the
show and we'd already talked casually after a few of his concerts, he
even spoke candidly about once having been addicted to heroin—a
subject he later told me he would have preferred not to discuss at all.

TERRY GROSS: You're a virtuoso performer, but you're known for practicing nearly every day.

SONNY ROLLINS: Monk said to me one time that if it wasn't for music, life wouldn't be worth living. You know, if I don't play my horn for a while, I actually begin to get sick. I wonder, "Well, gee. What's the matter with me?" Then I realize that I haven't played my horn for a few days.

TG: When you're improvising during a performance, are you thinking?

ROLLINS: No, no, I don't think. That's why I practice and I keep doing these exercises. When I'm on the stage and performing, the optimum condition is not to think. I just want the music to play itself. I don't want to have to think about it. If I have to think about what I'm doing, then the moment is already gone.

TG: Are you analyzing what you're playing, and thinking "Oh, this is good." Or, "Oh, I don't like this. I've got to find something that works better."

ROLLINS: When I'm playing at my best, I can hear what I'm doing, but [only] after it's done. I can't hear it while I'm doing it.

There are some occasions when I *can* stand back mentally and listen to myself play. The music plays itself. I'm just the person standing there, moving my fingers. Certain times it's an out-of-body experience, so to speak.

TG: What do you do when you practice now? You're a brilliant player. And you're a veteran player. Some people of your stature would just perform and not practice anymore.

ROLLINS: When you play a reed instrument you have to deal with your embouchure, which has to do with the position of your lips around your teeth and the mouthpiece of the instrument. This has to form sort of a cushion. If you don't play for a while, your lips will bleed when you play. Your lip might even split. It's happened to me when I've had to lay off for a period of time. So I like to play a certain amount every day.

TG: One of the things I love about your playing is the diversity of your repertoire. You play a lot of old pop songs that many people don't know or have forgotten, as well as old novelty songs like "Toot, Toot, Tootsie" and "I'm an Old Cowhand." Are these songs you grew up with?

ROLLINS: A lot of them are songs that I heard when I was a youngster. When I was growing up, the big thing to do every week was go to the movies on Saturday. We'd see Louis Armstrong and other musical personalities in pictures that I enjoyed a lot. Of course, I also heard music around the house. But those movies did provide much of the things I play today.

TG: Did you ever suggest playing something like "Toot, Toot, Tootsie" and have other musicians look at you like you were crazy?

ROLLINS: Well, they might have thought so. But they wouldn't dare to say it. It was my gig.

TG: Right. You grew up in Harlem. Your parents were from the Virgin Islands. What were their ambitions for you? Did they push you to excel when you were young?

ROLLINS: Yeah, well, I was the youngest child. I have an older brother who's a very fine classical violinist. He ended up being a physician. Then I had an older sister who sang a lot in church. I was supposed to follow in their footsteps. Of course, I didn't because I was somewhat of a black sheep. They were much more studious than I; I wanted to hang out and play ball. I was the guy that was out going to jazz clubs and all that. These things were frowned upon at that time.

TG: When you started to perform, for many musicians, heroin was part of the jazz life. You started using for a while when you were young. Do you think you would have tried heroin if it hadn't been such a big part of the jazz world in the fifties?

ROLLINS: I don't think I would have. There would have been no reason. I got involved with it because a lot of idols were doing it. So we thought that using drugs was the thing to do.

TG: **It must have been your parents' worst nightmare come true when you entered the jazz world and started using heroin.**

ROLLINS: Well, since I was a baby, my mother stuck by me regardless of what I did. She was really in my corner. But I had a lot of problems with the rest of my family. My father, my grandmother—they were pretty down on me. And my siblings didn't really understand where I was coming from, anyway. But I have to say that my mother believed in me all the way. I'm happy that I was able to get myself together before she left the scene. She saw me start to make records, so I made her feel that her trust wasn't exactly all in vain.

TG: **Were you ever arrested?**

ROLLINS: Oh, yeah, I was arrested. But I was lucky because I was always able to get involved with music programs in prison. In those days, there were other musicians there, too.

TG: **Did it scare you when you were in prison? Did you say to yourself, "What am I doing here?"**

ROLLINS: It scared me a lot. But again I was lucky because I could play an instrument. A lot of the other prisoners knew of me. So I immediately had respect from them. But being locked up is no joyride.

TG: **How did you straighten out?**

ROLLINS: It took a little while. I slid back a couple of times. Eventually I got down to the complete bottom. I couldn't have gotten any worse.

TG: **What was the bottom?**

ROLLINS: The bottom was sleeping in parked cars and garages. What we used to call in those days "carrying the stick." "Carrying the stick" meant that you were homeless. I did this mainly when I was in Chicago, where I was out there on my own. In New York, even though

I was persona non grata at home, I could always get by, or sneak in the house, or something. But when I was away from home, I had to pay a lot of dues, as we used to say.

TG: How would you protect your horn during the periods when you were homeless?

ROLLINS: Well, I didn't protect my horn. I didn't have a horn. I was borrowing other people's horns.

TG: What did you learn about yourself during that period?

ROLLINS: I learned that I had the strength to get over something really deep. But I had to struggle. One time, after I came away from the hospital and went back to the nightclub, it was the classic scene of the old drug pushers standing there saying, "Come on, man. Come on. This is good." I went through the classic scene of fighting myself, saying, "Well, gee, if I go with them it wouldn't be so bad. It's just one time. Maybe I should do it. Why not?" Then the other part of me was saying, "No. Don't do it." The real classic battle between good and evil, right and wrong. But I won out. That's one thing that I really feel good about. I went into the lion's den and came out alive. After that, it increasingly got easier and easier to say no to drugs, which are a terribly debilitating thing for people to do.

TG: Once you found that strength and knew you had it, how else were you able to use it in your life?

ROLLINS: I felt I could do anything. And I could get back to what I really wanted to do, which was my music.

TG: How do you use that strength in your music?

ROLLINS: I don't know. Actually, I think I always had strength in my music. Even when I was a kid, I used to practice for hours and hours and hours at a time. I always had something within myself that enabled me to be alone and play, and get into what I'm doing, and not think about anything else. So by getting rid of the negative elements, I was able to return to what I had in the beginning.

TG: Several times over the years, you've taken extended breaks from the music business and performing. During one now legendary hiatus, between the summer of '59 and the fall of '61, you used to practice on the Williamsburg Bridge in New York. Did you play on the bridge because you played too loud to practice in your apartment?

ROLLINS: Right.

TG: Why did you take these long breaks from performing in public?

ROLLINS: Well, there was a period when I ran into a lot of difficulty with the "powers that be" in the music business. I was looked upon as a person that was hard to get along with. Somehow I got that reputation. I guess because I tried to demand a certain amount of money, or I didn't want to be messed around with like some guys were—whatever. One way or another, I've dealt with that problem my whole career.

TG: When you took one of these long breaks, how would you know it was time to get back to performing?

ROLLINS: When I took my hiatus on the bridge, I was trying to accomplish something musically. I had gotten close enough to what I was doing that I felt that if I stayed there, it might turn into self-indulgence. That's not what it was about. At that point I realized, "Well, it's time to come back." I didn't accomplish everything that I wanted to. But I felt I had accomplished enough that I proved the point to myself.

TG: I'd love to know what it felt like to play your horn on the Williamsburg Bridge. You weren't making records or performing in clubs, but you were practicing a lot on the bridge. Was it in the middle of the night?

ROLLINS: We played in the night and the daytime, anytime. It was a beautiful place to play. You were on top of the subway; the trains that came across the bridge were underneath you.

TG: **You were on the pedestrian walk?**

ROLLINS: Yeah, the pedestrian walk. It's really a nice space up there. You're right in the middle of everything. You can see Manhattan, and on the other side, Brooklyn. The boats would be coming by at night. And you could blow as loud as you wanted. Nobody would even look at you. Every now and then, people would walk by. But nobody would even look—I mean, this was the sophistication of New Yorkers.

TG: **New Yorkers are immune to everything. Do you think your sound got bigger during that period?**

ROLLINS: Definitely. So, it did have certain good effects.

TG: **Do you feel now that you've designed the right life for yourself? Performing when you want to perform, living in the country in upstate New York, and keeping an apartment in Manhattan?**

ROLLINS: I do feel that I designed the right life for myself. However, as I'm getting older, I'm beginning to feel that I want to perform more. As Count Basie said, "It's four o'clock in the afternoon for me now." I might be off for six weeks or so, and I'm beginning to feel that I'd like to be playing a little more now because there's less time. There's less time for me to do everything that I want to do.

February 2, 1994

Send the Salami

Hal David

Bacharach and David's hits, because they were pop rather than rock, were anomalies in their own day—bridges across the generational divide, built by men born in the 1920s, whose musical sensibilities were formed before the onslaught of rock-and-roll. While competing for a rung on the Top 40 with Lennon and McCartney and with the Motown songwriting and producing team of Holland-Dozier-Holland, Bacharach and David were also competing for movie assignments with older writers such as Dimitri Tiomkin, Johnny Mercer, and Jimmy Van Heusen.

Francis Davis, *Like Young*

Although Burt Bacharach is revered, not enough attention has been paid to the lyricist Hal David, his songwriting partner from the late 1950s through the early 1970s. Among the hits they wrote together during those years were "The Look of Love," "Alfie," "This Guy's in Love with You," "I'll Never Fall in Love Again," "What's New Pussycat?," "What the World Needs Now Is Love," "Make It Easy on Yourself," "I Say a Little Prayer," "A House Is Not a Home," "You'll Never Get to Heaven (If You Break My Heart)," "(There's) Always Something There to Remind Me," "The Man Who Shot Liberty Valance" . . . I could go on and on, but you get the idea.

TERRY GROSS: **Dionne Warwick is the leading interpreter of the songs you wrote with Burt Bacharach. How did you first meet her?**

HAL DAVID: She was a background singer on recording sessions in New York with groups like the Drifters, and had asked Burt Bacharach and me if she could do some demonstration records for us. We invited her to our office in New York City, and she sang for us, and she just blew us away. We thought we ought to record her.

TG: **Warwick says that the song "Don't Make Me Over" was written for her after a little argument. What was that about?**

DAVID: Well, we were making a demonstration record with her of a song called "Make It Easy on Yourself." The publisher, Famous Music, is an arm of Paramount Pictures. They took the song to Jerry Butler, who recorded it, and it became a hit. Dionne was very upset, thinking that she should have been the one to record it for the commercial market because she had just made the demonstration record.

She said, "Don't make me over!" Meaning, "Let me record my own songs once you write them." So we went in the studio and we wrote this song, "Don't Make Me Over," and recorded it with Dionne. It was her first recording commercially, and it was a hit.

TG: **You and Burt Bacharach have both said that of all the songs you wrote together, "Alfie" is your favorite. Why is that?**

DAVID: Well, in writing songs, we're always trying to be as good as we can be. But we're not always at our very best. I think that's an impossibility for anyone. There are time constraints when there are recording sessions or films where the song has got to be produced in a given amount of time. And then there are theater pieces where it's gotta go very quickly.

Consequently, you sometimes let go of songs before they're every bit as good as you hoped they would be. "Alfie" came as close to being the way I wanted a song to be as any I've written.

TG: **In the bridge—does your lyric really rhyme? It goes, "As sure as I believe there's a heaven above, Alfie, I know there's** something much more—something even nonbelievers can believe in." Why did you decide to write that part of the lyric without a rhyme?

DAVID: Well, now that you ask the question, I hadn't even thought of it. That's just exactly how I heard the lyric. I wrote that lyric first, and Burt wrote the music afterwards. He wrote brilliant melody. I just heard those lines. And the structure of the lines was the way I thought it should fall in the bridge of the song. Now I know I didn't have a rhyme in the bridge, and that's interesting to me.

TG: If I were a lyricist, this is one assignment I don't think I would want: Write a title theme for a movie called *Alfie* about a womanizer who really mistreats the women in his life. Seems like a tough assignment. You did good. What did you think when you got this assignment?

DAVID: Well, I thought to myself, "My God, why do they keep giving me these terrible assignments?" It seemed such an odd phrase. "Alfie," it was not a name that spelled any romance whatsoever. It sounded almost like a British music hall song. It took me a while to find my way into the song, which was the opening line, "What's it all about?" Then suddenly, I had a sense of where I should go.

TG: One of your songs that I really love is "The Man Who Shot Liberty Valance." I'm a real sucker for these big Western themes. I've always loved the big Gene Pitney vocal. This song is not used in the movie *The Man Who Shot Liberty Valance*. It was just inspired by the film. Why did you write it?

DAVID: Well, we were asked to write it for Paramount. There was a John Ford movie called *The Man Who Shot Liberty Valance*. They were called "exploitation" songs in those days. The film companies had you write these songs in order to have a hit and exploit the film. Every time the "title song" was played on the radio, people would hear the title and think of the film.

"The Man Who Shot Liberty Valance" turned out to be a rather good song, and we made every effort to try to get it into the film. John

Ford resisted it because he didn't conceive of any song in the film. As much as Paramount pressed him to put it in, they were not success- ful. And we were not successful.

Then Gene Pitney recorded it, and he made a very good record, and it became a big hit. I suspect Mr. Ford might have been a little re- gretful that he didn't have it in the film.

TG: One of the lines that I really like in the lyric is "'cause the point of a gun was the only law that Liberty understood. When it came to shootin' straight and fast, he was mighty good." It's such a different style from your sophisticated love songs. How did you find the language for this Western anthem?

DAVID: Well, let's see. Over the years, I found myself writing hit songs that became big country hits, and I had never been down South. But I've never had a problem writing Western songs, country songs.

You know, most of the work we do as songwriters is really done in the imagination. You can do almost anything that you can imagine, and I guess I imagine things like "The Man Who Shot Liberty Valance."

TG: Your parents were from Eastern Europe. Your father opened up a delicatessen in Brooklyn, and your family lived upstairs from the deli. What was the best part about living upstairs from your parents' deli?

DAVID: Well, the best part was it was easy to go home from the store. And everyone knew us. It was a lower-middle-class area, maybe poor. But it was a very friendly atmosphere to grow up in.

TG: As a kid listening to music, did you pay a lot of attention to lyrics?

DAVID: Well, my oldest brother, Mack David, was a songwriter.

TG: I'm going to stop you right there, and name some of the songs that he wrote. He wrote the lyrics to "Blue and Sentimental," "Cherry Pink and Apple Blossom White," "Lili Marlene," "It Must Be Him" (that Vikki Carr hit), "I'm Just a

Lucky So and So," and the lyrics for the TV themes "77 Sunset Strip," "Hawaiian Eye," and "Surfside 6."

When did you start thinking that you wanted to write lyrics, too?

DAVID: Well, I don't know. I was always interested in writing lyrics more than music. We all studied music. We all played the violin. When I say "all," I mean my brothers and me. I had a band that used to play for weddings and bar mitzvahs in Brooklyn.

We used to work the Borscht Circuit in the Catskill Mountains during summers. Finally, I got a job writing advertising copy for the *New York Post*. And I thought I would wind up being a newspaper person.

TG: **You wound up with a showbiz job in the army. You were writing songs for the USO, was it?**

DAVID: No, not the USO—the Central Pacific Entertainment Section, which was an army special service unit based at the University of Hawaii in Honolulu. I was very lucky. I think the army was very lucky to have me away from guns, too. That's what I did for about three years. I worked writing shows, musical shows, songs, sketches. It changed my life, because when I came out of the army, I knew that's what I wanted to do.

TG: **Do you remember any of the lyrics that you wrote for the army?**

DAVID: The one I'm most proud of—and it was a hit in the Pacific, though I'm sure it's not known by your audience—was called "Send the Salami."

> *Send the salami to your boy in the Army.*
> *It's the patriotic thing that everyone should do.*
> *Send the salami to your boy in the Army.*
> *Don't just send him things to wear.*
> *Send him something he can chew.*

TG: **Oh, this was written by the son of a deli man.**

DAVID: Yes, and it was a hit. I remember being with my wife at some function, and somebody came over to our table and said, "Did you write 'Send the salami to your boy in the Army'?" He had been in the Pacific. I said I had. And he just wanted to shake my hand.

TG: I would like to give you the chance to choose the music that we're going to close the show with, since I've been hogging all the selections during the program. Do you have a song that you'd like to have us play?

DAVID: Yes, I would. I'm sitting here right next to my wife, Eunice, who's listening to this interview. I know the song that she loves is "To All the Girls I've Loved Before" with Julio and Willie. That's the one I choose.

TG: Maybe Eunice would like to tell us what she loves about the song?

DAVID: Let's put her on.

EUNICE DAVID: Hi.

TG: Hi. How are you?

EUNICE DAVID: First of all, I think you have a great voice.

TG: Oh, thank you.

EUNICE DAVID: What I like about that song is the rhythm and the happiness of it. I've never looked at it as a sexist song. I know some women have objected to it. I think it's got great verve and energy. I love the fact that the two men who are singing it—Julio and Willie—are so different, and yet they go together so well in that duet. It's just a super song.

TG: Well, I hope when you hear it, you don't think of your husband thinking of all the girls he's ever loved.

EUNICE DAVID: Yes, but that's in the past, don't forget.

October 22, 1997

LIKE RAW MEAT

Isabella Rossellini

She is clearly intelligent, creative, and a social creature. . . .
She is also a very sympathetic actress . . . who can rise to a
performance of great courage and psychic insight, such as her
Dorothy in Blue Velvet.

David Thomson, *The Biographical Dictionary of Film*

In her 1997 memoir, *Some of Me,* Isabella Rossellini acknowledged that she means different things to different people. To those sixty and over, she's Ingrid Bergman's daughter. To film scholars, she's the daughter of the Italian neorealist director Roberto Rossellini. People in their thirties know her from David Lynch's *Blue Velvet.* Women of all ages know her as the former model for Lancôme cosmetics. Reading *Some of Me* in preparation for my interview with Rossellini soon after it was published, I was surprised to learn that a woman so poised and beautiful had suffered from a crippling spinal deformity as a girl.

TERRY GROSS: When you were young you had scoliosis, a curvature of the spine, and yours was quite severe. You had surgery in which thirteen vertebrae were fused, and you were in a body cast for two years. How did you spend your time when you were in the body cast?

ISABELLA ROSSELLINI: Well, if you are in pain, most of the time you can't do much except sit there and wait till the pain subsides. Occasionally, I felt better and I tried as much as I could to go to school, take walks, and have a regular life. But obviously, it was incredibly disruptive. The hardest part was the pain. I could deal with everything else. I was a teenager and, of course, I was embarrassed to have a body cast and I was embarrassed to be labeled deformed. But those things seemed not to be major problems. The great problem was the great physical pain. I'm glad that I'm over it.

TG: How long did the pain last?

ROSSELLINI: It depended on the operation. They don't do that procedure anymore. But at the time of my operation, they used bone from my leg to fuse my vertebrae, so there would be no problem of rejection. I had to be immobilized for six months, and then I had a cast. The operation was very painful. The stretching and the correction of the spine—which is now done with metal rods while you're unconscious—was done instead while I was awake. They stretched you like the medieval torture. That was very painful, and that pain stayed for a long time. The cast was much bigger than I, so it put pressure on my spine. I had a machine in my mouth because the pressure was so strong underneath my chin, and on my hips, that my teeth could go back in my jaws. The machine kept my jaws separated, but still the pressure on the jaw was great. It took days before my body gave in to that lengthening and straightening.

TG: As an adult, you've been recognized as an international beauty. Was it odd for you to go from thinking of yourself as deformed to thinking of yourself as beautiful, and to realize that other people thought of you as beautiful?

ROSSELLINI: It was wonderful to have overcome all the odds. I remember people sending postcards to my doctor saying, "Can you imagine?"

TG: **Your mother was beautiful. Was it important to you to be beautiful? Were you insecure about your self-image because of the scoliosis and the surgery?**

ROSSELLINI: Not so much. I don't remember being young and wondering if I was beautiful or not. Even in my old age, I am not very concerned about it. I don't know if it is wisdom or if I'm spoiled. Maybe people did tell me, "You look so pretty." So I thought, "Oh well, then I don't have to worry."

When I had scoliosis, I didn't think of myself as ugly. I thought of myself as deformed—as having a deformed spine—which is different. I couldn't walk. I'd lost the ability to walk. The stakes were so much higher than just looking pretty.

TG: **Right. Right. How did you start modeling?**

ROSSELLINI: I started modeling by chance. I was twenty-eight and worked for the Italian television, but I lived in New York. Socially, I met a wonderful photographer called Bruce Weber who wanted to photograph me. I thought, "Oh, that'd be fun, maybe I'll save the issue of that magazine to show to my grandchildren. I'll be an old bag and say, 'Look, I was pretty when I was photographed once.'" But then, literally, I had an overnight success. Within a month, I was in Richard Avedon's studio working every day, having covers—and my life completely changed. I became a model and learned to love it.

TG: **You've been photographed by many great photographers. Do you respond to the camera differently, depending on who the photographer is?**

ROSSELLINI: Oh, definitely. The style of posing slightly changes with a different photographer. It can be more emphatic and artificial, or it can be real acting. You learn that as you go along.

TG: **Would photographers direct you to do certain things, or think in certain ways, that would help you develop?**

ROSSELLINI: Well, with Richard Avedon I couldn't have had a better school. At first when I was posing, I thought I just had to be obedient and wear the clothes and make sure I didn't wrinkle them and mess them up. I sat there obediently just waiting for every instruction—"turn a little bit left; turn a little bit right; look up; look down." And I just obeyed. Avedon would look at me and say, "Can you think of something?" And then when I thought of something, he'd say, "No, change your thought. I don't like what you're thinking." I said to myself, "What is he saying? He doesn't know what I'm thinking." So I went back to the thought I'd had, and he caught me immediately. He said, "No, no! I told you. I don't like what you're thinking. Change your thought."

If you concentrate, there is something that emanates from you, and that's what the great photographer photographs. Diana Vreeland says, "There is no beauty without emotion." I think that is the responsibility of a model. It isn't so much to look beautiful. That mostly is genetic. You're born like that. But you have to show your emotions—that's what makes a great photo.

TG: Is this something you think about when you're making movies, too?

ROSSELLINI: Yes, it is. People always differentiate between modeling and acting as being so categorically different. Instead, I think there is a lot in common. Of course, you don't have a dialogue when you are a model. You don't have to react to another actor. But sometimes you react to the photographer in the same way an actor would respond to the partner in acting.

TG: You say you wore very little makeup before you started modeling professionally. Why?

ROSSELLINI: I grew up like that. Nobody in my family used much makeup. And then, you use so much makeup when you work, and you are made up by such great makeup artists that you think you can never mimic the result created by these professionals.

TG: Once you started modeling for Lancôme, you had a contract that stipulated you had to wear makeup for public appearances.

ROSSELLINI: Yes. Well, obviously, I think they were right. You know, you have to celebrate and support what you represent.

TG: **What else did the contract stipulate?**

ROSSELLINI: The oddest part of the contract is the moral stipulation that if I was involved in any scandal, they could get rid of me—which reminded me of the contract in the forties that actors and actresses had with the studios. There were many, many similarities. The idea that a studio then, or a company now, works as a Pygmalion—they create you, so you have to obey that image, that persona that they have created. Even in modeling now, there is a greater liberalization. But when I signed the contract, which was almost seventeen years ago, the moral stipulation was still in.

TG: **I understand that another stipulation stated that you weren't allowed to gain weight.**

ROSSELLINI: Oh, well, that's obvious because they have to use your image and you become like a label. So you can't change too much. It also stipulated that I couldn't change hair color or hairdo, or that I at least had to have their approval. It's understandable. You have to create a certain continuity.

TG: **Did food become a big issue for you during those years?**

ROSSELLINI: No, it didn't, because I never was an anorexic model. I was the fattest, shortest, oldest of the models. I just watched not to become too fat, and that was it.

TG: **What about having a child without being married? How did they react to that?**

ROSSELLINI: Well, they didn't like that so much, but then they had to live with it, 'cause I'm tough, you know. I assert my freedom very strongly, so they understood that at the beginning.

TG: **How old were you when you lost the contract with Lancôme?**

ROSSELLINI: Forty-two.

TG: **Was it because of your age?**

ROSSELLINI: Yes. The truth of the matter is that in any fashion magazine or any film, a woman who is represented as beautiful and appealing is always between sixteen and thirty-two. Lancôme did keep me until I was forty-two.

There was an enormous debate within the company whether to keep me or not; finally they just succumbed to the tradition in spite of my protesting. It's their freedom, and I guess freedom is to be respected, so I do respect their choice. I still think that we lost an opportunity to break a prejudice. I do believe that it is a prejudice not to use older women to represent elegance.

TG: **Older women buy their share of cosmetics and want to see them displayed on a mature woman, not someone in their twenties, because there's no way a mature woman is going to look like a twenty-year-old, no matter how much makeup she uses.**

ROSSELLINI: Well, that is their point. The point is that when you do a campaign, you represent the dream in people. You do not represent a reality in people. They believe that the dream of women is to stay young, so they take the symbol of youth. They are careful not to take someone who's terribly young, because then you would feel alienated. The people that do the big cosmetic campaigns are generally in their late twenties or early thirties. They're generally brunettes instead of blondes, because brunettes are more accessible. But still, they have to be young enough to represent a dream of what you wish to be.

My point with Lancôme is that with the new generation of women, the biggest dream isn't to stay young, it's to be independent—to be free, to be powerful, to do what you like to do, to assert yourself. They considered that too avant-garde. It's not that they didn't recognize it. They said, "Yes, but we still think that it's only a minority of women with those values. Most women dream of staying young." That's why plastic surgeons are so successful, I guess. They had a valid point, and they're there to sell cream, not to do a social battle.

TG: What was your mother Ingrid Bergman's attitude toward getting older? Did it bother her to have wrinkles on her face?

ROSSELLINI: I don't remember ever discussing it with her, and I didn't think she was very affected by it. But one day I spoke to my stepfather, who said, "Oh, Mama was kind of worried about that." It surprised me. Then I said to myself, "Well, obviously, she must have been to a certain extent. She was an actress." But I don't think it was a great obsession.

TG: How much focus have you wanted to place on acting in your career?

ROSSELLINI: As a teenager, I wanted to do something different from acting, because not only was my mother such an established and adored actress but everybody else in my family was very successful in movies, including my father, who was a great filmmaker. Once I became a model, I realized that there were some similarities to acting, and I became curious about it. Unexpectedly, I loved modeling. Like everybody else, I went into it thinking that it was a stupid job. I had this stereotype in my head.

Tentatively, I started to take classes in acting. I got some parts and had the courage to do them, which isn't easy when you come from a family that has been so glorified in films. I like acting, but I think I like it somewhat less than my mother. My mother just adored it, lived for it. I don't. I like it a lot, but I think my mother liked acting above all.

TG: I want to ask you about *Blue Velvet*. You were so wonderful in that film. You played an exotic and mesmerizing nightclub singer who's in an abusive relationship with a psycho played by Dennis Hopper. What interested you about this part?

ROSSELLINI: To me, it was a chance to portray a battered woman who is also suffering from Stockholm syndrome—that situation where it's very hard for a victim to recognize that they are a victim. The victim feels guilty and does anything to please the person who's torturing them. It's an absolute strange twist our mind gives us, and it is recognized as a syndrome in people who are kidnapped, or rape victims.

I thought it was quite interesting to play that part. It was a wonderful way to portray the darkness of sexuality. I played a femme fatale who was beautiful, yet completely destroyed inside. Most of the time, femme fatale roles are portrayed as women who know exactly what they want, and sex is portrayed as something that you choose for yourself. We know the reality is often that it just happens, and we don't know what to do with it, or what to make of it.

TG: There is a scene in *Blue Velvet* that you play opposite Kyle MacLachlan. His character is a young man who's trying to solve the mystery of your identity, and he's also attempting to find out who Frank is—the character played by Dennis Hopper. You're trying to seduce the young man Kyle MacLachlan portrays. As you both begin to feel turned on sexually, you start asking him to hit you. Could you understand why your character asks to be hit?

ROSSELLINI: Yes, because I once was beaten. When I played that part, and I had to say that line, "Hit me, hit me," I remembered the time that it happened to me, the first blow to my head. You just see little stars, exactly like Donald Duck. There was a sense of bewilderment, and you don't know where you are. I wasn't panicked. I wasn't anything. I was just bewildered. I thought that this woman, who had so many torments in her mind, became the victim of abuse because she was raped and beaten by the character of Dennis Hopper. When she did get the first blow, the first punch, she would see stars, and her tormented thoughts could stop. That's why she asked to be beaten.

TG: What an interesting way of looking at it. Who beat you?

ROSSELLINI: I don't want to give the details of all that. I don't want to start looking like, "Oh, poor me, poor me." It happened, but I'm fine now.

TG: There's a scene in the movie where you're wandering around the street naked. Tell me about that scene, and what you wanted your body to look like. It's not a vanity scene.

ROSSELLINI: No, not at all. David Lynch told me that when he was a child, coming back from school, he saw a naked woman walking down the street. Instead of getting aroused or excited at that sight, he started to cry. It terrified him. And he wanted to convey the same terror. He wanted Dorothy to walk naked in the street of Wilmington, where we shot the film, and convey the same sense of terror, instead of the sense of sex appeal. When he was talking to me, I remembered a photo by Nick Ut of a young girl in Vietnam. She has been a victim of a napalm attack and her clothes have been completely torn off her body. She has skin hanging, she's completely naked, and she walks in the street with the arms outstretched. It's such a helpless gesture. I couldn't think of anything else but this absolute helpless gesture and walking like that. If I would have walked covering my breast or covering myself, it would have meant that Dorothy still had some sense of pride—still had something in her to protect her. That woman had to have lost everything. She had to walk completely exposed, just saying, "Help me." I took the gesture from that photo and used it. I hope I conveyed the same sense of despair. I wanted to be like raw meat. My nudity was like raw meat—like walking in a butchery and seeing a quarter of a cow hanging. That was the thing that I wanted to convey.

TG: **Many people say that you bear a strong resemblance to your mother. When did you realize how much you look like her?**

ROSSELLINI: I write about it in my book because I always thought, "Oh, people exaggerate. It's not true." Then my mother noticed it. I was working as a journalist, and she saw me once on television and said, "You know, I don't see it in life, but I see it when you appeared on television. It isn't just that we have similar features, but there is something in the voice and the way we move." I said, "No, Mother, you're wrong. I think you're wrong." I was the last one to be convinced.

One day I walked into an antiques shop, and there were beautiful things—tables and chairs and old mirrors. I was walking and a middle-aged woman came in, quite elegant, but she looked very reserved. Every time I walked toward her, I discreetly walked the opposite way so I wouldn't disturb her. As I was walking, I kept on thinking, "She reminds me of my mother. She reminds me of my mother." Then when I bumped into her, I looked up and it was a reflection of me in the mirror. I had not recognized myself because I didn't realize I'd grown so old. That's when I thought, "Well, people are right. I do look like her."

TG: You write in your memoir that your mother came out of Hollywood, and she had a Hollywood sense of entertainment. She liked entertainment. Whereas your father, the famous neorealist director, had a much more serious artistic approach to movies. Do you feel that you grew up with an integrated sense of both film as higher art and as an entertainment?

ROSSELLINI: I think so. I think I'm more indulgent. If I see a film that's silly, but I have enjoyed looking at it, I praise it, as I praised film that made me think or made me cry. And yet my father was a filmmaker who was a great innovator in cinema. He needed energy, or faith, and absolute belief in his ideas. If you are like me—too democratic and too open—I don't think you can assert yourself to the point you can break new ground. Often the great artists are pretty obsessive. Not all of them, but some of them.

TG: Well, you grew up around people who were obsessed with work, and you've been married to people who have been obsessed with work. Do you wish you had that obsession? Or are you glad you don't?

ROSSELLINI: Now I'm glad not to have it. For many years, I felt diminished by not having that same passion, because I thought that passion corresponded to talent. Even today, I have to say, when I see the ability for a passion for film, or passion for writing, or passion for anything that can completely absorb you, there is something incredibly enviable. Yet I have my children. And I'm really glad now not to have that obsession. If I have to pay for it by having less talent, well, then I'd rather have less talent but be with my children.

June 12, 1997

A LITTLE OUT
OF WHACK

Dennis Hopper

He's sort of the perfect American dangerous hero.
David Lynch in *Crazy About the Movies: Dennis Hopper* (Cinemax)

This combines excerpts of two of my interviews with Dennis Hopper. When I spoke with him in 1990, following the release of *The Hot Spot,* which he directed, I, like many other people, was still reeling from his menacing performance in David Lynch's *Blue Velvet,* the 1986 movie that (along with *Hoosiers*) brought him back into circulation after years lost to drugs and alcohol. He's played crazed characters similar to *Blue Velvet*'s Frank in many subsequent movies, including *River's Edge, Red Rock West,* and *Speed*. But when I did my second interview with him in 1996, he'd been cast against type in *Carried Away* as a withdrawn schoolteacher who lives on a run-down farm with his dying mother.

TERRY GROSS: **You grew up on a farm. Were you anxious to get away when you were growing up?**

DENNIS HOPPER: Yeah. I wanted to know where the trains were going. My mother ran the swimming pool in Dodge City, Kansas. My father was at war in the Second World War, and I lived with my grandparents on a small farm. My grandfather went out to work on a larger farm in Garden City, Kansas—a wheat farm where I would go work with him during the summer. I had a wonderful childhood on that level. I used to milk the cow before I went to school in the morning.

TG: While you were living there, was it fun to see movies about Dodge City?

HOPPER: I remember when I was about five years old, Errol Flynn came to town for the premiere of *Dodge City*. He starred in it along with Olivia de Havilland. That movie probably had a lot to do with me wanting to be an actor.

TG: Was that the only connection you saw between the movie world and your own life?

HOPPER: I grew up during the last days of the Dust Bowl, so I used to tell people the first light that I saw was not from the sun, but from a movie projector. My grandmother didn't drive a car. We lived about five miles outside of Dodge, and on Saturday mornings she'd fill her apron full of eggs, and we'd walk into town. She'd sell the eggs at the poultry place and get the money, and we'd go to see a matinee of the singing cowboys. Once in a while we'd see an Errol Flynn sword-fighting movie.

I knew I wanted to find out where they were making these movies. Kansas was a very flat place, so I wanted to know what a mountain looked like, what a skyscraper looked like, what the ocean looked like. It's one of the reasons I became so interested in the visual aspect of things. On the way to California, when I was thirteen years old, when I saw my first mountain in Colorado, and when I finally saw the ocean, I was really disappointed. The mountains that I'd imagined were so much bigger. The ocean in L.A. had the same horizon line that I'd seen in the wheat fields of Kansas. And I thought, "Wow. This is not what I had imagined." I don't know what I thought. I thought maybe you could see all the way to China or it would look different, it would be a different angle. But it was the same horizon line. I thought my imagination was a little out of whack, because buildings were bigger, mountains were bigger, and the ocean was bigger in my imagination than in reality.

TG: What was your first exposure to art?

HOPPER: I drew when I was a kid and studied at the Nelson Art Gallery on weekends. They had an underprivileged children's art class.

TG: You got a scholarship to the National Shakespeare Festival when you were young. Did you want to do classical theater? Or did you see theater as a way to get into movies?

HOPPER: I wanted to become a great actor. The great actors at the time were all Shakespearean actors.

TG: You first appeared on-screen in the 1955 film *Rebel Without a Cause.* Did the movie give you a sense of teenagers having their own culture—their own misunderstood culture? Or were you already feeling that way?

HOPPER: At that point, all I was concerned about was being an actor. I wasn't concerned about whether people were juvenile delinquents or not. I was only interested in acting. Working on *Rebel Without a Cause,* I saw James Dean act. Throughout shooting, I was trying to figure out what he was doing, because at that time I thought *I* was the best young actor in the world. Suddenly I ran into this guy who was some years older than me, doing work that was so far over my head. One time I actually grabbed him in the "chickie run" and threw him into a car and said, "What are you doing? You've got to teach me what you are doing."

TG: So what did he teach you?

HOPPER: He wanted to know what my motivation was for wanting to act. He asked me if I'd had a problem with my parents, if I'd actually hated my parents. I said that I had felt that. And he said that's what he felt also and that his mother died when he was very young. He used to go to her grave and cry and say, "Mother, why have you left me?" And that turned into, "I'm going to show you. I'm going to be someone." That was the drive that he brought into his acting. So this confused kind of drive and wanting to put these feelings to use in some imaginary circumstance became the key for acting.

But anyway, he said to me, "You must learn how to do things and not show them. You must learn how to smoke a cigarette and not act smoking a cigarette. If somebody knocks on a door, you go answer the door. Moment-to-moment reality. Never anticipate what the next moment is going to hold." Then he said, "You're a very good technical actor, so get rid of all that technique. Stop the line readings. Don't worry about how it's going to come out. Just let it come out."

TG: **Stop the line readings? What did you stop doing?**

HOPPER: Well, I came out of a classical theater background and there are fixed ways of reading lines. Even "Hello, how are you?" became a fixed way of reading a line.

TG: **Was James Dean the first friend you had who died? Did it scare you to have someone your age die?**

HOPPER: He was more than a friend; I think of him as a teacher. We did two films together that took about a year of our lives. He only made three movies in all. We did *Rebel Without a Cause* and then *Giant*. Then he died two weeks before we finished shooting *Giant*. I was nineteen. He was twenty-four. It wasn't like we went out and drank beers together and got high or raced cars. We talked about acting. When he died, it destroyed me, because I totally had this belief that people fulfill their destiny. I couldn't understand why James Dean had died so young. He had only been in three movies. He wanted to direct movies. It destroyed my whole concept of destiny and life for years. It still bothers me. I miss him.

TG: **How did you start collecting art?**

HOPPER: When I first arrived in Los Angeles, I'd worked at La Jolla Playhouse, and my friend who was my boss there was an interior designer. He was working with Mary Price, Vincent Price's wife, who was also an interior designer. They had a kiln at Vincent's house, where they did tile work. I went up there and made some tiles. Vincent was an art collector, and that's where I saw my first Franz Kline. My first Jackson Pollock, my first de Kooning, and so on, were at his house. I'd been painting abstractly, but I'd never thought that anybody really painted abstractly until I saw these things.

TG: **You started collecting art in about 1963 at a time when you'd been acting in a lot of TV shows like *Sugarfoot, Wagon Train, The Rifleman, Cheyenne, Naked City,* and *The Defenders.* Was it like living in two different worlds?**

HOPPER: It was strange because I was doing what I considered sophisticated work as an actor. I'd been in *Rebel Without a Cause*—which was a far-out flick of the day and very successful—and I'd done a film called *Night Tide,* which was made for $25,000. Curtis Harrington and I had shot it in the streets. In Paris it was well received, but we couldn't get it distributed because we'd made it nonunion. I was also doing television, but the television work was very formulaic stuff. But I was also living this other life. I was helping Andy Warhol make his first films, which had nothing to do with any professional thing, but involved just setting up a camera and watching the Empire State Building, and reloading the film.

TG: **It was in 1961 that your home burned down in the Bel Air fire. I know your photographs had been touring in an exhibition, and so were saved. But you lost just about everything you owned. Did that discourage you from collecting art? A lot of people would think, "Well, what's the point of collecting when objects you own can be so ephemeral?"**

HOPPER: No. I had a studio in the garage, it all burned down. So I lost over three hundred of my own paintings. I did have a photographic show that night that opened, so my negatives from my photographs were saved. My ex-wife Brooke Hayward lost all of her mother Margaret Sullavan's furniture.

My father had fought with Mao across China. He was in the OSS, Office of Strategic Services. He'd been one of the people that took the surrender from the Japanese. He collected some things when he was going back and forth between Mao and the Japanese getting artifacts out of China. He had these beautiful tapestries and other things that he'd brought back from the Second World War. Unfortunately, I lost all those in that fire. The only thing that I saved out of the house was a painting by Milton Avery. I carried it out on my back as the house was burning down.

When you lose everything, you have to start over again. It gave us an opportunity. That's when I started collecting. I had some money, and I started buying pop art. I fell into it right at that moment. I saw my first soup can painting. I saw my first Lichtensteins. I bought a soup can and I bought an Ed Kienholz—he was an assemblage artist. There was a mannequin, called *The Quickie*. It was a woman's mannequin head on a roller skate. She had her arm up, and she was picking her nose. I bought that for thirty dollars. Then I bought a big abstract wood relief in black and white, that Kienholz had done, for seventy-five dollars. My agent came in and looked at these things—the soup can painting, this mannequin on a roller skate picking her nose, and this big wood black-and-white construction, abstract thing, and he said, "You're wasting your life. You're wasting your money and your wife's money, and if you don't stop this foolishness, you're going to have to look for another agent." That's when my agent and I parted. I went on collecting. So it's funny enough.

TG: **You cowrote, directed, and starred in the 1969 film *Easy Rider*. You had worked with Roger Corman, and your costar Peter Fonda had done some biker movies and acid trip movies with Corman. Did you see *Easy Rider* as an exploitation film? Or did you want it to be a movie in the spirit of the counterculture?**

HOPPER: I wasn't really thinking about either one of those things. I wanted to win the Cannes Film Festival. I wanted it to be an art film.

The counterculture was becoming *the* culture at that time, so I thought I was making a film for everyone. What I did for the first time was show people smoking marijuana without going out and killing a bunch of nurses, and I used the music of the day rather than writing a score for a movie. It was the first time individual songs had been used for a film. The editing of the cemetery sequence was like a lot of experimental films of the day. I used a kind of cutting that I'd seen on television commercials. Those motorcycle rides that I edited to the music of Jimi Hendrix, and the Byrds, and to Dylan, were the first MTV music video things that were ever done.

TG: Were you already doing a lot of drugs when you made *Easy Rider*?

HOPPER: There was a lot of smoking of grass on that picture. Grass made me paranoid, and I didn't do it. I mean, I did it for the scene where Peter, Jack, and I are all smoking marijuana and Jack talks about space people. But most of the time I didn't smoke it, only because it made me paranoid. But I drank. I was a classic drinker in the great tradition of John Huston, Howard Hawks, and John Ford. I was an alcoholic. Even though I smoked pot a great deal of my life, I didn't do it while I worked.

TG: What form of paranoia would it bring out in you?

HOPPER: It would interfere with the work. Nothing that I did interfered with the work. The work was the only thing that was important to me. We didn't have any cocaine on *Easy Rider*. We just made it popular. That was baking soda that I chose to use in *Easy Rider*.

TG: How did it get to the point that you were doing drugs so much that you ended up not working?

HOPPER: There comes a point when, if you're not the most popular guy in the world and in demand, people suddenly start looking at your behavior, and not wanting to work with you. Drugs never interfered with the careers of some very big people—some of our biggest stars. I'm not advising people to use drugs, or not to use drugs. Drugs destroyed my life. But if my career had maintained a level where I was productive, I probably would have never gotten into the trouble I got into with drugs and alcohol, and never gotten straight.

TG: I get the impression that you've been working really manically since you've been straight.

HOPPER: I would have worked manically all my life if I had been allowed to.

TG: You mean, if you got offered enough?

HOPPER: Yeah. I was never offered anything. At a certain point, my using and my drinking became a question of what Jekyll or Hyde character is he going to be today? What emotional roller coaster is he going to take us on now? Unfortunately, that's what drugs and alcohol did for me. My personal life was a shambles. It never seemed to hurt what went on the screen. But it was the process of getting it on the screen that terrified people.

TG: I want to ask you about the role that I think of as your comeback role—Frank in *Blue Velvet*. It's ironic that you got sane to play this role that's absolutely crazy. You reportedly told David Lynch when you accepted the role that you *are* Frank. How did you mean that?

HOPPER: I meant that I really understood Frank. I didn't have a problem with Frank. I just understood him. I called David. He was down in North Carolina and had already begun filming. I'd never met David, and he'd given me the part. I said, "You don't have to worry about this. I am Frank. I really understand this role." So he got off the phone and told Isabella [Rossellini], and Kyle MacLachlan, and Laura [Dern], "My God, I just got off the phone with Dennis Hopper, and he said he was Frank. That may be great for the movie, but how are we going to have lunch with him?" I just meant that I understood the role. And I do understand Frank. I've known a lot of guys like Frank.

TG: Did you think that you were like Frank at some point in your life?

HOPPER: Well, I understood his sexual obsession. Even though David wrote that the stuff he was sniffing was helium, I'd always thought of it as some sort of drug, like amyl nitrate or nitrous oxide. I asked David if it would be all right to play it that way. He had helium on the set. All helium does is make you sound like Daffy Duck. So I tried it, and I said, "David, just hearing my voice, I'm not able to act. Couldn't I try to use something that disorients my mind?" And he said, "What?" And I said, "Well, watch this." And I'd do a sense memory of an amyl nitrate or nitrous oxide high. He liked what he saw. I told him, "If you want to dub the helium voice in later, we could do that." He said, "No. I don't think it will be necessary." Anyway, it did work. But since then I started thinking how strange it would be if I'd used that helium voice and not had it disorient my mind. What a strange character he'd actually written, even stranger than my portrayal of Frank.

TG: Do you like roles that allow you to bring the kind of intensity that you brought to your portrayal of Frank?

HOPPER: Well, I think that Frank is probably the flashiest role I ever had. I like it on that level.

TG: There's a pretty famous story about an incident that happened in your early career. Henry Hathaway was directing you in the film *From Hell to Texas,* and he was trying to get you to do the scene the way he wanted it. You wanted to do it your own way. This went on for twelve hours—with you doing takes and him insisting that you do it his way. He finally won. I think that you were exiled from Hollywood for a while because of your rebelliousness. Is that right?

HOPPER: Yeah for a long time—till he rehired me again [for the 1965 film *The Sons of Katie Elder*].

TG: Now that you are directing again, do you ever see yourself in Henry Hathaway's position of wanting the actor to do it your way?

HOPPER: I don't see myself any other way. I'm the director. I want them to do it my way.

TG: So if the young Dennis Hopper came in, and he insisted on doing it his way, what would have happened?

HOPPER: I would have probably been amazed by the young Dennis Hopper, and let him do it his way. I would have given him plenty of space to do it his way. Hathaway didn't. But if it comes down to doing it my way, it's got to be my way. I give actors a lot of room to work. The director is the boss. That's just the way it is. If you're in a director's movie and you don't do what the director wants you to do, it doesn't matter how good you are—you look like you are out of step with everybody else. There's no sense fighting him.

October 10, 1990, and April 1, 1996

THE WAY
PEOPLE LOOK

Chuck Close

They are not, in any sense, portraits of Beautiful People.
Every wrinkle, bulge and sag in their flesh is colossally
magnified: a face 9 ft. high is no longer a face but a wall of
imperfections that mock the convention of "good looks."
Robert Hughes, *Time*, April 27, 1981

Faces reveal so much, yet it's rude to stare at someone. That's what I find so fascinating about Chuck Close's work. His hyperrealistic, larger-than-life portraits allow us to stare at even blemishes and nose hairs without embarrassing anyone. But when you move in for a closer look, the face on the canvas breaks up into a grid of paint dabs.

Now considered one of our most important living artists, Close has been painting portraits since the 1960s. In 1988, a collapsed spinal artery paralyzed him from the neck down. He recovered only partially, but has been able to resume his work by attaching brushes to his arm.

TERRY GROSS: Why has the human face been your subject for so long?

CHUCK CLOSE: Well, initially I started making portraits. At that time I didn't even call them portraits, I called them heads, because it was as different as possible from what I had been doing before. My work had been abstract, and I was looking for something that was diametrically opposed to what I had done as a student. The first heads were just my friends, and I had no idea then, thirty years ago, that I would still be painting heads today. But over the years, I found that of all the subject matter that I could use, nothing interests me as much as people, and it offers the viewer an entrance into the work through life experience. We all look in mirrors and look at each other and look at images in magazines and film. And it's a great leveler. Whether a person is the most sophisticated person in the art world or a layperson, we all share that interest in the way people look.

TG: You've said that you try to see the faces neutrally, without opinion or subjectivity, without editorializing in any way about the face. And yet I see the faces very subjectively, even though you, as the painter, didn't. Could you explain why you try to avoid imposing any point of view on your subject?

CLOSE: Well, it's not that I'm uninterested in the psychological reading of the paintings. I just don't want to lobby for one reading over all others. I want to present them straightforwardly and flat-footedly, without editorial comment, without cranking it up for extra psychological readings, or without drawing big circles around things, saying, "Make sure you see it this way." I leave it to the viewer to read the image. I believe that a person's face is a road map to their life, and embedded in the imagery is a great deal of evidence if you want to decode it. If a person has laughed his or her whole life, they'll have laugh lines. If they've frowned their whole lives, they have furrows in their brow. It's not necessary for me to have them laughing or crying or anything in order to have people be able to read them.

TG: Your canvases are very large. You include every detail of a person's face, every line and wrinkle and pucker and pore, every flaw. And it's enlarged, because the painting is so large. Looking at one of your faces in a painting is like looking at yourself in the bathroom mirror with harsh lighting. You see everything. There's something so recognizable about the landscape of the faces, the way you paint them.

CLOSE: Well, yes, we don't stand close enough to each other, we don't invade each other's space enough to really be able to see the intimate level of detail that I typically put in one of these paintings, because they're in fact usually nine feet high. So if there's more information than you ever really wanted to know about someone, it makes it a more intimate experience. I try to make these big, aggressive, confrontational images that you can see clear across the room. You have one kind of relationship with it there. Then another relationship at a middle viewing distance, where you scan it, and you can't readily see the thing as a whole. Then hopefully I've sucked the viewer right up to the canvas, where you can see the individual marks and the methodology.

TG: You have a method of working with grids when you're painting a face from a photograph. What effect are you striving for with that technique?

CLOSE: Well, besides being one of the great modernist conventions, the grid has been around most recently because it's a flattening device. It's a way to restate the flatness of the canvas. But in fact, the use of a grid as a scaling-up method goes back to ancient Egypt and was, of course, used in the Renaissance as a way to take a small drawing or preparatory sketch and enlarge it, by having smaller squares on the preparatory sketch and bigger ones on the painting. All of my work, from the 1960s on, has been built with the use of a grid. I don't use a projector or anything like that. At a certain point I decided to let the grid remain a visible part of the image. Initially, I would get rid of the grid so nobody knew that I used it. But I began to let the incremental unit show. I found all kinds of ways, from using my own fingerprints to gluing on little wads of pulp paper, to let the individual unit show. One of the things I like about working that way is that there's nothing about the building block which says anything about what's going to be made from it.

TG: **Exactly.**

CLOSE: There's no mark that equals hair, there's no mark that equals skin or anything else. It's a little bit like an architect choosing a brick. The brick doesn't determine anything about what kind of building will be built from it. You stack up the bricks one way and you make a gas station, or you stack up the bricks another way and you can build a cathedral. Both of them will be very different experiences, but it wasn't the brick that determined the nature of that experience.

TG: **What suits your personality about working in these small units, one dot at a time?**

CLOSE: Actually, I'm a nervous wreck. I'm a slob. I have no patience. And I'm rather lazy. All of those things would seem to guarantee that I would not make the kind of works I make. But I felt I didn't want to just go with my nature and say, "Well, that's the way I am, I can only make big, sloppy, nervous, quick paintings." I thought to construct a situation in which I couldn't behave that way was also to address my nature. But I found that one of the nice things about working this way, working incrementally, is that I don't have to reinvent the wheel every single day. Today I did what I did yesterday, and tomorrow I'll do what I do today. You can pick it up and put it down. I don't have to wait for inspiration. There are no good days or bad days. Every day essentially builds positively on what I did the day before. In some ways, I think it's rather like what used to be called women's work, that is, quilting, crocheting, knitting, or whatever. The advantage of that way of working was that it allowed a person to just keep working. Women could knit for a while, put it down, go feed the baby, come back and pick it up and knit a little more, and then put it down, and go out and weed the garden. If you believe in the process, and you knit one and you purl two long enough, eventually you get a sweater. Given my nature, it was very good for me to have a way to work in which I was able to add to what I already had, and slowly construct the final image out of these little building blocks.

TG: How have you dealt with impatience? Don't you ever feel like, "Okay, it's going to take me another twelve months of making these dots to have a painting. I want to see it now."

CLOSE: Well, I do finish each area as I go, so I have a chance to see what it's going to look like almost from the beginning. Patience is a funny thing. I used to work every day and make a painting every day. Now I work every day and I make a painting every several months. But work is work, and it doesn't seem to take any more patience to keep working on one piece than it did to make a different piece every day. The big difference is that I used to enjoy painting, I loved the activity, but I didn't care very much about what I made. Now I have a way of working which is essentially positive building on what I already have, and eventually I get to something about which I care a great deal more. For me, that was a very productive trade-off.

TG: Ten years ago you had a terrible medical problem. I think it was a blood vessel in your spinal cord that broke—

CLOSE: Well, actually it's very funny—I don't know whether the listening audience knows that you're in Philadelphia and I'm in New York. But nine years ago I was in this very studio talking to Susan Stamberg about the National Endowment for the Arts. It was the last thing I did before I went up to Gracie Mansion, where I suffered this collapsed spinal artery and became, within a matter of a few minutes, a quadriplegic. So it's a little freaky to be in this studio, and I'm wondering about what's going to happen today when I leave.

But at any rate, yes, I did have this event in my life in which I ultimately became what's called an incomplete quadriplegic. I was initially paralyzed from the shoulders down, but I got considerable return. I am confined to a wheelchair, and I don't have the use of my hands. I paint now with brushes strapped to a brace, which is strapped to my arm. Essentially, I'm not doing anything that I don't think I would have been doing anyway. The work has progressed much the same way that it would have. Luckily, I had something to get back to that really mattered to me. If I hadn't already known how to paint, I don't think I could have learned to do it postinjury. But once you know how to do something, it's not so hard to equip yourself with what's necessary to be able to get back to it.

TG: **You don't have much movement now at all, and you have to paint with the brushes strapped onto your wrist. Have you thought about how much painting is something that happens in your mind, versus something that happens with your hands?**

CLOSE: Somebody told me in the hospital, "Oh, you'll be all right, because you paint with your head and not with your hands." And I thought, "Oh, easy for you to say!" I thought, "Gee, this is like something that came out of a fortune cookie." I was actually quite annoyed that they had this kind of throwaway answer for my very severe problem.

But, you know, they were right. Once you know what art looks like, you can figure out how to make it. It's just a question of adaptation. Part of my ability to get back to work is due to the fact that I am, and have been for thirty years, a very successful artist and have made a lot of money, and I can afford to equip myself with what's necessary to be able to get back to work. I have a totally wheelchair-accessible studio. I can hire assistants who can get me where I want to go. I still make the paintings entirely by myself. My assistants don't help me paint. But they help me with all the other things. If this were to happen to another artist who was not as celebrated as I was, and not as financially successful as I was, no matter how much they might have wished to get back to work, it may have been an impossibility. Again, I think that I'm very lucky.

TG: **Often when people lose the ability to move, it's through a traumatic accident, a car crash, or a fall. But for you it was a broken artery—**

CLOSE: I just collapsed.

TG: **When did you realize that you had lost the ability to move?**

CLOSE: I had tremendous pain. In fact, I had had the pain over the years. It would come and go. Nobody could ever figure out what it was. This time, I had massive seizures all over my body, and then all of a sudden—my whole body was still. It took them several days to figure out what happened to me. I remember my art dealer came in and he said, "Come on, get out of bed." He was convinced that I had some sort of hysterical paralysis.

TG: How did you come up with a system for getting your paintbrush attached to your arm in such a way that you could get the mobility and control that you needed?

CLOSE: After a couple of months of being in intensive care, I was moved to a rehabilitation hospital that was connected to the hospital. I began rehab, and I remember rolling down the hall one day and seeing a name on a door. It said, "Occupational Therapy." I said, "Oh, great, they'll help me get back to my occupation." But it was much more about stacking spools and making things out of pipe cleaners. The therapists were wonderful people and very helpful, but it took the active intervention of my wife, who really went to bat for me and made sure they understood just how important it was for me and my sanity to be able to get back to work. She convinced the therapist to stop working on things that I didn't need to do, and to get back to what really mattered. They found me a space in the basement of the building, and I equipped it as a studio and managed to start painting while I was still in rehabilitation.

TG: Were there times when you found yourself trying to make things out of pipe cleaners because that's what you were supposed to be doing in occupational therapy?

CLOSE: They tried to get me to do my laundry. I said, "Well, you know, I didn't do my laundry before. Why should I want to do my laundry now?" They tried to show me how to use a computer, and I said, "I have absolutely no interest in using a computer. And I really don't want to do it with a pencil stuck in my teeth." It was a fight, because they're trying to bring everybody along, and they have a general idea of what's liable to be helpful in a person's life. I was looking for very specific help.

April 14, 1998

It Gets Harder

Frank Stella

Stella wrings more pictorial feeling from abstract art than anyone else alive.

Robert Hughes, *Time,* November 2, 1987

In the late 1950s and early 1960s, Frank Stella's austere paintings helped to launch a minimalist movement in the visual arts. By 2000, when I spoke with him, Stella had become known for the wild color and exuberance of his paintings and sculptures. One of his most famous early statements, "What you see is what you see," implied that we should expect no explanations from him. Despite this, he speaks eloquently about his own art and about art history.

TERRY GROSS: You work on a very large scale now. You work not only in your studio, you have a foundry, you have a staff. You have to have a crew because the works are so large.

FRANK STELLA: Yeah. People make a lot of that, actually. It's not my foundry. I work at a foundry. I have a studio and I have people who work with me and help me out. From my point of view, there's a lot of work to do and we all work at it. It's not exactly collaboration because, by and large, they're supposed to be doing what I tell them to do. Sometimes they don't and the results are good, and sometimes they don't and the results are quite bad.

TG: I'm not an artist, but I would think that something might get lost in the process if you're not doing it all yourself.

STELLA: I suppose that people can mess things up, but by and large, one man can't do very much. Although Michelangelo did fire some of his assistants when he was working on the Sistine Chapel because they were annoying him, and he had to finish it himself.

TG: Has your role as an artist become something you never imagined it would be, because you run a business, pay a staff, and work with a foundry?

STELLA: It's changed, but it's just as hard to pay for yourself, or take care of your children, or whatever you do. The scale of it doesn't matter all that much to me. The one thing that hasn't changed is the problem. The problem is always the same—to get the work done. That's always hard. Money never made it easier, and now that I don't have so much money, it's still hard. Actually, I don't understand.

TG: You don't understand what?

STELLA: I don't understand how it came to be that you could be successful and so overwhelmingly unsuccessful at the same time.

TG: What's the unsuccessful part?

STELLA: The effort that it takes to make *anything*. The amount of effort that it takes to make something good doesn't change. Actually, maybe it gets harder.

TG: Your work has changed so much since the late fifties, when you first became known for your austere black-striped paintings that helped launch the minimalist movement. Later, you added color and often painted geometrical forms. Eventually, your work became wildly colored with drips and brushstrokes, then it became more sculptural, and you started working with hard materials like metal. Do you feel that you first stripped things down to a basic vocabulary, and then added to that vocabulary, to build it up again?

STELLA: I suppose.

TG: Were your early black canvases a dare?

STELLA: Yes, I think they were. They were pretty aggressive, yeah. But I felt very confident about them.

TG: What were they about to you? What were you trying to do or to say?

STELLA: Well, it was about being able to make an abstract painting that really wasn't based on anything but the gesture of making itself— so that the gesture of drawing, or the path of the brush on the canvas created the painting. Most drawing is outline, or edging, to create a form. The drawing and the painting in this work was one. It didn't create a form. It was the form.

TG: When you were in your twenties in the 1950s, some of the best-known artists, like Pollock, were famous not only for their work but for their bohemian lifestyle. That lifestyle was emulated by many young artists. Did that lifestyle mean anything to you?

STELLA: No, it didn't mean much, largely because I was so young and it was just very hard to keep yourself together, to keep working, to get money, to do whatever you have to do. I didn't have that much time to get drunk.

TG: You grew up in a pretty middle-class family. Your father was a gynecologist. Apparently he worked as a housepainter during the Depression to put himself through college. From what I've read, it sounds like you'd occasionally help him paint the house you lived in.

STELLA: Yeah. I was in paint all my life.

TG: **Did you enjoy the feel or the colors of house paint?**

STELLA: Yes, I did. I liked it. I always liked paint, the physicality of it, yeah. It was never a problem for me. My mother was an artist and she painted with oil, and my father painted with house paint. So I had paint pretty well covered. When I first saw a de Kooning and Kline, and even Pollock, I knew right away how it was done. It wasn't a problem for me to figure out how to make those kinds of paintings.

TG: **Did you have that knowledge more from house paint than anything else?**

STELLA: Yes. Even at the time that Pollock was doing it, there was a tradition for decorating, dripping paint on floors and on furniture. It's been around. It just hadn't been in the art world.

TG: **What connection did you see between house painting and the Pollocks?**

STELLA: Painting a wall is a big physical expanse. I could see that most of the time, if you stopped halfway through while you're painting your wall, it would be a lot more interesting. No one's going to let you stop and have it half white and half red. But it was beautiful, and I liked doing it. I could easily see that you could make paintings like that.

TG: **How did you get from painting walls to actually painting canvases?**

STELLA: I painted all my way through school. I went to Phillips Academy in Andover and I took art classes, and then when I was at Princeton, we had art teachers, and I took classes there.

TG: **Yet the impression I get is that you never studied the technique of representational art.**

STELLA: That's true. When I was at Phillips Academy, there was an introductory course to fine art, and that consisted of an art history course and a studio course. So you went to art history lectures, and then you went to the studio and you made paintings. As one of the prerequisites in the painting course, you had to make a fairly representational painting of a still life. You couldn't make a mess. You had to paint it in a realistic way. I didn't really like it. We had a class and they started showing us about Seurat and neo-impressionism and things like that. I said to myself, "Oh, that's kind of obvious." So I ran downstairs to do my painting and I just made it all splotches. I made a table with splotches, a cylinder with splotches, some ivy with splotches, and it all held together. It looked like a painting. Everyone else was doing the modeling, and the light and shadow, and having a wonderful time doing what they were doing. But I was done. I showed it to Pat Morgan, who was the teacher, and he said, "All right. All right," and he let me go. From then on, I just did whatever I wanted. I didn't have to do any more representational art.

TG: How much time did you spend on representational art before abandoning it?

STELLA: Well, I did about twenty minutes.

TG: How old were you?

STELLA: I was probably fifteen.

TG: I'm surprised that your teacher allowed you to dismiss technique just like that.

STELLA: Look, I was a wiseguy. A lot of teachers have to deal with kids who are wiseguys. But if you know what you're doing, what are you going to do? You're the tennis coach and the kid comes in and he hits the ball eighty, ninety miles an hour, and no matter what you do, he hits it back. You can say, "Well, that's not exactly the right way to do it," and you can talk to him, but you're not going to tell him to forget it. I mean, either you can hit the ball or you can't.

TG: What made you realize that you weren't going to do representational art? Was it a technical problem or an aesthetic lack of interest?

STELLA: I had representational art on my window. My mother painted Santa Claus on there. She was always making things. I saw representational art all the time. I wasn't very moved by it. But when I saw magazine reproductions of Franz Kline, and when I saw the Pollock painting, and Hans Hoffmann paintings in Patrick Morgan's house and in the Addison Gallery, I was overwhelmed by them. I just loved them and I wanted to make paintings like that. I wasn't going to let anything keep me from making paintings like that right away. I wasn't going to wait ten years and then make an abstract painting.

TG: Was there ever a point in your life where you said to yourself, "I wish that I had studied representational technique and had more of that technique available to me?"

STELLA: I didn't understand representational painting very much and I probably wouldn't understand representational technique, up to a point. But when I saw Caravaggio's the young *St. John the Baptist,* it really knocked me out. I really liked it, and it was very real and displayed the realist technique. I should have said, "Oh my God. But I can't do this," and I should have been very worried about it. But actually, the effect was the opposite. It was an incredible euphoria—that's it, that's what painting is about. I realized that Caravaggio's success, and what made this painting beautiful, was its sense of being very real, being very physically present. It had nothing to do with the technique, but with the fact that Caravaggio worked very hard at painting, and that he had wanted to make a painting. I realized that the goal is what counts, what you intend to do, what you want to make. Making things pictorial is what's important—the technique you use to make the pictoriality manifest and make it successful doesn't really matter. You get the job done, whichever way you can. They never had a problem in caves in Lascaux or wherever, Altamira. They got the job done.

TG: I want to—if it's okay with you—ask you about your finger.

STELLA: Yeah, it's okay.

TG: You have one finger that—

STELLA: Yeah. I have a crushed left hand. Yeah. Yeah, one finger is half, and a couple of other fingers are damaged. It's a crush injury from when I was ten years old.

TG: **What happened?**

STELLA: A concrete urn in the yard toppled over onto my hand—
that's all. It was a crush injury.

TG: **Were the parts of your finger amputated on the spot, or was
the surgery afterwards?**

STELLA: When it's crushed, it turns black. Eventually they had to cut
it off.

TG: **You do a lot of physical work. It's never interfered with that?**

STELLA: I'm right-handed, so it's not a problem.

TG: **Did your hand get you out of the military?**

STELLA: Actually, indirectly it did. There was a turning point in my
artistic career when I graduated from Princeton; I went to New York
and took a loft and started painting. I wasn't really that aggressive
about being a painter or being an artist, but I did it because that September I had to go home to Boston to take a physical examination.
We still had the draft. I expected to be drafted, so I thought, "Well,
you know, this is just a bad time. I'll paint for a while and then go in
the army. Then I'll worry about my career when I get out, after I do
my military service." I mean, it wasn't complicated. And I wasn't con-
flicted or anything. I was just painting and living in New York, meeting people and making paintings.

　　I went to take my physical examination, and I didn't really want
to go in the army, so I did all the things—I wet my bed, I sucked my
thumb—and they just laughed at me and they stamped all my papers.
There were three doctors in a row on a table, and the last guy looked
at me and said, "Well, let me see your left hand." And I said, "Yes, sir."
And he picked up an envelope and he held out the envelope to me.
He said, "Put this between your thumb and your index finger, your
third finger, your fourth finger, your little finger." I said, "Yes, sir." He
said, "You know, son, you have faulty opposition." And I said, "Yes,
sir." And he said, "You don't want to go in the army, do you?" And I
said, "No, sir," which I think is not exactly what I should have said.

And he said, "You went to Princeton, didn't you?" And I said, "Yes, sir." He said, "I don't think you'd make a very good soldier anyway." And he picked up the form and he stamped it, and I was out.

TG: **How did that make you feel?**

STELLA: Well, I felt weird actually. I was happy not to be in the army, and then I suddenly realized that I was going to go back to New York to my studio and that I didn't have a career ahead of me in the army. They kept telling me my tour of duty would be in West Germany or Korea, and I wasn't sure which fabulous place I wanted to go to, but I had these fantasies of going on tour. I mean, the army tour is a little bit different than my idea of touring. But anyway, I called up my father and I said, "Gee, I'm sorry, Dad. I have bad news. I failed my physical examination. I won't be able to go in the army." And he said, "Too bad. It would have made a man of you." And I said, "Well, I'm just gonna go back to my studio." And that was it.

TG: **Were there things you had to face in the studio that you didn't feel ready to face yet because you thought you were putting all of that off until after your tour of duty?**

STELLA: It wasn't a problem. I just went back to my studio and kept on painting. Life at that age was nice. New York was relatively gentle. There were artists around, and you could bum around, and it was okay. You could manage.

November 16, 2000

MOM, DAD, I WANT TO BE A TAP DANCER

Conan O'Brien

O'Brien seems a switch on the guest who won't leave; he's the host who should never have come. . . . Clearly he should be the head writer of the show, not the star.

Tom Shales, *The Washington Post,* September 15, 1993

Conan O'Brien, 33-year-old host of NBC's "Late Night," has gone through one of the most amazing transformations in television history. Rarely if ever has such a shiny silk purse been made of such a humble sow's ear. . . . Modest, wry, self-effacing and demonstrably the most intelligent of the late-night comics . . .

Tom Shales, *The Washington Post,* June 18, 1996

When Conan O'Brien replaced David Letterman as the host of NBC's *Late Night,* I was among the many skeptics who felt he didn't belong in front of the camera, despite the comedic gifts he had shown as a writer for *Saturday Night Live* and *The Simpsons.* Tom Shales wasn't the only one to change his mind about that. My husband was the first person to tell me he thought O'Brien was very, very funny. Unlike me, Francis stays up late almost every night, so he was in a position to know. Watching *Late Night* soon became one of the things I looked forward to about having a day off from work. I mean, how could I—of all people—resist the bit about the "emergency guest"? This was a tuxedo-clad mannequin in a big glass box with a sign that read, "Break in Case of Emergency"—i.e., when one of that night's big-name guests canceled at the last minute. The emergency guest was even programmed to say everything the scheduled guest might have: "I'm really excited about this movie," "Please don't talk to me about my relationship with Cher—that's strictly personal," and "If we don't do something, who will?"

I recorded my first interview with O'Brien in 1996, after public opinion about his show began to change in his favor. My second interview with him was in 2003, just before his prime-time tenth anniversary special. What follows combines questions from both of these interviews.

TERRY GROSS: **Congratulations on your tenth anniversary. Are you usually confident or insecure when you're facing a big event like your special?**

CONAN O'BRIEN: Here's my formula. I like to be extremely insecure, and then that insecurity drives me to work very hard and worry a lot. That's the formula I've used for everything that I've done in show business. Anxiety works for me when it spurs me to work and think hard. This is a terrible person to quote, but I'm gonna do it anyway. Someone told me that Charles Manson once said—

TG: **We get all of our self-help adages from Charles Manson.**

O'BRIEN: Yeah. Charles Manson once said about comedy—no, he once said, "Fear is a good thing because it makes you hyperaware." And I thought, "Well, that's interesting," because I found that anxiety and fear, to a certain degree, actually help you prepare and focus and help the creativity. The problem is that if it gets out of control, suddenly you're nervous, you freeze up, and you don't do your best work.

TG: **When you started doing *Late Night,* you didn't have a lot of experience as the person onstage at the microphone. Did you have any sense of how you would look on TV?**

O'BRIEN: No, but I did have a sense of how I would be in front of an audience, because for years, starting in 1985, I had been working on-stage as an improvisational performer, doing sketch comedy in front of audiences. At the time when I started on *Late Night,* it made a much more dramatic story to say, "This guy's a writer; he's never been a performer. In fact, he doesn't want to be a performer; he's being forced to do this by the government." It made the whole story much more compelling.

But the truth is I knew what I would be like in front of an audience. I knew that if we had a live studio audience, I could come alive in front of people. I'd always been that way. As to what I would look like on TV, I really didn't have that great a sense.

TG: **When the show was first on the air, did you watch yourself every night to get an idea of what was working and what wasn't?**

O'BRIEN: Yeah, yeah, I did. Once I got over the shock at just how fat my Irish head is, I started to make adjustments, a lot of them visual. Okay, the lighting's all wrong. I'm wearing too much makeup—I look orange. I'm a big rockabilly fan so I got into the habit of combing my hair up and out, like Eddie Cochran. For the first six months of the show, I had this giant pompadour that was knocking klieg lights out in the studio. It was frightening viewers, so I combed my hair down a bit.

TG: **When you were writing for *Saturday Night Live,* did you ever think, "I should be in front of the camera. I'm at least as good as these guys I'm writing for"?**

O'BRIEN: First of all, I was writing for people like Dana Carvey and Jon Lovitz. And they're just much better sketch players than I am. I don't have nearly the range they have as performers. So I didn't think I could do better than them. I'm not really an actor. I'm not really a stand-up. I'm not really a sketch player. What am I? I know that I'm kind of funny when I am just myself. And I know that I like to inter-act with people. Basically, I ended up getting the one job that I'm qualified to do, which is a little bit of everything.

TG: **I imagine when you started to do the show, you had to create a TV version of Conan O'Brien. Would you talk about the process of figuring out who you would be?**

O'BRIEN: A lot of the good stuff, if we want to qualify any of it as good stuff, is unconscious. These silly, weird abstract things that I do on the show, like pretending to pull my hips with string or licking my eyebrows or growling, it's stuff that I was probably doing on a playground when I was eight years old. It just comes out of me. If I have any persona on the show, it would be the guy who has mistakenly been given a late-night talk show, but he's going to do it anyway. I mean, I don't come out in an appropriate authoritative way. I jump around, I hiss at the camera, I hide from the camera, I start weeping openly. I do all these things that a talk-show host probably shouldn't do, and for some reason that seems to work for me.

TG: **You said you were probably doing a lot of the things that you do now back in your playground days, but I doubt you were rubbing your nipples then.**

O'BRIEN: Yeah, I don't think I had nipples then. They were added later. It's a surgery you can get in Sweden. But I was doing the Bob Hope growl very, very early.

TG: **This is the growl at attractive women.**

O'BRIEN: Exactly. I was doing that to girls when I was eight years old because I saw Woody Allen do it in one of his movies and later saw Bob Hope do it. I thought, "That's the funniest thing I've ever seen." I was playing the part of the bungling Lothario when I was ten years old. Any comedian, whether they know they're going to be a comedian or not, they're working on their act from the minute they're conscious.

TG: **So you knew as a kid that you weren't the leading man, you were the comic lead?**

O'BRIEN: Well, this isn't a moral choice or anything—but since I was five years old, my sense of humor has been to make fun of myself or to find myself absurd.

I think everybody subconsciously figures out very early how they fit into the puzzle. When I was very young, I think I said to myself, "Okay, what do I have and how do I fit into this? What's different about me?" I come from a big family, I'm one of six. I figured out that I could make people laugh.

TG: **Did watching Woody Allen movies lead you to Bob Hope movies?**

O'BRIEN: Yeah, it's funny, because my discovery of Bob Hope was backwards. For a lot of people in my generation, he's that guy wearing a blue blazer who's telling corny jokes in late-seventies TV specials. It was only much later that I discovered him in movies with Bing Crosby and saw that he had created this prototype character that a lot of people have borrowed from—the confident, cowardly guy on the make who will betray his best friend to get what he wants.

That was a comedic persona that always appealed to me. It tapped into my idea of who I was, which is: I'm the person who's going to growl at the actresses on my show and hiss at them; or if Harrison Ford's on, I'm going to have a mock bravado with him that completely collapses the minute he gives me one of those cold stares. It's a comedy dynamic that's old and tried-and-true, but in a talk-show format, it's a little different.

TG: **As a teenager, did you behave around girls the way you do around the attractive actresses on your show, growling at them and playing "the comic guy"?**

O'BRIEN: Sadly, yes, and I'm being serious about that because if you grew up the way I did—a fairly repressed Irish-Catholic—you're too scared to try anything. You're fascinated by women, you want to make them laugh, so there's the whole bag of tricks you do—but God forbid any of them ever made a move towards you. Then you'd run for the hills. That's where the whole persona came from. You always had that idea with Bob Hope that if he ever got Dorothy Lamour, he wouldn't know what the hell to do with her. He'd be panic-stricken.

TG: How much did the Irish-Catholic background figure into your identity? How repressed were you?

O'BRIEN: This is turning into a therapy session. I'm going to get a bill from NPR. The repression's there, it's real. It fuels the depression and the self-hate. It's a wonderful Rube Goldberg device. The depression drops down onto the self-hate, which triggers the self-loathing, which then fuels the anger, which curdles into comedy, and then it sadly leads to a slow, quiet drinking problem. It all fits. It's like a Swiss watch the way it interrelates. No, there's an element of truth to everything I say, and then I exaggerate. A little repressed, but I didn't take it too far. I had a good time, if you know what I mean.

[Laughter]

TG: Okay.

O'BRIEN: [Still laughing] I can't stop doing that. I'm sorry.

TG: Well, you have a whole repertoire of weird laughs. I figure some of those laughs must come from having watched a lot of horror movies.

O'BRIEN: Yeah, you know what's funny? I watched everything, and I took from everybody—commercials, jingles, a funny thing I'd see on a Christmas special. If you see something you like, you grab it and throw it into the stew and mix it up. I remember when we first started doing the show, one of the first characters that I did was called the Laughing Genie. I was a genie that laughed way too much—you know, that hands-on-hips Yul Brynner "Ha-ha-ha-ha-ha!" So, yeah, I collect all those things. If I pass a mirror—even if I'm brushing my teeth in the morning—I'm busting stuff out. I'm trying things. I'm always trying to make my wife laugh. It's a sad, never-ending cry for help. If there are any listeners out there who can, please help me. Someone, help me.

TG: You took tap dance lessons when you were about nine years old, didn't you?

O'BRIEN: That's right. Nobody forced me. That's the sad part. I think the story is much less frightening when you say, "Well, my parents made me." But it's scary to think that a nine-year-old boy says, "Mom, Dad, I want to be a tap dancer." You think, "What is with this kid?"

TG: **I find it really endearing that a nine-year-old would want to learn a form that's become pretty archaic.**

O'BRIEN: I knew when I was very young that I wanted to be in show business. My view of show business was based on the movies that they ran on Channel 56, which was the UHF station in Boston when I was growing up. They used to show movies from the forties, like *Yankee Doodle Dandy* and *On the Town*. As this little kid, I didn't have a sense of "Well, this movie was made a long time ago." I didn't know. I'm still, to this day, not that bright.

But I would watch these movies like *Yankee Doodle Dandy* with Jimmy Cagney, and he's singing and tap-dancing. I thought if you want to be in show business, you've got to be able to tell a joke, put a song across, but most importantly, you have to be able to break into a ten-minute tap dance at any moment. So I went to my parents and said, "I've got to take tap dancing lessons." They considered that for a few days and said, "All right, he really wants to do it." They hooked me up with a guy named Stanley Brown. He was this older black gentleman who had been the protégé of Bill "Bojangles" Robinson, the great tap dancer who'd been in all those Shirley Temple movies.

I really got hooked up with the master. And remember, I was this nine-year-old, really pale, round-faced kid with bright, bright orange hair. My dad would drop me off on his way to work on Saturday mornings in a part of Boston that's right near the Berklee College of Music. I would walk up this rickety, old ten flights of steps into his dance studio. And it would be all twenty-four-year-old black men and women, and then one orange-haired, freckled kid sitting there, holding his shoes in a box.

I did that for a number of years until Stanley Brown passed away. Then I got this huge growth spurt. I grew to six foot four in a day. It was like I was irradiated or something. I lost all my coordination, and tap dancing fell by the wayside.

TG: **Did you have a nice sense of rhythm when you were nine?**

O'BRIEN: Since we're on radio, I'll just say, yes, I did. And by the way, I'm extremely handsome right now, for those of you who can't see me.

TG: **You mocked your concept of show business on a *Late Night* parody of the Jerry Lewis Telethon, in which you appear as a telethon guest.**

O'BRIEN: Yeah, yeah. We took footage of Jerry Lewis introducing an act on his telethon, and then dropped my voice in, so that it looks like Jerry Lewis is introducing a wonderful new talent, Conan O'Brien. Then you cut to me, and we match the studio so it looks like I'm right there. I'm wearing a gold tuxedo jacket and a sparkling bow tie—and the band kicks into "Consider Yourself" from *Oliver!*. I go into this really over-the-top version of it, and we cut to actual footage of Jerry Lewis wincing. Then we cut to the board with all the tallies for the telethon donations plummeting.

TG: **When you were nine, did you think that you'd actually be on the telethon in a gaudy suit singing "Consider Yourself"? Was that your idea of what your future would be as an entertainer?**

O'BRIEN: Yeah, I used to host a television show in front of the mirror on the first floor of our house. That mirror is still there. I would stand in front of the mirror and say, "Ladies and gentlemen, welcome to the program. Good to have you here." And I would invite guests on. It was always my brother and my sister. They were actually very good shows. We got top guests back then in front of the mirror. We had Tom Cruise on when he was eight.

TG: **Did you sing on your show?**

O'BRIEN: Again, I had this very corny, antiquated idea of what show business is. You can see there's an element of that on the *Late Night* show. There is a lot of singing and performing and puppets—elements that really are from a bygone era.

TG: **Looking back, after ten years of doing *Late Night* has your style of doing the opening monologue changed?**

O'BRIEN: When we first started doing the show, I was trying so hard to do the monologue correctly and do a good job and be a professional. What's funny is that at a certain point, I gave up. I think that's when the monologue became compelling and original. The monologue relies on good jokes, and I have very good monologue writers who do a really good job.

But where I really come to life is when a joke completely misses. Other late-night shows have music play in between the jokes to fill it out if a joke misses completely. I always told the band, "Never play anything in between the jokes," because there's nothing funnier than a comedian saying something and then there's absolute silence—especially with me because I've built up this persona over time. The best monologues are when people see me backed into a corner, and I have to fight my way out. The most important thing to do is acknowledge that it didn't work. Don't pretend it worked and keep moving, because that's where you alienate people.

TG: **There's a lot of "ripped from the headlines" humor in your monologue. Do you read the newspaper every day?**

O'BRIEN: Yeah. I read *The New York Times*, because that's what gets delivered. And then I'll flip through, you know—

TG: **I like the way you're not taking responsibility for the fact you're reading the *Times*. You're reading it only because it's delivered.**

O'BRIEN: Yeah, it's delivered. I've asked them not to bring it. No, that's the one I get at the house, and so that's the one I read most thoroughly. And then I'll read *USA Today*, because they have the colored pie charts, and that really breaks it down nicely for me.

Of all the late-night shows, I think ours is probably the least topical of all of them. It's the most abstract. We do a lot of comedy that's just about people in bear suits and with puppets. We've created a little wonderland of characters and oddballs, and it's almost like a *Pee-Wee's Playhouse*. I often think we're more like a children's show than a late-night topical talk show.

TG: Well, let's talk about the most famous character that's come out of the show, which is the puppet Triumph, the Insult Comic Dog. Triumph was created by Robert Smigel, the original head writer of the show, who also does the voice for Triumph. At the MTV Video Awards last year, Triumph had a big fight with Eminem. Did Smigel tell you that he was going to take Triumph into the audience, where Eminem was sitting, and insult him? And did you say, "No! Eminem's going to fight you. It's going to be dangerous?"

O'BRIEN: I knew that Robert was going to do it. Most people react pretty well to Triumph. Triumph became so popular that we started getting celebrities requesting Triumph. Jon Bon Jovi called up and asked, "Please, can Triumph come over and insult me?" It was a high honor. Eminem was the first person to get angry at the puppet, which I love saying. I love that someone can get angry at a puppet.

TG: I figured he'd never seen your show, didn't know who Triumph was, and had no idea what was going on.

O'BRIEN: I have no clue. It's possible he thought he was being attacked by a man with a rubber dog on his fist. I love that his bodyguards intervened. That was the best part. It's a good thing that he had three bodyguards on hand to protect him from the rubber dog.

TG: Would you talk about the evolution of Triumph on your show?

O'BRIEN: The best that I can remember is that we used to do a recurring routine on the show about talented animals from the Westminster dog show. We would say, "You know, some of these animals are really talented, and we actually have some of them here in the studio," and cut to a little puppet theater, where these little dog and cat puppets would do silly little tricks like spinning a plate on a stick or doing card tricks. People seemed to like it. There was the idea to do an animal comedian. So Robert said, "Well, what if he was an insult comic?" Robert started playing around with that, and right away, it was very funny.

My favorite part about Triumph is that he has the voice of a Ukrainian woman. I have no idea why, but apparently, this is an immigrant who made her way to the Borscht Belt. When we started, Triumph just insulted me. Then we thought, "Let's bring Triumph back and have him insult celebrities sitting next to me." So after I was done interviewing them, I'd say, "Would you like to meet Triumph, the Insult Comic Dog?" And Triumph would start yelling at William Shatner, "Look at you, Shatner. What has happened to you? You're a fat pig, Shatner." We realized, "Okay, this is working really well. People really love this."

We sent Triumph to an actual Westminster dog show, where he attacked different dogs and started humping real dogs, and we got one of the dogs to hump him. We got thrown out. Those are not people with a sense of humor, so men in bow ties, who later ended up working for Eminem, converged on Triumph and threw him out. We snuck back in with fake credentials the next year and got thrown out again after shooting a remote.

There was a period of time where people thought, "Well, Triumph has run its course. It's not going to be that funny again." One of our writers noticed that there was a long line of fans all dressed as the *Star Wars* characters, waiting to get into the premiere of *Star Wars*. Someone had the idea, "Let's send Triumph there." So we sent Triumph with some of our writers, and everybody wrote lines. I am not an arrogant person, but I do think Triumph in line, attacking different *Star Wars* fans, is probably the funniest ten minutes of television that's been on the air in the last five, eight years. The reaction was amazing. And Triumph is just talking to a man dressed as Darth Vader.

TG: **What did he say?**

O'BRIEN: The guy as Darth Vader is explaining which buttons do what, like, "This button is my transporter." And Triumph says, "Yes, yes, and which button do you press to call your mother to come pick you up?"

TG: **You have guests on the show each night. And we have guests on our show all the time, of course. When we don't know much** about somebody who we're thinking of having on the show, one of the producers will often call them up and pre-interview them. We almost feel guilty about it, like we're auditioning them for the show. But we always say to ourselves, "Well, I bet the *Today* show does that and more. I bet David Letterman and Conan O'Brien do, too." How do you screen the guests you don't already know?

O'BRIEN: Well, we do have segment producers who talk to them on the phone. Some people think, "Well, but that's cheating, because shouldn't it just be a real conversation?" I believe that there's a happy medium. I don't believe in trying to turn people who aren't necessarily raconteurs or funny people into comedians. So I'm uncomfortable having people tell a prepared whopper of a story with a big punch line at the end, because a lot of people can't do that very well. You've seen people try, and I think it's painful, so what we like to do is have areas that seem promising. When you do a television or radio show, it should be a slightly heightened reality. It shouldn't just be the conversation that I would have with somebody if I bumped into him on the subway and we were going to ride forty blocks together. It should be better than that.

TG: I love your description about how the conversation you have on TV should be a heightened reality. It should be better than the conversation you'd have on the train with someone. But when you run into somebody on the train, do they expect that you're going to have that kind of heightened conversation that they're used to hearing on TV?

O'BRIEN: Well, first of all, let's get something straight: I will not ride the subway.

TG: I knew, as I was saying that, that you probably don't ride the subway.

O'BRIEN: It's ridiculous. I've had a strap handle put in my limo so I can have that subway experience, but in the comfort of a limousine. I don't even know—subways, are they steam-powered still? I don't remember. It's been so long.

Back to the misconceptions that people have about me: One is that for some reason, people think I'm not very big. Whenever I go anywhere, all I hear is, "Oh my God. I can't believe you're this tall. You don't look this tall on TV. Why do you look so small on TV?" And the other thing is that I'm so up. On television, I'm a cartoon character. I've got the big hair and the big grin. I jump around a lot. I'm kind of like this hyperactive Bob's Big Boy character. So when I'm walking down the street, people will ask me, "What's wrong? Are you okay? You seem sad." And I'm not sad. I'm just neutral.

TG: **Yes, yes, yes.**

O'BRIEN: My mouth is a straight line. There's no downward curve whatsoever. It's an exact straight carpenter's line, because I'm thinking. I'm wondering what I'm going to have for lunch, or where I'm going to take my dog for a walk, or where my wife and I are going to go on vacation. But when people know me from the television show, neutrality reads as depression.

TG: **So it's not so much the conversation, it's how you look that gets people.**

O'BRIEN: Yeah, it's funny, because I actually make an effort when I'm talking to someone, especially if they're laughing. I think that probably reveals how needy I am. If it's three o'clock in the morning and my car breaks down, and someone from AAA comes on a country road to fix it, and I say something and the person laughs, I start working it a little bit. I want to get that second laugh and that third laugh. It's the AAA guy, and he doesn't need to hear this, but it's hard to turn that off. I'm always killing with, like, Chinese food delivery guys.

TG: **You're married now, and I believe you're expecting a baby? Do you feel ready to be a father?**

O'BRIEN: I don't think you're ever ready. I'll report back, though, because the idea that I, along with my wife, will be responsible for a human life is very intense and crazy.

TG: **The interesting thing is that, let's face it, you got married just to prove you're not gay.**

O'BRIEN: That was my manager's idea. He said, "We've got to prove you're not gay." So we tried marriage, and that didn't work apparently. Then we decided, "Okay, now we got to crank it up, and we got to have the baby." So a baby was purchased and will be, quote, "born" on the fifteenth, 'cause I ain't having sex. That freaks me out.

TG: **How did you end up doing jokes on your show about not really being gay?**

O'BRIEN: It just seemed so absurd. There are a lot of people who are uncomfortable with the idea of someone even implying for a second that they might be gay. I'm not uncomfortable about it at all. It sort of fed into my insecure, bumbling guy who's constantly trying to convince the ladies that he's got it going on. Every now and then, in the monologue, there'll be a huge news story that's going on that day, and I'll say, "Of course, folks, you all heard the big news." Then I'll just pause and say, "I'm straight." For whatever reason, people just laugh. But who knows? It's going to be years before I really know what my sexuality is. Ultimately, it's not important. We're all people.

October 30, 1996, and September 8, 2003

NOTHING ELSE
WOULD MATTER

Eric Clapton

CLAPTON IS GOD

Graffiti said to have first been spotted on the walls
of a London tube station in 1965

Eric Clapton was one of the first of the British rock 'n' roll "guitar heroes." In common with Mick Jagger and Keith Richards, he was an avid collector of American blues records, and you can hear him dealing with this influence—absorbing it and gradually finding his own identity—in his work with the Yardbirds, Cream, Blind Faith, Derek and the Dominos, and under his own name. When I spoke with Clapton in 1989, a good deal of the interview was devoted to a discussion of these formative influences. Two years later, Clapton experienced tragedy—his five-year-old son, Conor, fell to his death from the window of a New York high-rise apartment building. "Tears in Heaven," which Clapton wrote in memory of his son, won a Grammy as Record of the Year for 1992.

TERRY GROSS: You've said that your music is inspired by the black blues performers you heard when you were a boy living in England. How did you discover their music?

ERIC CLAPTON: I heard a couple of records on the radio by blues musicians from America, when I was a little boy of about nine years old. One was quite popular in England. It was called "Whooping and Hollering" by Sonny Terry and [Sticks] McGhee, and was an instrumental thing with harmonica and guitar—fast country blues. I also heard Big Bill Broonzy. He was a fantastic guitar player and a great folk artist who was quite popular in Europe during the fifties and early sixties. I was immensely attracted to the sound and the spirit of the music. I decided to examine it and became a blues collector, buying export records. I got into people like Muddy Waters and Robert Johnson, and all of the country blues players. That's really where I got all my influences.

TG: Did you teach yourself guitar?

CLAPTON: Yes. There was no one else interested in the kind of thing that I was interested in. It was quite lonely, but I loved that music and wanted to play it.

TG: What were some of the greatest frustrations of being self-taught?

CLAPTON: Not knowing, for instance, when I picked up a six-string guitar, how to tune it. In a quite arrogant way, I refused to buy those "teach yourself how to play basic guitar" books. So I had to learn how to tune the guitar on my own. Then, the next step was to put your fingers on different frets and try to make a chord. I preferred to do it on my own, because I felt like I was discovering it all. I was under the impression I was inventing all this stuff, you see. In actual fact, it had all been done before.

TG: As a white Englishman, you were learning the blues far removed from the lives of the bluesmen whose music you were emulating. Was there an element of romance in your mind about a blues musician's life?

CLAPTON: Yes, it was incredibly romantic. I could identify with some aspects in that I came from a very poor, country background. Except it wasn't a racial situation. But we were very poor and I can imagine it would be similar to somewhere in Mississippi. At a very early age, I dreamt of myself as being this lonesome blues singer.

TG: **Do you remember the first time you actually performed with a black blues musician?**

CLAPTON: It would have been Sonny Boy Williamson. I was eighteen, and in a professional band called the Yardbirds. Sonny Boy had just done a tour with a country blues festival through Europe. He decided that he would like to stay in England and make some money. It was possible then for a blues performer like Sonny Boy to make an incredible amount of money in Europe—more than he could dream of making in America. I met him and was scared of him. He was a very, very frightening man. I mean, a nice man, but he had an attitude he could adopt that was quite terrifying. Apart from that, musically, he was so inspiring. It was the first taste I had of the real thing.

TG: **What was your reaction to it?**

CLAPTON: My reaction was very mixed. First of all, I was very possessive about the blues. Around that time in my life, I tended to think that I owned the blues. To meet someone who was "real" doing it made me feel a little bit ashamed, a little bit resentful about the whole situation. At the same time, it was all mixed up with overawe. It was a bewildering experience.

TG: **When you use the phrase "playing with someone who was real," it makes me think that you thought of yourself as "not real."**

CLAPTON: Well, it was a bit of a phony situation. I was English. I was white. I was dedicated to playing the blues, or what I thought were the blues. But it was all an unreal situation—derived from records that I'd bought or listening to the radio—and quite contrived, really. I deliberately was trying to live what I assumed would be a bluesman's lifestyle. You know, bumming around with a guitar on my shoulder.

To meet the real thing—to see Sonny Boy—blew a lot of the myth away because he was incredibly interested in money and women. I set myself up to think that a bluesman was far, far above these kinds of earthly pursuits. I thought a bluesman would be dedicated to his music and nothing else would matter. It really wasn't like that at all. It was all flashy suits and fast cars. And it shook me up.

TG: So how did it change you?

CLAPTON: Well, I started to adopt those attitudes myself. Musically, it meant that I had to get my act together.

TG: Early in your career, you were with the Yardbirds, playing a mix of blues and pop. You left shortly after the band had a big hit with "For Your Love." My understanding is that you quit the band because you thought that song was too pop, and the group was getting too commercial, moving away from an emphasis on the blues. I wonder what you think listening back to that record now. I mean, I think it's a really good record, whether it's blues or not.

CLAPTON: I think it's a good record. If I hadn't been part of the band, I probably would have liked it then, too. But at the time, it seemed a huge threat to me.

TG: Because it was taking you away from what you wanted to do?

CLAPTON: It was kind of like going out with a girl and then finding out that she likes Sly Stallone when you like Robert De Niro. Do you know what I mean? Your tastes suddenly start to diverge. It was heartbreaking, and one of the first real big disappointments in my life, because at first the band was very unified in our likes and dislikes. Then I noticed that they became more interested in what Freddie and the Dreamers were wearing onstage, and things like that. It really floored me. For a while after I left that band, I considered packing it all in because I didn't think anyone else cared about music the way I did.

TG: After you left the Yardbirds, you joined the Bluesbreakers with John Mayall, and then you formed Cream with Jack Bruce and Ginger Baker. You said that you liked Jack Bruce's irreverence; you liked him for not trying to be an authentic bluesman.

CLAPTON: Yeah. He was a musical rebel. He came from a jazz background. He was one of the first fusion players I'd ever met who was willing to cross jazz into blues and rock 'n' roll. He didn't see a musical boundary. He was deeply into classical music and modern classical music. For quite a while, I was under Jack's spell because he seemed to have the most unique and avant-garde attitude towards music.

TG: What did Cream bring out in your playing that you hadn't expressed before?

CLAPTON: Freedom. I was constantly urged by Jack and Ginger to throw off all the inhibitions I'd spent years honing with the Bluesbreakers. When we played live, we would simply improvise, and it would be very hard for me to get rid of my ideas of framework and structure.

TG: What was it like for you to learn to take sustained solos in concerts? Were you used to doing that before Cream?

CLAPTON: Yes. John Mayall would encourage me to play as long as I liked, but I had a much more controlled idea about what it should be then. With Cream, it came out of a very basic kind of necessity. With the first gig we ever played at a big jazz festival in England, we ran out of material after about an hour. The crowd wanted more, and they weren't going to give up. So we literally had to jam. That became the most popular part of our act. We would just play off the top of our heads. And it worked. A lot of the time, it really worked.

TG: I'm wondering if there were times at concerts when everyone in the band was really high, and nearly everybody in the audience was really high, and it would lead to this almost self-indulgent faith in solos. Did you ever feel that way?

CLAPTON: Yeah. I can remember playing at the Fillmore West many times when it was just like being in someone's front room with everyone smashed out of their brains listening to the stereo.

TG: Was that a good feeling or an alienating feeling?

CLAPTON: Well, I'm not going to pretend it was anything but great. I think it was fantastic.

TG: A couple of years ago, you did an interview with Robert Palmer. You told him that Jon Landau had written a review of a Cream concert and gave it a really bad review. You said that when you read that review, the ring of truth literally knocked you backwards. Why did that review have such a profound effect on you?

CLAPTON: It was tied in with an in-depth interview I had done in Sausalito. If my memory serves me right, I had been flying high, and we'd been playing the Fillmore West stoned and thought we were God's gift to music. I was blathering on about all this. On the next page was this review, and I was summed up as being the master of the cliché. Juxtaposed with this interview, the effect was astonishing. I remember reading the article in a restaurant. I was with some friends in Boston, and I read the whole thing in silence. I stood up to go to the loo and passed out. I was carried out of the restaurant and put in someone's house, and woke up thinking, "What the hell is going on?" and immediately thought, "I've got to get out of this. I've been playing this awful musical game for too long, and I've got to leave that band and plan a new life." It had a devastating effect on me.

TG: Was it because you were embarrassed, insulted, or because you felt that you needed to be moving in a new musical direction?

CLAPTON: I was ashamed because inside I had known for quite a while that we were selling the audiences short. We were going onstage stoned. We were playing meaningless, endless solos. And people were swallowing it.

TG: Did you leave Cream because of that?

CLAPTON: Yes, I did. We talked to the manager about it, and he decided we should do one farewell tour and make a farewell album. Funnily enough, we suddenly became much closer. During our farewell concert at the Albert Hall, there was a great deal of regret and nostalgia on my part. I wasn't sure if I was doing the right thing.

TG: Looking back, what do you think?

CLAPTON: Yes. I think I had a lot of other things to do that I couldn't have done if I'd stayed with that band.

TG: After that you went on to form Blind Faith with Steve Winwood, but eventually you took a hiatus from music and spent a couple of years doing a lot of drugs.

CLAPTON: Yeah. Basically doing a lot of drugs. I've always had a leaning toward addictions, an obsessive personality, to say the least. Even when I was sixteen, everyone was taking amphetamines or drinking wine. During the early seventies, I got as close to killing myself with drugs as I could get. For some people, it escalates very quickly. For me, it took a long time. But I got there. I danced with death for a while. I regret it, that's for sure.

TG: Did you have a bottoming-out moment where you figured, "This is it; I've got to change"?

CLAPTON: At some point, I remember seeing myself sitting in my car at dawn, totally naked, trying to start it. I was trying to escape from my own house, where these people were trying to look after me. Thank God, one of the guys had taken out the rotor of the engine. I don't know where I was going to go. But I had a flash that things had gone too far. That was when I decided to start doing something about it.

TG: What did you do?

CLAPTON: I went to an acupuncturist in London who used a fairly revolutionary form of treatment. She passed a small electric current from one ear to the other, and it induced a mild natural narcosis that took away the withdrawal symptoms you get when you stop taking heroin. I'd never taken heroin intravenously, so it wasn't that hard a habit for me to kick.

TG: Did you ever think that an addiction and obsession with drugs is related to the same kind of obsession that allows you to spend as many hours as you must in developing your guitar playing?

CLAPTON: Absolutely. One is a natural kind of dedication, and the other one is a very unnatural dedication. I like to think of my love for guitar playing as being dedicated. But it's not far removed from being obsessive.

TG: You've said that your mother wasn't married when you were born. She left when you were a baby, and your grandparents brought you up. They told you they were your parents. At first, when your mother returned, you were told that she was your sister. What effect do you think all this had on your public identity?

CLAPTON: It's very complicated, isn't it? As a result of that upbringing, I think there's a side of me that dreads rejection, dreads abandonment. And there's another side that loves solitude.

TG: Is your mother still alive?

CLAPTON: Yes, she is. And we're great pals. We're more like brother and sister than anything else. When I was born, she was only fifteen. It's difficult to say what kind of family members we are.

TG: You said that at some point in your career you got bored with virtuoso musicianship. What was the turning point for you?

CLAPTON: Well, that might have been a glib way for me to say that I couldn't get it any better. I had actually reached the end of my capabilities. A lot of people were taking it further on. I suppose I had to develop some kind of attitude about it. It was probably a way of saving face to say that I was getting bored. I realized that technically my potential had come to its end. I'm not that nimble, really. I don't think

I can compete in the fast, furious guitar championships. So I tended to go the other way.

TG: By going the other way, you mean singing more?

CLAPTON: Yeah. Singing more, or refining my technique to simplify it, and get more out of it—with doing less.

December 7, 1989

A Large
Feminine Side

Steven Tyler and Joe Perry

After thirty years of big rock, hard drugs, wasted fortunes and
seesaw chart rides, singer Steven Tyler, guitarists Joe Perry and
Brad Whitford, bassist Tom Hamilton and drummer Joey
Kramer should either be dead or babbling incoherently.
Instead, Aerosmith are our most treasured and reliable warrior
clowns . . .

David Fricke, *Rolling Stone*, April 12, 2002

Hard rock and heavy metal bands rarely do shows like *Fresh Air,* because public radio just isn't on their map. But when Aerosmith's book, *Walk This Way,* was published in 1997, the group's lead singer and lyricist, Steven Tyler, and its guitarist and songwriter, Joe Perry, made themselves available for an interview—and I just couldn't resist. I had so much fun talking with them that five years later I thought talking with Gene Simmons of Kiss might be fun, too (it wasn't, and yet somehow it was).

TERRY GROSS: I know you feel that your music has been given short shrift compared to the attention that's been paid to the image of the band. I'll take that as my cue to talk about the image of the band.

Steven, as the lead singer, you're the visual focus of the group, so it's important for you to have an onstage style. This is particularly true in the era of the stadium concert, which is your era. Tell me a little bit about creating your stage persona.

STEVEN TYLER: It kind of created itself. I couldn't just stand there when Joe and the guys were playing. It made me want to dance. I started out as a drummer, so I had some sense of beat and time. I used to have a tambourine before I had my scarves and my microphone stand and all that.

TG: **How sixties.**

TYLER: Yeah, really—and a fur vest. One thing led to another. I remember being down in the East Village, and buying a couple of scarves and hanging them on the mike stand.

I like to dance, I like flowy things, and I like to look like a peacock and strut around. It goes hand in hand with our style of music.

TG: **Another part of your visual style has been the open shirt, the bare chest. I find it an interesting paradox that your image and the band's image is a mix of the real macho and something that would be considered very female. Like the scarves, flowing garments, tight-fitting satin pants.**

TYLER: It's my Russian roots. In today's "men are from Mars and women are from Venus" way of talking, I've got a large feminine side which I pay homage to. I love my sensory perception. I love my feeling and my passion so much that I call it life itself. My ability at songwriting is as natural as a woman's ability to give birth. It goes hand in hand, and it's all just grown from that.

TG: **I'll just point out women can write songs, too. But we'll let that go.**

TYLER: And don't they all.

TG: **So did you wear makeup onstage, too? Lipstick?**

TYLER: It's interesting, you go right to lipstick. No, I'm more a rouge man. My lips are big enough already. I don't need any more accentuation there.

TG: **Do you accentuate the cheekbones?**

TYLER: No, I go to town on my eyes. I used to paint a tear on. I like to have fun up there.

JOE PERRY: In that whole era in the late sixties and early seventies, the androgyny thing was really big with the English bands, too.

TG: **True.**

PERRY: Everybody from the Stones on down was trespassing on that weird ground.

TG: **Well, since your image and the music itself were so sexualized, and since it was mostly men in the audience early on, do you think there was a homoerotic thing going on there? Or that men wanted to *be* you?**

TYLER: I don't know. I never took it that far in thinkology. I just always thought that in rock 'n' roll, when you love something, you don't question why others do, too. It's got its roots in the whole blues thing. A lot of the posturing and chest puffing that the hard rockers do—the roots are directly in blues. If you listen to the lyrics in blues, it's all "I'm a man" and "I'm going to Chicago to find my woman," and all that stuff.

The roots are very close. It's still about guys getting onstage and blowing a lot of hot air.

TG: **In some ways, Aerosmith led the way in rock 'n' roll excess with sex and drugs. The band helped create, forgive me for saying this, some of the most unappealing images of rock stars as satyrs—as spoiled, selfish, excessive, destructive, sexist.**

I wonder if you've reflected on your contribution to that image of rock 'n' roll? It's an image that a lot of bands reacted against. Punk rock reacted against that. Roots rock and garage bands reacted against that.

PERRY: I don't know. I see a lot of those guys doing the same things now.

TG: **Do you?**

PERRY: I mean, Sid Vicious lived it to the end, right? You're right, there was some rebellion against our style of rock 'n' roll, but we came out of it, and we're still here swinging.

The thing is, in that era, we were standing toe-to-toe with a lot of bands doing the same thing. Like Zeppelin. A lot of the stuff that we did, we learned early on from the English bands. Who was it— Mott the Hoople—smashing things and putting everything in the hotel room through the TV? It was quite a feat. Plus it takes up time. It gets pretty boring in those hotel rooms.

TG: **Doesn't that kind of behavior disgust you?**

PERRY: Well, we don't do it anymore. It's pretty juvenile. Back then, it was fun to do.

TYLER: That sense of "How bad can you be?" is thrilling.

PERRY: And to get away with it. You get in the car and go, and the road manager's stuck paying for it.

TYLER: It's something that people go through in life. Most children do—there's that rebellious young age of six to nine. But when you're doing drugs, it keeps it going.

Doing a lot of cocaine, some people say, is God's way of telling you you have too much money, especially when you're a rock 'n' roller. The money's coming in, and the women are there, you're out on the road, people are screaming, you're going from town to town, and everything becomes a big blur. We did it to the max. My role model was Keith Richards. Early on, I would go see him. I remember once I gave him my Walther PPK for his birthday and a tab of methadone. It was kind of like going to the Wailing Wall and paying homage to my god.

I never want to blame him for what I went through with my drugs. However, I lived the same lifestyle he did, and I can't say "unfortunately" got caught up in it, because I wouldn't trade those years for anything.

TG: One of the drugs you did was heroin. Heroin is the kind of drug that doesn't exactly enhance the sex drive. I know that you both had very hearty sexual appetites and fulfilled them every chance you could on the road. But I'm wondering how you can do heroin and have a really active sex life?

TYLER: I wasn't as promiscuous as most people would think. The vision of me gallivanting around the country, raping and pillaging everybody's daughter—it wasn't that. When you do the kind of drugs that I did, you really stay to yourself. You live in a bathroom. You live in your hotel room with the curtains drawn. When I got sober, I realized how much sex I had missed while I was actively using in my drug addiction. As far as heroin goes, it also afforded me to be able to sleep a lot, and heroin also keeps a lot of water in your flesh; that's the upside. The downside is that it will kill you in the end. Heroin makes you feel so good.

September 10, 1997

TOO MUCH FOR
YOU TO TAKE

Gene Simmons

CRACKPOT OF THE YEAR—MALE: *Kiss bassist and memoirist Gene Simmons, who returned NPR host Terry Gross' salutation with "I'm afraid you're also going to have to welcome me with open legs."*
Entertainment Weekly, December 20/27, 2002

GENE SIMMONS STORMS NPR
Does he kiss groupies with that mouth?
"The Ten Biggest Disappointments of the Year," *Rolling Stone Rock and Roll Yearbook 2002*

"Asked about codpiece."
Caption under photo of Terry Gross, *New York Post,* February 6, 2002

Honestly, I thought it might be fun to talk about the Kiss phenomenon of the 1970s with the group's bass player, Gene Simmons. You'd think that a man who dresses for the stage in breastplate and codpiece, paints his face white with black bat wings around the eyes, and wags a superlong tongue (meant to suggest the great size of another organ, needless to say) would have a sense of irony about himself—right? Nope. He certainly wasn't kidding when he told me that he wanted Kiss to be not just a rock 'n' roll band but a rock 'n' roll *brand*. The Kiss logo appears on all sorts of products, including condoms and a beer cooler in the shape of a coffin.

This is an excerpt of an interview I recorded with Simmons in 2001, following the publication of his memoir, *Kiss and Make-up*. He begins the book by explaining that he was born Chaim Witz in Israel, in 1949, and became Gene Klein after moving to New York City with his mother at the age of nine (Gene sounded more "American" than Chaim, and Klein was his mother's maiden name). He took the name Gene Simmons on cofounding Kiss in 1972.

TERRY GROSS: **Let's talk about your stage makeup. Do you like having your face covered up onstage? Does it make you feel any less vulnerable or any less like Gene Simmons, or Gene Klein, or Chaim Witz, your birth name?**

GENE SIMMONS: Close, but no guitars. It's [pronounced] Chaim *Vitz*.

TG: **Oh, thanks. Okay.**

SIMMONS: You said it. Well, the name came out through a gentile mouth, so it didn't quite have the flavor. It came out bland.

TG: **Well, it's not a gentile mouth.**

SIMMONS: Ooh. Maybe it's a discussion we can have. What was the question about makeup?

TG: **Do you like being covered up by makeup?**

SIMMONS: I don't feel covered up any more or less than any girl feels covered up when she wears makeup. The makeup is simply an extension of a personality. Colors, clothing, makeup, all express something. Getting up onstage was a chance to sort of live out—oh, I don't know—sort of "scream therapy meets a rock 'n' roll band." I wanted to put together the band I never saw onstage. I wanted to be in a band that gave bang for the buck. I wanted to be in the band that didn't look like a bunch of guys who should be in the library studying for their finals. I wanted stars up onstage. Regular people just didn't look big enough. So we wore eight-inch platform heels, put on more makeup and higher heels than your mother, and made more money than your banker. It all kind of works out.

TG: **Did you pattern your makeup on comic book heroes?**

SIMMONS: My makeup came as a result of a lot of things, all things Americana: Godzilla, horror movies, science fiction, Black Bolt from the *Inhumans* Marvel comic book, and science fiction. The rest of the guys in the band had different notions. Paul put on the red lips and the star over his eyes, an exaggeration of what he thought a rock star looked like, because he always wanted to be a rock star. I was never interested in being a rock star. I always wanted to be Boris Karloff. And Ace, who's the spaceman in the group, has delusions of grandeur and perhaps gravity doesn't quite affect him in the same way, which is to say that he doesn't have good equilibrium—which is a big word, come to think of it, just like gymnasium. This is NPR. That's why we are using big words.

TG: **How would you describe the pattern on your face?**

SIMMONS: A banker's pattern. When you look at it, it says, "Boy, that guy's got a lot of money." You know why I'm pulling your leg? Because I can't touch it from where I am. This is a serious kind of—

TG: **We'll get to that a little later.**

SIMMONS: Yeah. I'm not going to play the serious game, because after all, it means very little. I'm in a weird band. We've done very well. The American dream is alive and well. In terms of what it all means, it's sort of academic really. But what you can't argue with is the American notion, which is: "Of the people, for the people, by the people." They vote with money. You and I, we sit here and we just talk and toss the ball around. That doesn't mean a lot.

TG: **Are you trying to say to me that all that matters to you is money?**

SIMMONS: I will contend, and you try to disprove it, that the most important thing as we know it—on this planet and this plane—is, in fact, money. Do you want me to prove it?

TG: Go ahead.

SIMMONS: The first thing you need besides air—which so far is free and by the way, if you went scuba diving, you're paying for air—is food. It's what we need to survive. I don't know what other tool I would use besides money to buy it. Although as a woman, of course, you have the ability to sell your body, then get the money, and then get food. But ultimately money is part of it.

TG: You are weird.

SIMMONS: Really? How do you get food?

TG: Well, not by selling my body. But—

SIMMONS: That's a choice you have that I don't. But getting to the money part, money is the single most important thing on the planet, including the notion that love gives you everything.

TG: Well, let's cut to the chase. How much money do you have?

SIMMONS: Gee, a lot more than NPR.

TG: Oh, I know. You're very defensive about money, aren't you?

SIMMONS: No, I'm not. I'm actually just trying to show you that there's a big world out there. And reading books is wonderful. I've certainly read—well, perhaps, as many as you have. But there's a delusional kind of notion that runs rampant in—

TG: Wait, wait. Could we just get something straight?

SIMMONS: Of course.

TG: I'm not here to prove that I'm smart.

SIMMONS: Not you.

TG: And I'm not here to prove that you're not smarter, that you don't read books or can't make a lot of money.

SIMMONS: This is not about you. You're being very defensive. Why are you doing that?

TG: **It's contagious. Can we get back to your makeup? What do you use to paint your face? And do you ever break out from it?**

SIMMONS: No. It's actually oil-based. Steins makeup is one of the brand names. But you can use lots of different things. I don't think I've ever been asked that question. My skin is more beautiful than yours. I would be quite more popular in jail, if I so chose.

TG: **What do you use to take the makeup off?**

SIMMONS: I use Ponds, the same stuff women do. Or you can use a Steins concoction which is similar but more industrious—industrial in strength. Industrious means sort of ambitious.

TG: **Now, clothes that you've worn onstage include fishnet stockings, spike platform shoes—**

SIMMONS: That's actually untrue.

TG: **No?**

SIMMONS: No. Better research needed. Fire your research person. No fishnet stockings. Never. Not in this band.

TG: **Oh. I'm sure I saw you with fishnet—**

SIMMONS: We catch fish with fishnets.

TG: **I was sure I saw you in them. But that's all right. I trust you. I trust you on that.**

SIMMONS: Don't ever do that. I'm a man.

TG: **Let's get to the studded codpiece. Do you have a sense of humor about that? I mean, does that seem funny to you?**

SIMMONS: No. It holds in my manhood. Otherwise, it would be too much for you to take. You'd have to put the book down and confront life. The notion is that if you want to welcome me with open arms, I'm afraid you're also going to have to welcome me with open legs.

TG: **That's a really obnoxious thing to say.**

SIMMONS: No, it's not. Why should I say something behind your back that I can't tell you to your face?

TG: Has it come to this? Is this the only way that you can talk to a woman—to do that shtick?

SIMMONS: Let me ask you something. Why is it shtick when all women have ever wanted ever since we have crawled out of caves is "Why can't a man just tell me the truth and just speak to me plainly?" You can't have it both ways.

TG: You really have no sense of humor about this, do you?

SIMMONS: Oh, I'm laughing all the way, you know—

TG: Oh, to the bank, right?

SIMMONS: Well, of course. Don't I sound like a happy guy?

TG: Not really, to be honest with you.

SIMMONS: I was going to suggest you get outside of the musty place where you can count the dust particles falling around you, and get out in the world and see what everybody else is doing.

TG: Having sex with you?

SIMMONS: Well, if you chose. But you'd have to stand in line.

TG: You write in your book you've had forty-six hundred sexual liaisons over the years.

SIMMONS: You're supposed to say "so far."

TG: So far.

SIMMONS: Right.

TG: To you, this will be asking the obvious, but why have you wanted so many encounters?

SIMMONS: I can only spell it in three letters: M-A-N.

TG: Forty-six hundred—you actually count? I mean, do you have a book in which you attach marks for—

SIMMONS: Almost thirty years ago, I started taking photos, Polaroids. And I still have them to this day. So when the book was being written, Crown Publishers, who published my book, wanted to know. You can't just say, "I did this, and I did that." You've got to give specifics. So I sat down and started counting—one, two, and so on—and arrived at around forty-six hundred and change.

TG: Are you interested in music, or is the goal of being in a rock band to have sex a lot?

SIMMONS: I believe in my heart that anybody who gets up there and says what they're doing is art is on crack and is delusional. In point of fact, their modus operandi, initially—perhaps it changed, but clearly initially—was to get laid and make lots of money. Anybody that tells you otherwise is lying to you. We really get off on the notion that the opposite sex, the fairer sex—that's you—like what we do. And perhaps if we do it really well, you'll think, "Gee, he's not only talented and bright, but he's kind of cute, too." That's what we're hoping for against all odds. And in music, it's the great aphrodisiac that says that even though I'm short, fat, ugly, bald, and I'm hung like a second-grader, if I'm in a rock band, I've got a better-than-average chance of bedding you down than if I was a dentist. I didn't make those rules. I come from Israel. I'm simply a student at your feet. This is what I've noticed.

TG: Are you interested in music?

SIMMONS: Don't you love this interview? Tell me the truth.

TG: Well, I think it's kind of a drag because you're making speeches. And you're being intentionally obnoxious.

SIMMONS: That's right. No, I'm not. I'm being a man.

TG: That's what I mean. You're being intentionally obnoxious by defining everything that you're saying as "being a man."

SIMMONS: What bothers you is you're finally hearing a man tell the truth instead of, "You're the only one I'll ever live with and you're the—" He's lying. He's lied ever since he was twelve. "I promise I'll pull out." He's lying. I refuse to play that game. I refuse to stand up in front of a rabbi and my friends and the woman I love—who I will tell you, I can love with all my heart—and promise that she's going to be the only one I will ever have until the day I die. That's a lie.

TG: Let's talk about your background. You were born in Israel several years after World War II ended. During the war, your mother was in a Nazi concentration camp. Do you have any memories of life in Israel?

SIMMONS: I do. Six months after the independence of Israel, as recognized by the UN and who knows who else, I popped out. Growing up in Israel was like being in a box where you are not aware that the outside world exists. I certainly never saw a television set. I didn't know about Kleenex or supermarkets, or anything. All I knew was you heard stories in school about David and Goliath, and all these wonderful great superheroic stories—"the sea is splitting open and our people go through it; then it crashes again on the Egyptians." All these great stories. Then slowly, people started to tell me, "This is the place it happened. You're actually living in it." So it was tough to take in. At eight and a half years of age, when I came over to America with my mother, it was like being thrown into another dimension. I'd never heard of Santa Claus or Christ or Christmas. Never knew anything about Christians, or if there were other kinds of people. From then on, I became a sponge. I wanted to just take it all in. It was way beyond anything I could ever imagine. And television, rock 'n' roll, horror movies, science fiction, and comic books were my education. I thank God that those were what I learned instead of having to read *Jane Eyre* at an early age, because it wasn't anything I could relate to.

TG: I know you went to Yeshiva as a boy. Were you from an orthodox family?

SIMMONS: No. Nobody in the family was orthodox. But when I came to America, my mother, being a single mother, had to go out and work from six in the morning until seven at night. So she put me in a Yeshiva, which is a Jewish theological seminary. In other words, you're studying to be somebody. I was studying to be a rabbi. They fed me and clothed me. You take care of your child that way. You don't have to worry that your child is on the street. While I was there, I saw one world, the closed world. When I turned on television, people were flying through the air, and they had capes. There were cartoons and amazing things. I wanted to go there. I thought that was a lot cooler than yarmulkes.

TG: **What's your mother's reaction to Kiss?**

SIMMONS: Well, it's interesting. Good question. My mother is probably the wisest person I've ever known. She's not schooled. She's not well read. Yet she has a philosophy about life that makes well-read people seem like morons. She doesn't talk a lot. Uses very few words to express herself, unlike myself, who likes the sound of his own voice. Here's a woman who'd been through the German Nazi concentration camps of World War II and still thought that there was goodness in humanity and thought about the fact that the glass was half-full instead of half-empty. When asked, "Well, what about your son? He's in this weird rock band. He dresses weird, and apparently has lots of liaisons and girls and stuff, what do you think about that?" She goes, "Well, as long as he doesn't use drugs and alcohol and doesn't hurt anybody, I don't care about the rest." You know what? She's right.

TG: **Well, you've said that you don't use drugs.**

SIMMONS: Never have.

TG: **And you've never had a drink of alcohol.**

SIMMONS: That's not true. I've never been drunk. At parties when somebody says, "Toast," I try to take a sip. But it's true. As soon as I smell alcohol, I start to gag. I may be blessed with some kind of chemical reaction against it. I won't go near the most beautiful woman who's got my name written all over her, if she opens her mouth and smells like a truck driver who just drank Bud. I'm out of there. Gone. It always struck me as bizarre that women are willing to paint their mouths beautifully with lipstick, and yet smoke and drink and make their breaths smell like garbage heaps. I can't do that. I can't be around people who numb their senses. Everybody's allowed, as far as I'm concerned, to take their own life or numb themselves to oblivion. I could care less. I have no sympathy for anybody who lives in America and decides, "I'm going to numb myself with drugs, alcohol, cigarettes." I'm happy to be alive every single day. I want my senses working twenty-four hours a day. And if you were in my room and we were going to have a liaison, and you were high, you'd be out on your butt before you could spell your last name. Because if you don't want to experience me with all the senses God gave you, you don't deserve to be with me.

TG: You know, you've said you don't have sympathy for that proverbial guy on the roof who keeps saying, "I'm going to jump—"

SIMMONS: None.

TG: But my impression is you don't have much sympathy for anyone. You're so into yourself, you're so deep into yourself.

SIMMONS: Well, I think everybody should be. If it sounds like admiration coming out of you, I accept it. I think life is too short to have anything but delusional notions about yourself. You should really like yourself more than you deserve to, because the alternative isn't very good. You should think you are better looking than you are, because the alternative is some bad notions. I'm aware, as a sane person, that I'm not the best-looking guy in the world. I'm aware of it. But when I go into a party, I will walk out with your girlfriend.

TG: Just one more question before we wrap up.

SIMMONS: As many as you want.

TG: I would like to think that the personality you've presented on our show today is a persona that you've affected as a member of Kiss—something that you do onstage and before the microphone—but that you're not nearly as obnoxious in the privacy of your own home or when you're having dinner with friends.

SIMMONS: Fair enough. And I'd like to think that the boring lady who's talking to me now is a lot sexier and more interesting than the one who's doing NPR—studious and reserved. I bet you're a lot of fun at a party.

TG: Well, we'll leave it at that.

February 4, 2002

Dramatic Beats

Samuel L. Jackson

If you think about what Sammy does in the last scene, he's
doing this almost Richard III storm sequence kind of thing—
except he's in a coffee shop, bent over, sitting in a booth. . . .
He's dominating the entire room, while never getting up from
the booth.

Quentin Tarantino to Chris Willman, *Los Angeles Times,*
October 9, 1994

Tarantino watched hundreds or possibly thousands of movies before writing and directing them; he's good at describing the things
we respond to on an unconscious level in movies—in this case, the
way that Samuel L. Jackson refuses to let us take our eyes off him in
his role as a serene, Bible-quoting hit man in Tarantino's *Pulp Fiction,*
arguably the most influential American film of the 1990s. Pauline
Kael, who could be stinting with her praise, once said of Jackson, "I
think the audience is alert when he's on-screen, and that's all you can
ask of an actor." But Jackson was in his early forties before anybody
really noticed him: His performance as a crackhead in Spike Lee's
Jungle Fever was so electrifying—though in a relatively small part—
that the jury at the Cannes Film Festival created a supporting actor
award especially for him. I interviewed Jackson for the first time in
1991, when *Jungle Fever* opened in the United States. We spoke again

nine years later, when he starred in a sequel to *Shaft,* the 1971 blax-
ploitation classic. Between these two interviews, Jackson hit it big as
Bruce Willis's reluctant sidekick in *Die Hard: With a Vengeance,* but
he also gave eye-catching performances in an impressive variety of
movies both big and small, including *Pulp Fiction, A Time to Kill,
Eve's Bayou, Hard Eight, Jackie Brown,* and *The Negotiator.* He is one
of our busiest actors, and easily one of our most enjoyable.

TERRY GROSS: **Have you known people who are addicted to crack
like Gator, the character you play in** *Jungle Fever?*

SAMUEL L. JACKSON: Yes, I know people who are addicted. And I
know people who are in recovery. In talking to them, and to drug
counselors, I discovered that using drugs usually cuts off your emotional growth. I stopped Gator's emotional growth at about sixteen.
When he reacts to things, he reacts as a sixteen-year-old. He wants
what he wants, when he wants it, kind of like a baby, and that leads to
a certain amount of vulnerability.

TG: **Did your part in** *Jungle Fever* **give you a new empathy for
addicts?**

JACKSON: I always had that. In college, I had a roommate who was a
heroin addict. I've always had friends who were involved in drugs and
the drug trade. Even in my formative years, in Tennessee, I lived in a
kind of alcoholic neighborhood. The drug of the day was alcohol. We
had a neighborhood drunk. People in my neighborhood sold bootleg
liquor. I saw people who were drunk all the time. Then, I knew people who did pills. In the sixties, I did all the things that all the people
of my generation did. So I had my own drug experiences, at that time,
with marijuana and other things. You just outgrow them. I did. Some
people don't.

TG: **When you were starting out as an actor, didn't you spend a
couple years on TV as Bill Cosby's stand-in?**

JACKSON: Not on TV, actually. Just on the set. We had a whole stand-
in family. We were the junior Huxtables, I guess. We would watch
them rehearse the show and write down the blocking. On Wednesday

mornings, we would go in and do the whole show for the crew to plot out their camera shots and get the color palette down for the lights. Bill's larger than I am, so I wore his clothes over my clothes. I did that for two and a half years and never got on the show. Well, actually, I did. Every time they show an exterior shot of people walking down the street outside their house, that's me and a girl who was a stand-in. We'd walk past each other. That's the only time I was ever on that show.

TG: **As a stand-in for Cosby, you must have spent a lot of time sitting on a couch, making jokes and being wise.**

JACKSON: Yeah. I imitated him quite well. It was fun. It was like taking a "how to act on TV" course for free and being paid for it.

TG: **Did this lead to any breaks for you as an actor?**

JACKSON: No, that was always what was dangled in front of us to keep us coming back to do that job. I never really worried about it. I didn't wait for my big break on *The Cosby Show* because realistically I didn't think that was ever going to happen. And it didn't. I don't know anybody who's done that job who's ever been hired for the show.

TG: **In Spike Lee's movie *School Daze* you play a townie who's very hostile to the college students from out of town.**

JACKSON: Leeds. He had a name, Leeds.

TG: **Thank you. But you were not a townie. You were a college student and went to—**

JACKSON: No, I was not a townie. Yes, I went to Morehouse. But my freshman year, I actually hung out with the "black boys." That was what we called them. Not townies, but "black boys." I hung out with them, and for about six months they didn't know I was a college student.

TG: **Were you hiding that from them?**

JACKSON: Not really. But I was with them when they were robbing college students and beating them up. They didn't know I was a student until they saw me at a dance one night and I had on some Morehouse gear. They said, "Slim, you actually go to college?" It changed their image of the Morehouse guys, and they didn't beat them up so often.

TG: **Oh, so you were performing the role of Good Samaritan?**

JACKSON: That wasn't my purpose. What happened was this: When my mom first dropped me off at the college, I saw a basketball court up the street. I bought a quart of beer, went up to the basketball court, asked who was up next, and played with them. They just assumed that I had moved into the neighborhood because I was there most days. They assumed I was one of them. And I hung out with them like I was.

TG: **What kind of things would they say about the college students?**

JACKSON: Oh, they were stuck-up. A lot of them did think they were "better than." We were taught that we were "better than" by the administration of the school. We were told that we were in the top 10 percent of the black race and were going to lead everybody out of the darkness into the light. Morehouse men were "leaders of the race." A lot of them really believed that.

The guys would just say "hello," the students wouldn't speak back, and that would be cause for a beating. The guys would run them back to campus mainly because they wouldn't speak. The students ignored those people who lived in the community. They invaded the community and felt that they were there to run it. And that wasn't the truth.

TG: **Were you ever with your friends while they were robbing a college student you happened to know?**

JACKSON: Yeah.

TG: **So what happened?**

JACKSON: Nothing. He looked at me, and before he could say anything, somebody hit him, and by that time, they'd taken his stuff, and we left. As a result, I ended up in the dean's office. The guy did recognize me, and he reported the robbery and said that I was with them. I was put on probation a few times because I refused to identify the people who did it.

TG: Did it ever bother you that they were doing that?

JACKSON: No.

TG: Why not?

JACKSON: Because 90 percent of the time, they were correct in thinking that the person they were robbing could afford to have it taken. Those students had petit bourgeois ideas and needed a lesson in reality.

TG: I understand that when you were in college you were part of a group that held some of the trustees hostage? What were the issues?

JACKSON: That there weren't any student representatives on the trustee board. And there weren't any community representatives, either. We were right in the middle of this community, and these people should have had a say in what went on in their area.

There weren't enough black faculty members. And there was no black studies at the school. We were trying to change some of these policies. The head of the trustee board said we were absolutely correct. But it was these men in the administration who were trying to make us "perfect Negroes," who thought we were upsetting their applecart. They told us that we were the kind of people that they never should have let in to Morehouse in the first place. People like me were let in more or less as an experiment. We turned out to be just what they thought.

TG: Did your radical politics go along with a radical sense of theater?

JACKSON: I wasn't even doing theater then. I was just a student.

TG: So you can't call this guerrilla theater?

JACKSON: Well, that didn't happen until I came back to school in '71. That's when I started my theater major in earnest. Besides the Morehouse Spelman Players, the proper theater group where we did all our school productions, we had our own theater company, the Black Image Theater Company. That was our "hate whitey" revolutionary thing. We did revolutionary poems and skits about the supremacists. We had a singing group that was like the Supremes, but we were called the Supremacists. We sang racist tunes and new nation poems.

People were paying us to do this. We were traveling all over, going to Tulane and Florida State and all kinds of big white schools. They were like, "Yes. Yes. Denigrate us. Denigrate us. Do it. Do it." We enjoyed it. It was great fun.

TG: What led you out of the radical theater period?

JACKSON: I didn't have time to do it anymore. Times changed. People became very apathetic. Everybody was out trying to make a buck. Black Power just died, for some reason. People stopped wearing Afros and dashikis, nationalism wasn't so fashionable, and the theater changed into a mainstream thing. The Black Image Theater had started to do scripted plays that were by, for, and about black people, but it wasn't that "die whitey" or "hate whitey" theater. It was about the black human condition.

TG: This may sound like an odd question, but this summer has been terrific for young black directors and actors. I'm wondering if you think that there will be room for actors who are, gosh, already in their forties?

JACKSON: Like me? Sure. I think I'll be able to work with these kids. This will give me a chance to do things I've never been able to do. I'll be able to play a father with the true sensibilities of a father because I am a father. If they really want a good actor, then they'll ask me to do those things that forty-year-old people do in films. I'll be the teacher at the school, the principal, or a mentor. Who knows? I'll do something.

July 19, 1991

TG: As you probably know, you have enormous screen presence. Is that something that just exists, or is it something that you are conscious of and can work with? Are you able to turn it on and off?

JACKSON: It's something that exists in me. Through my theater training, I've learned how to take dominant positions or submissive positions through body language, or by positioning myself inside the framework of a scene. I do it without thinking now. If I'm the dominant person, I try to make myself as large as I possibly can. When it's time for me to be in the background or just be around, I find a way to make myself almost invisible.

TG: Would you talk a bit about how you find that dominant position?

JACKSON: You find a way to be taller in the foreground. Or you change your body position and make it stronger than the person you're talking to or reacting to, by having straighter shoulders, a more upright posture. You find a way to put yourself in a position that makes that other person have to sit, or look up, or face away from you, so that you are the dominant person. It's a purposeful upstaging.

TG: I love the way you speak and the way you do your lines in film. There's a scene in *Pulp Fiction*, toward the end of the movie, when you have a religious awakening. You believe that only the intervention of God could explain why you weren't killed in a shoot-out.

Later, you're at a diner with your hit man partner, played by John Travolta, when two people pull out their guns and demand that everyone hand over their money. You manage to get the gun away from the guy. Then the question is, will you shoot him? You quote a passage from Ezekiel 25:17—the same passage you used to quote before killing somebody. It's a great scene.

There's such an interesting contrast between the Bible reading with lines like, "The path of the righteous man is beset on all sides by the inequities of the selfish and the tyranny of evil men," and your slangy biblical analogies, like, "Mr. Nine-millimeter here, he's the shepherd protecting my righteous ass in the valley of darkness." Would you talk about how you developed your line-reading style for this scene? Do you decide in advance where you're going to breathe and which words you're going to emphasize? Or do you do it in a more improvisational way?

JACKSON: Well, I do a lot of things. I break down scripts into dramatic beats, in the context of a scene. I try to understand what one particular thing is attempting to accomplish, then what the next thing is trying to do, and what explains what, and why. This leads me to understand which things have to be spoken together without a breath, and which things I can breathe between.

It's not a science. It's good, old-fashioned theater training. You learn to understand the purpose of each particular scene, and what a sentence does in terms of moving that scene along, or defining what came before it or what's going to come after it.

TG: One of the things you do so effectively is use pauses.

JACKSON: Quentin's one of the few guys who allows you to do stuff like that on-screen. I was channel surfing the other day and *Jackie Brown* was on television. It was the scene in the van with De Niro when we discover the money is gone, and I stop to think about what happened.

When we were doing that scene, I would look in the bag, think for a second, then say, "It's Jackie Brown."

But Quentin would say, "No, take your time."

I'd do it again. I'd count to five and he'd say, "No, no, no. Go through the whole thing, and think about what's happened. Then, realize it's Jackie Brown. Take as much time as you want."

This led me to that almost twenty-second pause, which he left in. It's amazing that he trusts the audience to stay with you and go through the process that long. A lot of times, people don't want dead air in a film, especially for a thought process. They want to feed the audience the idea, then feed the audience the answer quick before they lose concentration. But Quentin trusts audiences, like I do.

TG: In action movies, you've had to use a gun on-screen. You briefly worked as a security guard when you were younger. Did you have a gun? Were you in any real-life action scenes? Did you ever display the bravado that you can turn on in your movie roles?

JACKSON: I didn't have a gun when I was a security guard; I had a nightstick. I didn't want to carry that either, because I didn't want to pose a threat to anyone. As I told my superiors, I was out there as a reporter. If I saw something happening, I would call them on a walkie-talkie, or wait until it was over, and then tell them what had happened. I didn't want to walk up on anybody doing anything criminal. It was just a security job.

In real life, I don't try to be the characters that I am on-screen. I will defend my house, and my family, and my friends, and I've been in confrontations with people because of that. But I don't walk around looking for trouble. I will walk away from trouble before things escalate to that point, the way it does in movies. Life's too volatile and people are too crazy out there now.

TG: Something happened to you in 1988 that would have been the stuntman's job, if it had happened in a movie. You were getting off a train in the New York City subway and your leg got caught in the closing door.

JACKSON: The door closed on my ankle and the train took off, yes.

TG: You were dragged across the platform?

JACKSON: I was in the middle door of the last car and was dragged to within a car length and a half of the tunnel.

TG: What went through your mind as you were being dragged along?

JACKSON: That it was going to be a very sad Christmas. I was trying to figure out how I could grab ahold of something on the train and get as close to the train as I possibly could, as the wall approached swiftly. But I couldn't find anything to hold on to. There were people in the train trying to pull my shoe off, people pulling on the door, people pushing on my foot.

Then, it was, "Okay, this is it. I'm not going to make it." I started thinking about how sad it was going to be for my family. Who was going to call my house and tell them what had happened? My life never flashed before my eyes, so I should have known I wasn't going to die. People always tell you, "Oh, your life flashes before your eyes." Well, none of that happened. I was thinking of ways to survive.

TG: **So the train stopped in the nick of time.**

JACKSON: Someone pulled the emergency cord.

TG: **Have you drawn on anything from that experience in your acting—like what real terror is?**

JACKSON: Well, no. I never felt terrorized. It was a very calming, slow-motion thing. It's the way people describe car accidents, where everything goes very slowly until it's over and then—*boom*—everything comes back to real life. I never experienced that element of terror. But I don't terrorize very easily.

TG: **You were born in 1949 in Washington, D.C. Your parents divorced when you were less than a year old, and you went to live with your grandparents in Chattanooga. Your mother eventually joined you. Were your grandparents or your mother strict with you?**

JACKSON: Yeah, I had a lot of restrictions. I had to be at home at a certain time. I had to make certain grades. I had to treat people with respect. I was a lot more afraid of my family than I was of peer pressure. I did what they wanted me to do, and not what everybody else wanted me to do.

TG: **Were you afraid of your family's disapproval, or was there a more physical kind of punishment that—**

JACKSON: Well, all of that. I didn't want to embarrass or disappoint them, and I grew up in the age of corporal punishment. There's something about getting hit and whipped with switches that makes pain a motivator, especially when you're small.

People always say corporal punishment is bad. But for every spanking I got, there was a hug that came along with it that explained to me how much they loved me, and that they were sorry they had to do it.

By the time I was bigger than all of them, they didn't hit me. They couldn't make me cry anymore. Punishment was bizarre. I would much rather have been whipped and gotten it over with than be restricted—like, "You can't go out, you can't use the phone for a month."

TG: I think I've made it clear that I love the way you speak. Did your family ever try to correct your enunciation? Did you ever have a teacher who gave you a sense of diction?

JACKSON: My aunt was a schoolteacher. She taught fourth-grade English and performing arts. When I was very small, things like grammar and learning how to conjugate verbs were ingrained in me. When people say, "Well, that's what he should have did," I go, "No, no, no."

TG: Did you know your father?

JACKSON: We met.

TG: What was he like?

JACKSON: I met him to talk to him in Kansas City. I was on the road doing a play in Wichita. He was in Kansas City at his mother's house, my grandmother, who had always kept up with me. She sent me Christmas cards, birthday cards, graduation gifts. Every year there was something from her. I went to see her because I'd never met her. I took my daughter who was six or seven months old with me. And he was there.

It just so happened he had a daughter younger than my daughter, by some seventeen-year-old kid, which was kind of disgusting to me. We talked about that, and at one point, he said, "You can't talk to me that way. I'm your father." And I went, "Wait a minute, we're just two guys talking. We can't go to this father-son space."

TG: Did you think that he hadn't earned the right to call himself your father?

JACKSON: Having a kid, or supplying the sperm to fertilize an egg, and then not being around to offer support or guidance, doesn't give you the right to say, "I'm your father." You can say, "I'm the guy who made you," but that's about it.

TG: You were an understudy for Charles Dutton in *The Piano Lesson,* the August Wilson play. You've said that you were frustrated having to wait in the wings, when you were the one who had originated the role.

JACKSON: Well, I did originate the role at Yale. But Dutton did it on the road and on Broadway because the play was written for him. The only reason I did it at Yale was because he was off doing *Crocodile Dundee II.*

TG: During that time you developed a pretty heavy cocaine habit.

JACKSON: It's frustrating, listening backstage and hearing the audience response every night, knowing that you used to be out there, and the audience had been responding to you. Then there's the disappointment and frustration of "Oh my God, he got a Tony nomination now. Oh my God, the play's won a Pulitzer Prize, and I wasn't out there doing it." And there were the high-profile job opportunities missed. The mounting frustration of knowing how well you did something, then watching someone else reap all the benefits of doing it, combined to make me a bit crazier than I normally am.

TG: How did you learn to cover up your drug use?

JACKSON: I wasn't covering it up. People saw me in that state for so long, they just assumed that was my state. If they caught me first thing in the morning when I was sober, before I left home, that might have seemed unusual to them.

TG: How did you get off cocaine?

JACKSON: Rehab. I did my twenty-eight days. All the men in my family have died from some form of alcoholism. It's a family disease. Like all of them, if I bought a six-pack of beer, I drank six beers. I never saved anything for the next day. That's my personality.

TG: **Having been a cocaine user, were there things that you felt you understood firsthand, that you could use in your role as Gator in *Jungle Fever*?**

JACKSON: Definitely. I understood that it was easy to play the effects of being high. I also knew that family dynamic was an important element in that role. Gator ruined his relationships by alienating everybody around him. He collapsed every bridge that he had to humanity. We all did.

TG: **Did you burn a lot of bridges?**

JACKSON: Definitely. I used up everybody's friendship by saying, "Oh, man, I'm broke. I need some money." People knew that "Okay, he's gonna buy drugs." Everybody in my house was scared to talk to me.

It was important to me to show that this character was personable. He abused those friendships, so that in the end, he was alone. By the time he died, it was not so much a tragedy as a relief. After seeing that film, people I met described Gator as reminding them of a brother, their husband, sons, or somebody close to them. Because they all had been abused that way.

TG: **You're kind of a sex symbol now.**

JACKSON: No kidding!

TG: **Do you see your body differently now that so many people desire you? Now that so many people are, you know, imagining you? I don't have to keep going, do I?**

JACKSON: No, I know. I see myself as the same guy I always was.

TG: **Do you ever sit home alone, thinking, "Well, I may be bored, but I know a lot of people are probably thinking about me"?**

JACKSON: No. But, to be honest, I'll sometimes walk through crowds of people to see who will notice me. I do that. I'm not crazy enough to think that people aren't going to notice me, and I'm not so confident or bored or bothered by the attention that I try to avoid it. Sometimes I just walk around, trying to see what'll happen if somebody sees me.

June 27, 2000

STOP ACTING

Dustin Hoffman

There's no such thing as a Dustin Hoffman role. What Dustin really is is a character actor as leading man. Compare Benjamin in The Graduate *to Ratso Rizzo in* Midnight Cowboy. *Or Raymond in* Rain Man *to Stanley Motts in* Wag the Dog. *They're night and day. Who takes risks like him?*

Barry Levinson (who directed Hoffman in *Rain Man* and *Wag the Dog*) to Bernard Weinraub, *The New York Times,* February 17, 1998

When interviewing movie stars, I sometimes find myself at cross-purposes with them. They come on *Fresh Air* to talk up their latest movie, and they wonder why I'm asking them questions about their childhood. I realize that movie stars have good reason to be suspicious of the press, but I resent it when they act as if I'm just another snoop trying to dig up dirt on them.

It isn't always asking about a star's personal life that's considered going "off topic." At least once, it was a star's *movies* he refused to talk about. This was when Ralph Fiennes did the show, in 1999, along with his brother, Joseph, and his sister, Sophie, to promote their late mother's last novel (published under her pen name, Jennifer Lash). I agreed to the interview only because I was eager to talk with Fiennes, but his mother was the only topic he was willing to discuss. In a futile attempt to steer the conversation toward his own work, I found myself asking absurd questions like, "What did your *mother* think of your performance as a Nazi in *Schindler's List*?"

Dustin Hoffman, on the other hand, was a pleasure. I spoke with him in 1999, when he came on the show to promote *A Walk on the Moon,* a movie he produced but did not appear in. Set in the summer of 1969, *A Walk on the Moon* stars Diane Lane as a young Jewish wife and mother who's vacationing at a Catskill bungalow colony and finds herself drawn to the alternative culture represented by the Woodstock festival, which is going on a few miles away. Though I was hoping that the subject matter of the movie might lead Hoffman to discuss his film debut in *The Graduate,* and how being Jewish has affected his life and career, I half expected him to limit the discussion to *A Walk on the Moon.* He fooled me by turning out to be an amiable and generous guest.

TERRY GROSS: **Your new movie, *A Walk on the Moon,* is set in 1969. It was the year of Woodstock, it was the year of *Midnight Cowboy,* and just a year after *The Graduate.* What was the summer of 1969 like for you?**

DUSTIN HOFFMAN: I was doing *Little Big Man,* and we were on location in Billings, Montana, where Little Big Horn happened. At the conclusion of *Little Big Man,* I flew to Chicago to catch another great event of the time—the last week of the Chicago Seven trial.

I missed Woodstock. I was a little old for that. You know, I was thirty when I did *The Graduate.* I was too old to be drafted and too old to be in college.

TG: **Why did you want to go to the Chicago Seven trial?**

HOFFMAN: I heard it was the best show in town, and it was.

TG: **Because of *The Graduate,* you were seen as a representative of your generation. I wonder what that experience was like for you.**

HOFFMAN: I wanted to be honest in those days. If I had to do it again, I would have learned the art of selling out early. I was twenty-nine going on thirty, and I went from being an actor on the unemployment line to doing *The Graduate*. Suddenly I was thrust into stardom. The next thing I know, I'm supporting McCarthy for president and flying around the country with one of his daughters in a little airplane to all these colleges, trying to get votes for Eugene McCarthy.

I remember being in a college somewhere in the country watching kids' eyes glaze over as if they were thinking, "Oh, the new icon has arrived." I systematically set out to dethrone myself. I said, "Guys, I'm an actor. I'm not your age. I'm thirty years old. That's just a character I played and he has very little to do with me." After that, I did *Midnight Cowboy* to further dispel the image. I had a great desire to be known as an actor.

It's all changed now. In those days you didn't even admit it if you were on a soap opera. B-movies were really C-movies. Today, B-movies are legitimized. A-movies won't even get done. Back then, no one went to the Academy Awards or the Golden Globes. When I showed up as the "most promising newcomer," I was the only one that came. There was a whole antiestablishment thing going on. Now the kids embrace the establishment. They embrace fashion, embrace making money. I really wanted to avert the curse of being called a star. I just wanted to be this actor.

TG: **What else might you have done differently?**

HOFFMAN: Well, I would have taken advantage of it. I wasn't brave; I was just being in vogue. It was the vogue to be antiestablishment. It was the vogue to be pure. I would probably lie about my age. The first thing I'd do is tell them I was twenty-two and—

TG: **And the second thing you'd do is tell them that you were better than they were.**

HOFFMAN: Yes. And "Follow me, follow me."

TG: **Was being Jewish an important part of your family's identity?**

HOFFMAN: My father was an atheist. Not a professional atheist, but when you asked him he just said, "Kid, it's all—" Tell me the word I should use on the radio. It was one of the first and last things he said to me. When he turned eighty, shortly before he died, he reiterated it once again on a walk on the beach. He said, "Let me tell you something, kid, it's all—" For the air, we can say, "It's all 'horse puckey.'" My brother and I were not bar mitzvahed. We were circumcised, but I'm sure that was the city.

My mother's mother lived with us and she spoke Yiddish. When they didn't want us to understand what they were saying, my mother, my father, and my grandmother would speak Yiddish.

I was born in '37. The Second World War ended in '45, so in a sense, I went through the Holocaust without knowing it was going on. I never got a chance to ask my parents if they consciously kept it from me. I do know that I lived in an atmosphere of a family that desperately wanted to make it, to be successful, to be American. What American meant was "don't get stuck with an ethnicity that's going to hold you back." I'm sure that's the way the Italians felt and the Jews felt. Unfortunately, the blacks couldn't deny what they were. Sometimes I wished that I had some insignia on me that would have—well, I guess I did. There was a kind of virulent anti-Semitism in the part of Los Angeles where I grew up. I remember the words *dirty Jew* and *kike*. Even as an adult, I would get a little pit in my stomach if someone said, "So what are you?"

And you know what? I'd always say, "What do you mean?"

They'd say, "Well, what are you?"

And I would say, "What do you mean?" If they finally said "religion," I would say, "I'm American."

"No, what religion?"

I would keep pretending like I didn't understand.

TG: **Earlier in your career, when you were auditioning for parts, did anyone ever tell you you looked too Jewish for a certain part?**

HOFFMAN: They would never say it in those words. I think it still exists, maybe not in film so much, but if you turn on the soap operas, the look is still the same. And in those newspapers that actors buy to look for work, they have "available types." And it's "leading men." Now that automatically means non-Jewish and nonethnic. It means white Anglo-Saxon Protestant, and in a sense it means all-American. "Leading ladies," the same thing. If they wanted someone who looked ethnic they would say "character leading man." "Character" or "character juvenile" as opposed to just "juvenile," and as opposed to "ingenue." "Ingenue" was not Barbra Streisand. "Ingenue" is Gwyneth Paltrow. I don't think that's really changed yet.

TG: To what extent were you able to make your own rules, and how often do you think you were turned down for roles because of your looks?

HOFFMAN: When I was twenty years old going on twenty-one, I left Los Angeles and ran to New York. For me, New York meant a place where someone could get a job without looking like the people on *Bonanza,* which was being cast at about the same time.

When Mike Nichols cast me in *The Graduate,* it was a really courageous thing on his part. His friends thought he had made the most self-destructive move of his life. He called these guys who had blond hair and blue eyes and were getting all the work "walking surfboards." In fact, he purposely hired someone who looked like the actors that got all those roles for the guy that Katharine Ross is supposed to marry at the end of the movie.

TG: I've read that your father wanted to be a movie producer, but the closest he came was supervising props at Columbia. He made his living as a furniture salesman.

HOFFMAN: By the time I was born he was no longer working at Columbia. There was a recession, and he got fired with a number of other people. Anyway, at Columbia he went from the prop assistant to head of props to head of the set-dressing department. This was before I was born. He worked on Frank Capra films—*Mr. Smith Goes to Washington.* He did some of the set dressing for that. Then he was fired. And I was born. I guess he took his expertise from set dressing to furniture. I always thought of him as being a successful person all my life. He did not.

TG: **I think your mother once auditioned to be a dancer, but her mother forbade her to take the job when she got it. Is that right?**

HOFFMAN: Now that my parents have passed on, I guess I have more freedom to talk. I won't get phone calls from them saying, "How could you say that?"

There was a skeleton in my closet, which I discovered not too many years ago. My mother had been married before she was married to my father. She was sixteen or seventeen and she ran off with a jazz drummer. She wanted to be a Ziegfeld girl. She did inspire a lot of *Tootsie*. In fact, I was making it when she was ill, and I was hoping that she would survive long enough to see it, but she didn't. I had to bear a lot of her genetic heritage. But yes, there's a flapper inside me.

TG: **With your parents both living on the edge of show business, did you see theater and the movies as a gated kingdom that you knew would be very difficult to get into?**

HOFFMAN: No, I have an older brother and he was pushed into being an extra. My parents were both very Hollywood. My mother and my father came to L.A. from Chicago in a Model A Ford with only fifty dollars. My father worked as a laborer building the Hollywood Freeway. I have a wonderful photograph of him standing with a shovel. I know that he loved George Raft and Edward G. Robinson, all these short guys—my father was only five foot two—and he emulated them.

Before I was born, when my father was working at Columbia, they took my brother to tap dancing lessons. He was an extra in a couple of those Capra movies. He hated it. At one recital he fell into the orchestra pit on purpose so he could end his career as an actor. By the time I was born, they weren't about to repeat that mistake, so I never heard about acting. My father was already a furniture salesman by that point.

But they did stick a piano in front of me when I was five, and I was told I was going to be a pianist. I grew up in Los Angeles studying piano and wound up enrolled at the Los Angeles Conservatory of Music. I was trying to do that and be a regular kid. I tried to break into jazz piano, but I just didn't have an ear for it. I didn't read music easily. We had a little combo and the other kids in the combo could pick up tunes. It was laborious for me.

I took an acting class when I was nineteen simply to get through junior college, because I was such a bad student. For the first time, working on a scene with somebody, ten hours went by like ten minutes. I said to myself, "This is what I want to be. This is not like working."

TG: **So you knew you had found it.**

HOFFMAN: I knew I found what I wanted to do for the rest of my life—strongly believing that I would fail at it. In retrospect, had I known I was going to be a successful actor, I never would have become an actor. I was sure I was going to fail at it. When you're starting out, to fail at being an actor is a kind of romantic life, because it means you're going to be in a community of actors and you're just going to hang out. You're going to be bohemian for the rest of your life.

TG: **Hanging on to those ideals.**

HOFFMAN: Yes. Yes. Then I thought, well, if this doesn't work I'll go back to college and get a degree. If worst comes to worst, I'll teach acting at one of those colleges where the acting teacher has a lot of on-campus relationships. It can't be all bad.

TG: **What's the best acting advice you were ever given for a movie?**

HOFFMAN: Probably Mike Nichols in *The Graduate,* who told me two things almost every day. One was "Stop acting."

TG: **Oh, I thought you meant, "Get a new career."**

HOFFMAN: He probably thought that. But he would say, "You're acting. Don't act. Don't act. Don't do anything. Because you're doing so much in front of a camera by not doing anything. I mean, you're on seventy feet of screen. You're already interesting. The audience is doing a lot of work for you. You don't have to do their work for them." And if I did something, he'd say, "What did you do in that take?" I would tell him. And he would say, "Why?" And I would tell him the reason. And he would look at me and say, "Oh, I get it. Okay, on this next take when you get an idea in the middle of the scene, do the opposite." That was really the smart thing to say. Then the second thing, which he did five or six times a day, was to tell me to clean the inside of my nose—which has kept me on the marquee all this time.

TG: Is that important? Has a good take ever been ruined by an embarrassing "you know what" in your nose?

HOFFMAN: Yes, but now with digital, it's costly, but they can take out a lot of boogers they couldn't before.

April 19, 1999

In That Hurricane

James Baldwin

He named for me the things you feel but couldn't utter.
Jimmy's essays articulated for the first time to white
America . . . what it meant to be American and a black
American at the same time.

Henry Louis Gates, Jr., to C. Gerald Fraser, *The New York Times,*
June 22, 1989

James Baldwin's frank discussion of racial issues—in such novels as *Go Tell It on the Mountain* and *Another Country,* as well as in *The Fire Next Time* and his essay collections *Notes of a Native Son* and *Nobody Knows My Name*—made him one of the most significant literary voices to emerge after World War II. *Another Country* and his earlier novel *Giovanni's Room* became important to the emerging gay-rights movement for their daring exploration of sexual identity. Baldwin lived in Paris for most of his adult life. I interviewed him in 1986, a little more than a year before his death from stomach cancer at the age of sixty-three.

TERRY GROSS: **You grew up in Harlem, where your father preached in a storefront church.**

JAMES BALDWIN: Daddy was an old-fashioned fire-and-brimstone hellfire preacher, very direct, very chilling sometimes. His orders were not only coming from him but from the Almighty. In a way, to contest him was to be contesting the Lord, to be fighting the Lord. My father was not slow to point this out. There was something very frightening about it.

TG: Why did you become a preacher when you were fourteen?

BALDWIN: It was almost inevitable, being raised that way, and actually not doubting anything my father said, not doubting the Gospel, not doubting the church. At the time of puberty, everybody goes through a storm—the storm of self-discovery, the storm of self-intent, the terror of "Who is this self which is suddenly evolving?" And the sexual question. All of these things coalesce into some kind of hurricane. In that hurricane, what did I do? I reached out for the only thing that I knew to cling to, and that was the Holy Ghost.

TG: By being a preacher, were you able to put off confronting your sexuality and entering adulthood?

BALDWIN: Well, it didn't work. I mean, I was in the pulpit for three years, and all of the elements which had driven me into the pulpit were still there. I was not less menaced. In those three years in the pulpit, there was a kind of torment in it, but I learned an awful lot. And my faith—I lost all the faith I'd had. But I learned something else. I learned something about myself, and I learned something through dealing with those congregations. After all, I was a boy preacher and the congregations I addressed were grown-ups. A boy preacher has a very special aura in the black community. That aura implies a certain responsibility and the responsibility above all to tell the truth. As I began to be more and more tormented by my crumbling faith, it began to be clearer and clearer to me that I had no right to stay in the pulpit. I didn't know enough. The suffering of those people, which was real, was beyond the ken of a boy of fourteen, fifteen, sixteen. You could respond to it, but I had not yet entered that inferno. They knew something about being a nigger, which I was only just beginning to discover, and it frightened me. For those reasons and a complex of reasons, I left. I left home, and I left the church.

TG: **What did you do to try to get your foot in the door as a writer?**

BALDWIN: Oh, I wrote all the time. I worked all day, and I wrote all night. And I learned a lot. I began to be published when I was twenty-two. I had a fellowship when I was twenty-one. Something else was happening, though I didn't quite see it. I was defined as a young Negro writer, and that meant that certain things were expected of a young Negro writer. And what was expected, I knew I was not about to deliver. What was expected, putting it very brutally, was to accept the role of victim and to write from that point of view. From my point of view, it seemed to me that to take such a stance would simply be to corroborate all of the principles which had you enslaved in the first place.

TG: *Go Tell It on the Mountain* **was a fairly autobiographical novel, and it won you a lot of attention and prestige in America. Your book of essays** *The Fire Next Time,* **which was published in 1963, was perceived by many whites as an attack against whites, like, "He's threatening us with the fire next time." Did some white people see it that way, and did it change your reputation and make you more controversial?**

BALDWIN: Yes, but that had begun to happen already without my quite noticing it. It was long before *The Fire Next Time,* which wasn't written as an attack on white people. They flatter themselves.

Long before that, when I first went south, I went as a reporter. When I came back, the first few magazines did not want to publish the reports, because they accused *me* of fomenting violence. I was *describing* violence—violence for which I was in no way responsible. I thought that people should know what is going on and why it's going on. In the battle to do this, I became notorious. In any case, the battle I was fighting, it seemed to me, was not simply about black people. My position as concerns white America was "It's your country, too. It's your responsibility, too." And *The Fire Next Time* is probably a combination of all those years. It was when I was being called the "angry young man" on the white side of town, and being called "Uncle Tom" on the black side of town.

TG: You've been very outspoken about civil rights issues in America, but you've been much less outspoken about homosexual issues. Homosexuals have been marginalized in both the white and black parts of American culture.

BALDWIN: Well, there's no point in mixing the two questions, because it only leads to terrible confusion. In America, in any case, the homosexual question is tied up with the whole American ideal of masculinity, the whole infantile idea, according to me. And absolutely untrue. To be a man is much more various than the American myth has it. Love is like the lightning, and your maturity is signaled by the extent to which you can accept the dangers and the power and the beauty of love.

TG: Some of your writing has been very important to gay people in America. I wonder if the gay liberation movement had any effect on you, or if it was important to you that there was such a movement.

BALDWIN: No, no, no, no. I left the church when I was seventeen. I have not joined anything since. I had to go away someplace and get rid of all these labels and find out not what I was, but who. Do you see what I mean? So it was a very simple matter for me, in any case, to say to myself, "I'm going this way, and only death will stop me. I want to live my life, the only life I have, in the sight of God."

November 7, 1986

A PLACE OF
PROTECTION

Carol Shields

*Carol Shields, the Pulitzer Prize–winning Canadian novelist
who captured and illuminated the ordinariness of life—
"domesticity, the shaggy beast that eats up 50% of our lives," as
she put it—died on Wednesday in Victoria, British Columbia.*
Christopher Lehmann-Haupt, *The New York Times,* July 18, 2003

As you'll see, Carol Shields accurately predicted what the lead would be in her *New York Times* obituary. Shields came on *Fresh Air* to talk about *Unless,* her tenth and final novel, in 2002—four years after being diagnosed with stage IV breast cancer. Shortly before *Unless* was published, we got a call from her book publicist telling us that Shields was willing to do *Fresh Air,* and gravely warning that this might be our last chance. I confess I felt some ambivalence about saying yes. I knew that if I talked to Shields, the subject of her impending death would be unavoidable, and I was worried that this might introduce an element of exploitation into the interview. At the same time, I wanted to make sure that Shields was willing to discuss her mortality and not pretend that this was a typical book interview.

In retrospect, I realize I would have been a fool to pass up an opportunity to talk with such a reflective and articulate woman. The mother of five, Shields was forty-two when she published her first novel. In addition to her novels, she was the author of two collections of short stories and a biography of Jane Austen. The most celebrated of her novels is *The Stone Diaries* (1995), whose success took her by surprise—it won a Pulitzer Prize and a National Book Critics Circle Award and was a national best seller. She began work on *Unless* shortly after learning she had breast cancer. She died at the age of sixty-eight, fourteen months after this interview was recorded.

TERRY GROSS: *The Stone Diaries,* your novel that won the Pulitzer Prize, follows the life of a woman who was born in 1905 and lives to the age of eighty-five. For her, sex was a mysterious duty more than anything else. Was it difficult for you to relate to and express her point of view?

CAROL SHIELDS: Oh, I had a mother born in 1902, and she did very well talking about such things compared to most mothers. I remember that she took us to the Art Institute in Chicago and very carefully told us before we went in that we would be seeing statues of un-clothed men and women, and that the human body was a beautiful thing. But at home, she dressed in the closet. I never thought of this as hypocrisy. I thought she was trying to work this out in her own mind and just had a little trouble getting it all together. She did very well in talking to us about sex. She did better than I did with my chil-dren, in fact. But there was a lot that she missed. I don't know if I should say this, but I can remember when I was packing for my hon-eymoon, this would be 1957, she wanted to make sure I had seven nightgowns, because the honeymoon was a week long, and she said rather obliquely, "It's actually awfully messy." That was the message that I got about the sexual life that awaited me.

TG: Over the years, has writing about sexuality become more comfortable for you?

SHIELDS: Well, I don't do it as well as some people do. But I do real-ize that it is part of all our lives and you really can't miss it out alto-gether.

TG: In your new book, *Unless,* the main character is very comfortable with sex and really seems to enjoy it with her husband. It's not at the center of the book, but it's almost a sanctuary for them in a terrible time.

SHIELDS: Yes. Yes. So perhaps you're saying it has gotten easier. And, of course, my children have grown up, and we're living in a different era.

TG: Many reading groups and book clubs have chosen to read your books. In fact, at the back of one of the paperback editions of *The Stone Diaries* there are questions for reading groups to use as discussion points. How do you feel about that?

SHIELDS: Very negative. Anyone who picks up a book should not have to get a quiz at the end of it. I never had it again and never want to. They do book club guides now over the Internet. But I don't like the idea of them being bound into the book. It changes the book as we know it, the shape of the book, the arc of the book. I belong to a book club, but we wouldn't have used a reader's guide for anything in the world.

TG: Why not?

SHIELDS: Well, we set our own agenda. We had our own questions, our own experiences to bring to the reading. We would have felt put upon to use a reader's guide. But I also know people who welcome that kind of direction.

TG: You were married when you were twenty-two, and you had five children in ten years. Did you fall in love with motherhood?

SHIELDS: Yes, I loved motherhood. People were having large families then; this was through the sixties. I loved children. I was interested in children. I would say it was a wonderful period of my life. I thought it would go on forever, but of course it doesn't. I've had an empty nest since 1985.

TG: How did you discover feminism?

SHIELDS: I came to feminism late. I knew there was something wrong, I just didn't know what it was. But, of course, like many American women, I read Betty Friedan's *The Feminine Mystique,* and I have to say it was like a thunderbolt. I was astonished. I had no idea women thought like that, or that women could be anything other than what they were. I read that book in the early sixties, and it did change the way that I thought about myself. I did begin to do a graduate degree part-time, and thought about doing some writing. It gave me courage.

TG: **As much as you loved being a mother, did you ever resent all the responsibilities of motherhood? As a mother of five, you were discovering feminism and also discovering that you liked to write and had a gift for writing.**

SHIELDS: No. I can't think now why I didn't resent it. You know, the lives of middle-class women of my generation were rather predictable. The idea that even those of us who had a degree would marry, would have children, would have dinner parties, was completely accepted. I didn't know women who did anything else, so I expected that I would do this. But it was a very happy period of my life. My women friends, my coffee klatch friends, were all doing this, too. I sometimes think that the old coffee klatch idea is belittled, but for many of us this was the beginning of feminism. This is where we talked about these things for the first time.

TG: **How did you find time to write as the mother of five, particularly when your children were young?**

SHIELDS: Everyone asks me this, including my own children. What my children forget is that I did not have a job. They're all raising children and having jobs, but I didn't have a job. I didn't write until they went to school, and I didn't write on weekends, and I didn't write in the evening. None of this was possible. But I used to try to get that hour just before they came home for lunch, eleven A.M. to twelve, you know, got all those socks picked up and then I tried to write a couple of pages. That was all I ever asked myself to do. Sometimes in the afternoon, before they came home from school, I would get back to those two pages and maybe have a chance to do them over again. I really only had about an hour or an hour and a half a day, but it's funny because now I have the whole day and my output is no more than it was then. This was how I organized that time: I would give myself one to two pages a day, and if I didn't get to my two pages, I would get into bed at night with one of those thick, yellow tablets of lined paper, and I would do two quick pages and then turn off the light. I did this for nine months, and at the end of nine months, I had a novel. I never wrote as quickly again. I never wrote in such an organized way again. But I could see how it could be done in little units. I thought of it like boxcars. I had nine boxcars, and each chapter had a title, starting with September, and then October, November, December. It was a very easy structure for someone writing a first novel to follow.

TG: **Is this the novel *Small Ceremonies* that was published when you were forty?**

SHIELDS: Yes. Yes.

TG: **I know that now you have stage IV breast cancer. May I ask how your health is?**

SHIELDS: Well, I'm not in very good health. I'm under care here in Victoria. My cancer was discovered rather late, and I've had several recurrences, so I'm not in particularly good health now.

TG: **Was it an act of faith to start a novel and expect to live at least until the end of it? Or were you given a good enough prognosis that it wasn't an issue?**

SHIELDS: I wanted something to do. I wanted work to do. I didn't think I could finish it. My last few novels have been rather long. This one is a little shorter. Then I had a surgical procedure that gave me three excellent months where some of my old energy came back to me. I had those months to finish the novel. I was astonished that at the end of August, one day I looked up and realized I had finished the novel. I was so happy, I wanted to run out in the street and give people money and take in their mending. I don't remember ever finishing a novel and being so happy about it. It was a marvelous blessing.

TG: In the face of illness, some people find a deeper religious faith; some lose their faith. In *The Stone Diaries*, while talking about the religious impulse, the main character says, "There are ecstatics like my father, who become addicted to the rarefied air of spiritual communion, and then there are cooler minds who claim that religion exists in order to keep us from feeling our own absurdity." Where do you fit in? Has having cancer changed your attitude toward faith and religion?

SHIELDS: I was brought up in the Methodist Church in the United States, and then the United Church in Canada, and then became a Quaker, and then became nothing. I still call myself a Quaker, although I don't go to meetings any longer. I feel a certain kinship and nostalgia for my Protestant background and those that shared it, that whole community. But I haven't been a believer for a long time, and I think I always knew, in one way or another, that the Old Testament was this metaphor of beginning, and the New Testament a metaphor for beginning again. I think I always knew that. I wasn't able to manage the other beliefs.

TG: I want to read you another sentence from *The Stone Diaries*. This is from a chapter that takes place in 1985, when the main character is eighty years old. "Suddenly her body is all that matters. How it's let her down. And how fundamentally lonely it is to live inside a body year after year and carry it always in a forward direction, and how there is never any relief from the weight of it, even when sleeping, even when joined, briefly, to the body of another." How does that read to you now?

SHIELDS: It's something I would say today. The body that we live in— the changing body, the aging body, the ailing body—I think we're very conscious that we can't really get away from it. I suppose we have to find a place of protection and think as well of ourselves as we can during this particular period.

TG: A lot of people are very concerned with having a legacy, an artistic output that will outlive them. Now that you are ill, does it matter any more or less to you that you will have your books as a legacy?

SHIELDS: You know, people think that would make a difference. People say to me, "At least you've written your books," the kind of people who say, "What have I done in my life?" But the fact is I don't think that. I'm a realist and I know the shelf life of a book is about four months. The day that I got the Pulitzer Prize, I met Margo Jefferson and she said, "You know what this means, don't you?" And I said, "No, what?" And she said, "You already know the first line of your obituary." And, of course, I do. And I found that rather frightening. But someone sent me a list of all the Pulitzer Prize winners since something like 1915, and I'd never heard of half of them. I don't think literary reputations live on—very few of them. Books fall out of the public eye. I don't have a sense of leaving anything permanent at all. I suppose one thinks of one's children as what you leave permanently, and their children. Naturally I like to write books that people enjoy reading. But the literary legacy? No, it's very unimportant to me.

TG: Are you afraid of death?

SHIELDS: I've had three years, kind of bonus years, really. No, I'm not afraid of death. I think it's just one instant away from being alive. I don't think it's far away at all, and I'm not afraid of it at all or anything involved with it.

May 1, 2002

A FRAUDULENT ANGEL

Maurice Sendak

Sendak belongs, not with sensible, sociologically oriented concocters of edifying kiddie books, with audience age ("5 to 8") coded on the jacket, but with the great eccentric visionaries like Lewis Carroll and George MacDonald who simply wrote books they had to write.
Walter Clemons, *Newsweek,* May 18, 1981

I was going to say I fell in love with Maurice Sendak's work as an adult, when I discovered *Where the Wild Things Are, In the Night Kitchen,* and *Outside Over There,* all of which he both wrote and illustrated. Then I remembered his illustrations for Ruth Krauss's *A Hole Is to Dig,* a book I had my mother read to me I don't know how many times when I was a child. I recorded this interview with Sendak in 1993, following the publication of *We Are All in the Dumps with Jack and Guy,* a departure for him in that it wasn't about the fantasies and fears of middle-class kids—the children in this book are facing poverty, homelessness, illness, and hunger. In 2003, Sendak collaborated with the writer Tony Kushner on *Brundibar,* an illustrated children's book about tyranny, based on the 1938 Czech opera of the same name, which was first performed by children in Terezin, the Nazi concentration camp.

TERRY GROSS: *We Are All in the Dumps with Jack and Guy* deals with real-world fears, like homelessness, that affect kids now. What were the big events in your life that you found frightening as a child?

MAURICE SENDAK: Being sick and being expected to die, and knowing at a very early age I might. This was spoken; my parents were very indiscreet. My parents came from a foreign country. They were immigrants. They didn't know about Freud, they didn't know about what to say, or not say, in front of children. They loved us—me, my brother, and my sister. But I suffered a good deal from very severe illnesses, not untypical in the thirties when there were no sulfa drugs and no penicillin. You went through all the dire illnesses, and sometimes you just croaked. At a very early age the awareness of mortality pervaded my soul, apparently, and provided me with the basic ingredients of being an artist. That was critical. Knowing that I was vulnerable, and knowing that other children were vulnerable.

TG: What did you have? What was the sickness?

SENDAK: Oh, you know, scarlet fever, pneumonia twice, and whooping cough. It was the pneumonia and the scarlet fever that really nearly did me in.

TG: Were you carefully watched over by your parents when you were sick?

SENDAK: I was so carefully watched over, they practically killed me with watching over me. Because I was delicate, I was not allowed to participate in street games, so a lot of my early childhood was spent in inventing and imagining. Happily I had superb—and still have, thank God—siblings. My brother, who is five years older, spent a lot of time with me that he might have spent having fun outside in the street, drawing pictures for me and telling me stories, as did my sister, as did my parents. I was well provided for in terms of human companionship. But it left a very severe mark.

TG: When you were sick and everybody was worried about you dying, did you have any sense of what death was?

SENDAK: I don't remember that. But I do remember I was a very close companion to death. I remember a game my father played with me, which was not exactly called a death game but did move in that direction. I remember in one particular place we lived in Brooklyn, if I lay in bed, which I spent a lot of time doing, just opposite the foot of my bed was a window looking out in the backyard facing a very boring brick wall. Dad said, "If you look and don't blink, if you see an angel, you'll be a very, very lucky child." So I did that frequently. And, of course, I would always blink, because it hurt not to blink. I didn't see any angels, and he'd say, "Well, you blinked, didn't you?" I'd say, "Yes." Once I didn't blink, and I saw it. Or I imagined I saw it. But the memory of it is so vivid I can even describe it to you.

TG: Would you?

SENDAK: Well, I was lying in the bed, staring out the window, my eyelids aching, my eyes aching, staring, staring, staring. Something very large, almost like a dirigible, but it wasn't a dirigible, floated right past my window. It was a slow-moving angel. She, he, whatever, moved very gracefully and slowly, coming from left, going across to right, not turning to observe me at all. I don't have a memory of the face, but I remember a memory of the hair, the body, and the wings. It took my breath away. It moved so slowly that I could examine it quite minutely. Then I shrieked and hollered, and my father came in, and I said, "I saw it." And he said I was a very lucky kid. You will have noticed angels in *We Are All in the Dumps*. I love angels. I'm not obsessed with angels, but I do adore angels. I've never drawn them in a book before, but they do appear in the new book, primarily because so many people have died recently that I have populated my book with their spirits floating around. And they're all reading *The New York Times*, because even up there, you've got to figure out what's going on every day.

TG: When you saw the angel, did you think it was a sign that you were going to live, or that something wonderful was going to happen?

SENDAK: Well, I think it put me in alliance with death things, with important things. I can't really describe it. I really can't tell you what it meant. It was a very internal feeling. But it came out of a complex awareness, as a child, of the fragility of life. There is a story that I can't prove, but I was told that at a very early age, my parents dressed me all in white from top to toe, so that if God was watching, He would have thought me already an angel and would not pluck me. It's a religious custom or superstition from the old country. I wouldn't die, in other words. I would be a fraudulent angel. This is a superstition, and it does occur in villages in the old country. I don't know that it happened to me. But it's significant that it was a family story. That told me how forcefully they were concerned about me.

TG: **Did you see your mother and father as parents who could help fend off death or whatever problems you had?**

SENDAK: No, no, because they were so vulnerable themselves. They caved in to problems all the time. This is not a criticism of them, their lives were extremely hard. But no, no, I did not see them that way.

TG: **I understand they were from Poland. Did they flee Europe before World War I?**

SENDAK: Yes, they did, just before World War I. But they didn't flee. My father left on a lark.

TG: **Oh, what was that?**

SENDAK: He had no cause to come here. My grandfather was a rabbi. My father was the youngest son, and he was obviously the spoiled younger son of my grandmother. He fell in love with a young woman, it became a little bit scandalous, and she was put on a boat and shipped off to America. He sulked and pouted and got money out of his siblings and got on another boat to follow her here. His family was appalled at his behavior. Because of that trivial behavior, he was the only survivor of his entire family. I mean, all of my uncles and aunts and all the children were destroyed in concentration camps. My father's grief his entire life was that his survival was based on such a trivial impulse. It really caused him a lot of grief, especially when he became older.

TG: **You grew up before the Holocaust. Was your father deeply regretful then?**

SENDAK: Oh, he was terribly regretful, guilty. He had survivor guilt, as did my mother, who had much less cause, because she was shipped off when she was about seventeen to come to America. She was un-educated, untrained in anything. She was a girl. My grandfather on her side, also a rabbi, had died at a very early age of a coronary, and there was no money to take care of everybody. So she was sent here to work hard, earn money, and then bring them over, which was typical. She met my father, they married. All their first income was spent on bringing one aunt, then an uncle, then another uncle, then another aunt, then my grandmother, till finally all but one brother on her side were all here. Then they were going to turn to my father's side, but it was too late. That was in the thirties. There was no getting Jews out of Europe at that point. Growing up during the war was tough, having to live through that in all its complexity. It colors your life forever.

TG: **Did your parents talk to you much about the old country?**

SENDAK: Oh, yes, thank goodness. The last year of my father's life, paradoxically, we had a wonderful time. I took down his biography, which was wonderful. A lot of it was fantasy and a lot of it was reality, but I don't intend to have it published. It's a private family chronicle. We didn't hear much of my mother's life. My mother was silent about that period of her life.

TG: **Did your family speak more Yiddish around the house than English?**

SENDAK: Yes, they spoke more Yiddish. I spoke Yiddish as a child. My parents spoke English very, very late and very poorly. We lived in a part of Brooklyn which was teeming with immigrants, either other people from Eastern Europe, Jews, or Sicilians. I couldn't tell the dif-ference. We lived next to the Sicilians, and it sounds like a coy con-ceit, but it's a fact. I was confused because at one place we lived, right across the hall was my best friend, Carmine, and his sisters and brothers, and his huge mother and huge father. And I used to run across the hall, because they had un-kosher food, which was much better, much better than kosher food because it was pasta. It was great Italian cooking. They laughed, and they drank wine, and they grabbed me, and I sat on their laps, and I had a hell of a good time. Then you'd come back to my house and have this sober cuisine and not-so-rambunctious family life. And I really thought that Italians were happy Jews, that they were a sect, and that I would have a choice after my bar mitzvah to belong to either the sober sect or the happy sect.

TG: And they went to a different synagogue where they had pasta.

SENDAK: Yes, I was a dumb kid, let me tell you.

TG: When I interviewed you about eight years ago, something you said really stuck with me. You were talking about the monsters in *Where the Wild Things Are*, and you said that when you were young, the monsters were just adults, they were people with moles on their faces and hairs growing out of their noses.

SENDAK: Yes, old relatives, actually.

TG: Yes, old relatives, exactly, exactly. That really struck a chord. Then I started thinking, "Well, I'm one of those people now." I mean, I don't know if I actually have hair growing out of my nose. But, you know, I have some of those characteristics that I'm sure scare kids. Do you have a sense that, in some ways, you're a monster to kids?

SENDAK: Of course I am. I see it in their eyes when I'm autographing books, which I don't like to do much anymore. Children are shoved at me. They have no idea why they're on the line. They'd much rather be in the bathroom. They're standing on line, and they're being told something which is so frightening and confusing, which they're being told by Mom or Dad. "This is the man you like so much, honey. This is the man who did your favorite book." They clutch their book even closer, because that really means he's going to take it away, because if this is the man's favorite book, then he's going to take your book. The look of alarm and the tears—and they stare at me with pure hatred. Who is this elderly short man sitting behind a desk who's going to take their book away? On top of that, the parents say, "Now, give him your book, honey. He wants to write something in it." Well, they've been told, "Don't write in a book." Okay, then why is it all right for a perfect stranger to write in their book? It's horrible for them. I become horrible. Unwittingly, I make children cry.

TG: **They cry?**

SENDAK: They cry when they meet me because they don't know what I'm doing. There's only one child who ever had the courage, when his father was urging him forward, urging him forward. I can see the hesitation. I felt so bad for the kid, I put my hand on the book to help draw it away from him. He literally screamed and said, "Don't crap up my book!" It was the bravest cry I've ever heard. I nearly wept.

TG: **What did you do?**

SENDAK: Well, I took the father aside, because I think the father was going to kill the kid because he'd embarrassed him and made everybody laugh. I had to sit down and say how great I thought his kid was and not to be angry with him, because the child just didn't understand what this whole nonsense—this social nonsense of autographing—was all about.

September 22, 1993

ACKNOWLEDGMENTS

So many people come together to make *Fresh Air*—and by extension, this book—possible that my list of acknowledgments risks becoming as long as the closing credits of a *Star Wars* movie. Even so, I expect to face many sleepless nights remembering the names of people I've inadvertently neglected to mention here. For now, I can only offer my sincerest apologies.

The interviews in this book were edited by Margaret Pick, who also did most of the work involved in actually putting together *All I Did Was Ask.* I put off beginning work on this book for several years because I couldn't fathom how I'd ever manage to complete it without taking an extended leave of absence from *Fresh Air,* which was something I was unwilling to do. The obvious solution was a collaborator, but I was afraid of choosing the wrong one. As soon as Margaret agreed to work with me, I knew that everything would turn out fine.

She's a public-radio veteran, the original producer of *A Prairie Home Companion;* and her company, PVPMedia, is responsible for *Riverwalk Jazz.* My one regret about finally putting this project behind me is that we'll no longer be working together. She could not have been more conscientious or resourceful, and the same goes for Melody Sober, PVP's project coordinator. Thanks also to Terry Bronson and Kathryn Weber for their assistance.

I stole the title *All I Did Was Ask* from the title that Kathy Levine gave a lecture I presented in Syracuse, because I loved it and knew I wasn't likely to come up with anything better.

I would have no interviews to choose from without my colleagues on *Fresh Air.* I've already told you a little bit about what each person on our staff does, but I haven't come close to expressing my gratitude to them not just for the excellent work they do in putting the show on the air but for willingly going out of their way to make my job more manageable. Their day-to-day jobs are difficult enough, often requiring them to work overtime to plug a last-minute hole in the guest calendar, land that hard-to-get guest, or edit a problematical interview. But they turn their lives upside down without complaint in times of national crisis, so that we can respond with timely interviews.

Danny Miller, our executive producer, holds us—and himself—to the highest ethical standards not just when it comes to programming but in our dealings with one another. Part of what makes him such a pleasure to work with is that he's so generous, even-tempered, and forgiving, though you might not guess this from his taste in movies and Broadway musicals—*Taxi Driver, Scarface, The Godfather, At Close Range, Sweeney Todd,* and other dark epics of murder and revenge. Just as long as he doesn't start acting out his Travis Bickle fantasies, he's the best executive producer I could ever hope for, and one of the truest friends.

Amy Salit joined Danny and me in 1985, when *Fresh Air* was still a local show. She quickly proved herself indispensable and became even more so when the show went national a year later. Phyllis Myers and Naomi Person were taking a big gamble by joining us in 1987, when *Fresh Air* became a daily national show. There was no guarantee the show would last; their dedication helps to explain why it has. Amy, Phyllis, and Naomi have spent more than fifteen years scouting out the most interesting books, movies, recordings, and guests. This sounds like a dream job, but only someone who does it knows how difficult it can be. And only someone who works alongside Amy, Phyllis, and Naomi is in a position to appreciate how hard they work.

In 1997 we expanded our staff without expanding our office space. This meant that Monique Nazareth had to spend her first few years as an associate producer for *Fresh Air* in a cinder-block closet, which she somehow managed to make look cheerful. Now, as our issues producer, she's relentless in tracking down guests who can explain our chaotic world. Monique's closet was spacious compared with the smaller one that we converted into an editing booth and then gave Ann Marie Baldonado for an office when she joined us as an associate producer in 1998. Fortunately, that didn't scare her away: She's since graduated to producer of *Fresh Air Weekend*. She's creative and conscientious, and I'm happy to say the added responsibility hasn't made her any less fun to work with.

On top of her other duties, Dorothy Ferebee manages to come up with good ideas for interviews and was the first member of *Fresh Air*'s staff to publish a book. The newest members of our staff, Patty Leswing, Jessica Chiu, and Ian Chillag, bring a vitality to their work that has prevented us longtimers from burning out.

Whenever one of us is late with a tape or a script and the show is on the verge of crashing, it becomes a problem for our director, Roberta Shorrock—but she never loses her cool or plays the blame game, and her expertise usually prevents listeners from realizing there was a problem.

The show is infinitely better for the insights of our critics and commentators: David Bianculli, Maureen Corrigan, David Edelstein, Milo Miles, Geoffrey Nunberg, John Powers, Lloyd Schwartz, Ken Tucker, Ed Ward, and Kevin Whitehead.

Our engineers, Audrey Bentham and Julian Herzfeld, keep things running smoothly in the control room. (We miss Bob Perdick.) Luckily for us, Joyce Lieberman, who helped design our studio, is still on staff at WHYY and there to lend expert assistance when our equipment gets the better of us. Because most of my interviews are long-distance, we also rely on the professionalism of engineers at the various NPR bureaus and member stations, and other studios around the country.

I've learned much from the guest hosts who've taken over during my absences. I'm especially grateful to David Bianculli, Barbara Bogaev, Marty Moss-Coane, and Dave Davies for filling in for me so often, sometimes bailing us out at the last minute.

A result of having been a daily national show for more than sixteen years and a local show for more than twenty-five is that we have a distinguished list of alumni. The honor role includes Deborah Begel, Lisa Brooten, Peter Clowney, Ed Dougherty, Nancy Greenlease, Meagan Howell, Lauren Krenzel, Fred Landerl, Maeve McGoran, Chris Spurgeon, Tracey Tannenbaum, Joan Toohey Wesman, Alan Tu, Nancy Updike, Sue Weinstein, and Kathy Wolff. Sue Spolan is a longtime member of our extended family who often fills in as director.

WHYY has always been our home. Bill Marrazzo, the station's president and CEO, has helped us in numerous ways, including renovations that have made WHYY a more comfortable home. Thanks also to the many people at the station who help keep the show afloat, many of whom assisted in some way with this book, especially: Art Ellis, Ken Finkel, Bruce Flamm, Nessa Forman, Paul Gluck, Kyra McGrath, Elisabeth Perez-Luna, and David Woo.

Fresh Air would never have developed into a national program without Bill Siemering, who became our station manager in 1978. Managers everywhere like to say they lead by example, their door is always open, et cetera, et cetera. Usually this is just talk, but Bill was as good as his word. In 1985, Bill had enough faith in *Fresh Air* to help us add a weekly half-hour edition, which he convinced NPR to distribute. Then he took on the massive job of helping us go national with a daily show. As NPR's first vice president of news, Bill had written the network's mission statement and created *All Things Considered*. Throughout public radio, his name was synonymous with innovation and integrity, and his confidence in us gave us instant

credibility at NPR and with local program directors. Bill left WHYY in 1987, just before *Fresh Air* made its debut as a daily national show, but he's never stopped cheering us on, even while helping to start community radio stations in such faraway places as Mongolia and South Africa. We hope he hears his influence in our best work.

Other people formerly at WHYY who were instrumental in the development of our national program include Mark Vogelzang, Katherine Ball-Weir, Rick Breitenfeld, and David Othmer. Thanks also to Anna Kosof and Fred Brown.

At NPR, Robert Siegel, Carolyn Gershfeld, and Joe Gwathmey helped us launch the national editions. Many other people at NPR have also offered us guidance and support over the years, including Jay Kernis, Margaret Low Smith, Joyce MacDonald, Bill Buzenberg, Alex Chadwick, Neal Conan, Jeffrey Dvorkin, John Dinges, Liane Hanson, Murray Horowitz, Renee Montaigne, Scott Simon, and Joanne Wallace.

Thanks to the Corporation for Public Broadcasting and to the late Rick Madden, the former director of its Radio Program Fund. Under Rick's leadership, the fund awarded us a start-up grant to initiate a daily national edition. Thanks also to David Giovannoni and Leslie Peters.

My sincerest thanks to the program directors who've had the confidence in *Fresh Air* to schedule it on their stations, and to every listener who has ever made a pledge during a *Fresh Air* broadcast. I'm indebted to my former colleagues at WBFO, in Buffalo, who taught me about radio—especially the producers of *Womanpower,* the show I got my start on. For commiseration and/or inspiration: Marcia Alvar, Alan Baratz, John Barth, Doug Berman, Jim Campbell, Wayne Conner, Rosemary D'Anella, Donald Elfman, Mark Fuerst, Ira Glass, Sydney Goldstein, Harriet Harris, David Karpoff, Karen Miller, Ann Mintz, Carol Pierson, Paula Randolph, Jennifer Roth, Mary Schobert, David Sedaris, and Judy Stein. I'm lucky to have as a friend Corby Kummer, an editor at *The Atlantic Monthly,* who read parts of this manuscript and offered valuable suggestions.

As I've said, I put off doing this book for years. Leigh Haber first approached me in 1994, just after becoming a book editor. I spent the next few years refusing to actually sign the contract we'd agreed on, while protesting—or, more precisely, whining—that I was much too busy to commit myself. As Leigh's career took off, it would have been understandable if she'd given up on me, but she wasn't going to let me off the hook that easily—her commitment to the book never wavered, even though she was leaving Hyperion by the time we delivered the manuscript. I'm grateful for her guidance, her practical suggestions, and her confidence in me.

I'd also like to thank William Strachan for his work on the book in its final stages. Others at Hyperion to whom I am indebted are assistant editor Ben Loehnen and publicity director Katie Wainwright.

My years of stalling also must have tested the patience of my book agent, Jonathon Lazear. But nothing I did—or didn't do—stopped him from being gracious and good-humored about the whole thing. He had faith that I would eventually not only start the book but finish it. My deep thanks to my agent, Tom Wiese, for his clarity and resolve, and for managing to keep me laughing. My lecture agent, Steven Barclay, has helped me in ways above and beyond booking me for speaking engagements. My thanks to his always helpful associates, Kathryn Barcos and Eliza Fischer.

I owe a lifetime of thanks to my family. My mother, Anne Gross, was always a reader. She taught me by example that books were a source of pleasure. Although she didn't believe in buying them, she always had one on loan from the library. I know she would have wanted her own copy of this one. I wish she were here to read it—I just wish she were here. Irving Gross, my father, who misses my mother beyond description, has always been my champion and someone I know I can count on to give me his honest opinion. He has helped me in innumerable ways, always putting my interests before his. Leon Gross was the greatest older brother a girl could have when we were growing up, and I still look up to him. There are many things I am thankful to Lee and my sister-in-law, Ellyn, for—not least, for making me the aunt of Jessica and Alison.

I miss Dorothy Davis, my mother-in-law and dear friend, whose death in the spring of 2001 followed my own mother's by just six weeks.

My deepest thanks go to my husband, Francis Davis. His writing about music and popular culture (which I've quoted several times in this book) has had an enormous influence on my own thinking. Reading his eloquent prose fills me with pleasure—and envy. Luckily for me, he took on the job of editing the introduction, the remarks that precede each of the interviews, and even these acknowledgments—in spite of the fact that he had a book of his own due. He helped me clarify my thoughts, reminded me of things I've said in conversation that belonged in the introduction, and donated more than a few of his own insights. Every sentence that I've written here and in the interview introductions became more graceful through his efforts—with the possible exception of this one [*Don't bet on it—FD*]. But the way he improved my prose is nothing compared to how he's enriched my life.